NEW YORK TIMES BESTSELLER

D0028579

AMERICAN FASCISTS

The Christian Right and the War on America

"*American Fascists* ... is a call to arms against what Hedges sees as the efforts of Pat Robertson and the operators of Trinity Broadcast Network, among others, to turn the United States into a Christian nation. Hedges reports in fascinating detail what goes on inside churches, conventions, and meeting halls of the Christian Right."
—*Los Angeles Times*

Featuring a Q&A with the author

CHRIS HEDGES

Author of *War Is a Force That Gives Us Meaning* and *Losing Moses on the Freeway*

PRAISE FOR *American Fascists*

"Chris Hedges may be the most credible figure yet to detect real-life fascism in the Red America of megachurches, gay-marriage bans and *Left Behind* books. *American Facists* is at its most daring when it enunciates . . . the perversities that are obvious to those of us not beholden to political exigencies."

—*New York Observer*

"Throughout, Hedges documents, and reflects on, what he feels is the bigotry, the homophobia, the fanaticism—and the deeply un-Christian ideology—that pose clear and present danger in our previous and fragile republic."

—*O*, the Oprah magazine

"This is a powerful book that looks inside some of the darkest movements on American soil."

—*Time Out New York*

PRAISE FOR *Losing Moses on the Freeway*

"Telling his own story, Mr. Hedges writes better than anyone else in the game, without sentiment but full of love and hate. . . . He walks out of these pages as a good enough man—better than most, perhaps—but best of all, he emerges as a teller of human tales with the unusual capacity to get them right."

—*New York Observer*

"At a time when the mere mention of religion can excite so much passion, anxiety, and discord, Chris Hedges' *Losing Moses on the Freeway* offers a sane and bracing way to think about, and rethink, the whole subject of faith. Each of the deeply felt essays finds spiritual lessons in the most unlikely places. Hedges reminds us that the point of religion is not to make us disdain those who think differently but rather to help us become decent, responsive, and moral human beings."

—*O, the Oprah magazine*

"Hedges brings a broad and secular perspective to a deep examination of the principles of the Ten Commandments. He turns a sharp eye toward a variety of human experiences touching on elements of the commandments in ways that are uncommon and insightful. The commandments bind us together and provide guideposts against excessive human temptations. A deeply insightful and moving book."

—*Booklist*

PRAISE FOR *What Every Person Should Know About War*

"A straight-faced study of how war works and what it looks like on the ground. Without any polemics, *What Every Person Should Know About War* is one of the most powerful antiwar statements in recent memory. The unadorned and brutal facts speak for themselves."

—*New York Observer*

PRAISE FOR *War Is a Force That Gives Us Meaning*

"A brilliant, thoughtful, timely and unsettling book . . . it will rattle jingoists, pacifists, moralists, nihilists, politicians and professional soldiers equally . . . Abounds with Hedges' harrowing and terribly moving eyewitness accounts . . . Powerful and informative."

—*The New York Times Book Review*

"[A] powerful chronicle of modern war . . . A persuasive call for humility and realism in the pursuit of national goals by force of arms . . . A potent and eloquent warning."

—*The New York Times*

"The best kind of war journalism: It is bitterly poetic and ruth-lessly philosophical. It sends out a powerful message to people contemplating the escalation of the 'war against terrorism.'"

—*Los Angeles Times*

"No one is in a better position than Hedges to pronounce on the revolting things war does to everyone caught up in it. . . . A con-fession of rare and frightening honesty."

—Slate.com

"As the 'war on terror' continues on its . . . potentially catastrophic course, America would do well to heed Hedges' . . . warning."

—Salon.com

"I highly recommend Chris Hedges' splendid little book. . . . His understanding is profound and was earned on the ground."

—Molly Ivins, *Fort Worth Star-Telegram*

"If . . . I thought Bush and Blair would give it time I would hap-pily send them a copy to read."

—Jonathan Power, *The Toronto Star*

"[Hedges] doesn't tell us that war is hell. He escorts us through the streets made slick with the blood . . . of innocents."

—*The Dallas Morning News*

"A compelling read and a valuable counterweight to the more an-tiseptic discussions common among strategic analysts."

—*Foreign Affairs*

"Small but readable . . . [Hedges] is a brilliant reporter . . . It's the book to read now."

—Liz Smith, syndicated columnist

"Rarely is a book so timely as Hedges' latest . . . a refreshing jolt of cerebral and emotional clarity to war's all-encompassing destruction . . . "

—*Willamette Week*

"This should be required reading in this post-9/11 world as we debate the possibility of war with Iraq."

—*Publishers Weekly*

"Chris Hedges has written a powerful book, one which bears sad witness to what veterans have long understood . . . [A] somber and timely warning to those—in any society—who would evoke the emotions of war for the pursuit of political gain."

—General Wesley K. Clark, former Supreme Allied Commander, Europe, and author of *Waging Modern War* _f_**P**

ALSO BY CHRIS HEDGES

Losing Moses on the Freeway
What Every Person Should Know About War
War Is a Force That Gives Us Meaning

AMERICAN FASCISTS

THE CHRISTIAN RIGHT AND THE WAR ON AMERICA

CHRIS HEDGES

Free Press

NEW YORK LONDON TORONTO SYDNEY

FREE PRESS
A Division of Simon & Schuster, Inc.
1230 Avenue of the Americas
New York, NY 10020

Copyright © 2006 by Chris Hedges

All rights reserved, including the right to reproduce this book or portions
thereof in any form whatsoever. For information address Free Press Subsidiary
Rights Department, 1230 Avenue of the Americas, New York, NY 10020

First Free Press trade paperback edition January 2008

FREE PRESS and colophon are trademarks of Simon & Schuster, Inc.

For information about special discounts for bulk purchases,
please contact Simon & Schuster Special Sales:
1-800-456-6798 or business@simonandschuster.com

Designed by Paul Dippolito

Manufactured in the United States of America

1   3   5   7   9   10   8   6   4   2

The Library of Congress has cataloged the hardcover edition as follows:
Hedges, Chris.
American fascists : the Christian Right and the war on America / Chris Hedges.
p. cm.
Includes bibliographical references and index.
1. Fascism—United States. 2. Fundamentalism—United States.
3. Conservatism—Religious aspects—Christianity. I. Title.

JC481 .H38 2007
322/.10973—dc22   2006047123

ISBN-13: 978-0-7432-8443-1
ISBN-10:   0-7432-8443-7
ISBN-13: 978-0-7432-8446-2 (pbk)
ISBN-10:   0-7432-8446-1 (pbk)

The author gratefully acknowledges the kind permission of Harcourt to reprint
Eternal Fascism: Fourteen Ways of Looking at a Blackshirt by Umberto Eco from
Five Moral Pieces. Copyright © 2001 by Umberto Eco.

*For Chris Marquis, a gifted writer, a courageous reporter
and a generous friend whose loss has left a hole in my heart.*

Men never do evil so completely and cheerfully as when they do it from religious conviction.

—*Blaise Pascal*

Eternal Fascism: Fourteen Ways of Looking at a Blackshirt

By Umberto Eco

In spite of some fuzziness regarding the difference between various historical forms of fascism, I think it is possible to outline a list of features that are typical of what I would like to call Ur-Fascism, or Eternal Fascism. These features cannot be organized into a system; many of them contradict each other, and are also typical of other kinds of despotism or fanaticism. But it is enough that one of them be present to allow fascism to coagulate around it.

•   •   •

1. The first feature of Ur-Fascism is the cult of tradition. Traditionalism is of course much older than fascism. Not only was it typical of counterrevolutionary Catholic thought after the French revolution, but it was born in the late Hellenistic era, as a reaction to classical Greek rationalism. In the Mediterranean basin, people of different religions (most of the faiths indulgently accepted by the Roman pantheon) started dreaming of a revelation received at the dawn of human history. This revelation, according to the traditionalist mystique, had remained for a long time concealed under the veil of forgotten languages—in Egyptian hieroglyphs, in the Celtic runes, in the scrolls of the little-known religions of Asia.

This new culture had to be *syncretistic*. Syncretism is not only, as the dictionary says, "the combination of different forms of belief or practice;" such a combination must tolerate contradictions. Each of the original messages contains a sliver of wisdom, and although they seem to say different or incompatible things, they all are nevertheless alluding, allegorically, to the same primeval truth.

As a consequence, there can be no advancement of learning. Truth already has been spelled out once and for all, and we can only keep interpreting its obscure message.

If you browse in the shelves that, in American bookstores, are labeled New Age, you can find there even Saint Augustine, who, as far as I know, was not a fascist. But combining Saint Augustine and Stonehenge—that is a symptom of Ur-Fascism.

2. Traditionalism implies the *rejection of modernism*. Both Fascists and Nazis worshipped technology, while traditionalist thinkers usually reject it as a negation of traditional spiritual values. However, even though Nazism was proud of its industrial achievements, its praise of modernism was only the surface of an ideology based upon blood and earth (*Blut und Boden*). The rejection of the modern world was disguised as a rebuttal of the capitalistic way of life. The Enlightenment, the Age of Reason, is seen as the beginning of modern depravity. In this sense Ur-Fascism can be defined as *irrationalism*.

3. Irrationalism also depends on the cult of *action for action's sake*. Action being beautiful in itself, it must be taken before, or without, reflection. Thinking is a form of emasculation. Therefore culture is suspect insofar as it is identified with critical attitudes. Distrust of the intellectual world has always been a symptom of Ur-Fascism, from Hermann Goering's fondness for a phrase from a Hanns Johst play ("When I hear the word 'culture' I reach for my gun") to the frequent use of such expressions as "degenerate intellectuals," "eggheads," "effete snobs," and "universities are nests of reds." The official Fascist intellectuals were mainly engaged in attacking modern culture and the liberal intelligentsia for having betrayed traditional values.

4. The critical spirit makes distinctions, and to distinguish is a sign of modernism. In modern culture the scientific community praises disagreement as a way to improve knowledge. For Ur-Fascism, *disagreement is treason*.

5. Besides, disagreement is a sign of diversity. Ur-Fascism grows up and seeks consensus by exploiting and exacerbating the natural *fear of difference*. The first appeal of a fascist or prematurely fascist movement is an appeal against the intruders. Thus Ur-Fascism is racist by definition.

6. Ur-Fascism derives from individual or social frustration. That is why one of the most typical features of the historical fascism was the *appeal to a frustrated middle class*, a class suffering from an economic crisis or feelings of political humiliation, and frightened by the pressure of lower social groups. In our time, when the old "proletarians" are becoming petty bourgeois (and the lumpen are largely excluded from the political scene), the fascism of tomorrow will find its audience in this new majority.

7. To people who feel deprived of a clear social identity, Ur-Fascism says that their only privilege is the most common one, to be born in the same country. This is the origin of nationalism. Besides, the only ones who can provide an identity to the nation are its enemies. Thus at the root of the Ur-Fascist psychology there is the *obsession with a plot,* possibly an international one. The followers must feel besieged. The easiest way to solve the plot is the appeal to xenophobia. But the plot must also come from the inside: Jews are usually the best target because they have the advantage of being at the same time inside and outside. In the United States, a prominent instance of the plot obsession is to be found in Pat Robertson's *The New World Order,* but, as we have recently seen, there are many others.

8. The followers must feel *humiliated by the ostentatious wealth and force of their enemies*. When I was a boy I was taught to think of Englishmen as the five-meal people. They ate more frequently than the poor but sober Italians. Jews are rich and help each other through a secret web of mutual assistance. However, the followers of Ur-Fascism must also be convinced that they can overwhelm the enemies. Thus, by a continuous shifting of rhetorical focus, the enemies are at the same time too strong and too weak. Fascist governments are condemned to lose wars because they are constitutionally incapable of objectively evaluating the force of the enemy.

9. For Ur-Fascism there is no struggle for life but, rather, life is lived for struggle. Thus *pacifism is trafficking with the enemy*. It is bad because *life is permanent warfare*. This, however, brings about an Armageddon complex. Since enemies have to be defeated, there must be a final battle, after which the movement will have control of the world. But such "final solutions" implies a further era of peace, a Golden Age, which contradicts the principle of permanent war. No fascist leader has ever succeeded in solving this predicament.

10. Elitism is a typical aspect of any reactionary ideology, insofar as it is fundamentally aristocratic, and aristocratic and militaristic elitism cruelly implies *contempt for the weak*. Ur-Fascism can only advocate a popular elitism. Every citizen belongs to the best people in the world, the members or the party are the best among the citizens, every citizen can (or ought to) become a member of the party. But there cannot be patricians without plebeians. In fact, the Leader, knowing that his power was not delegated to him democratically but was conquered by force, also knows that his force is based upon the weakness of the masses; they are so weak as to need and deserve a ruler.

11. In such a perspective *everybody is educated to become a hero*. In every mythology the hero is an exceptional being, but in Ur-Fascist ideology heroism is the norm. This cult of heroism is strictly linked with the cult of death. It is not by chance that a motto of the Spanish Falangists was *Viva la Muerte* ("Long Live Death!"). In nonfascist societies, the lay public is told that death is unpleasant but must be faced with dignity; believers are told that it is the painful way to reach a supernatural happiness. By contrast, the Ur-Fascist hero craves heroic death, advertised as the best reward for a heroic life. The Ur-Fascist hero is impatient to die. In his impatience, he more frequently sends other people to death.

12. Since both permanent war and heroism are difficult games to play, *the Ur-Fascist transfers his will to power to sexual matters*. This is the origin of machismo (which implies both disdain for women and intolerance and condemnation of nonstandard sexual habits, from chastity to homosexuality). Since even sex is a difficult game to play, the Ur-Fascist hero tends to play with weapons—doing so becomes an ersatz phallic exercise.

13. Ur-Fascism is based upon a *selective populism*, a qualitative populism, one might say. In a democracy, the citizens have individual rights, but the citizens in their entirety have a political impact only from a quantitative point of view—one follows the decisions of the majority. For Ur-Fascism, however, individuals as individuals have no rights, and the People is conceived as a quality, a monolithic entity expressing the Common Will. Since no large quantity of human beings can have a common will, the Leader pretends to be their interpreter. Having lost their power of delegation, citizens do not act; they are only called on to play the role of the People. Thus the People is only a theatrical fiction. There is in our future a TV or Internet populism, in which the emotional response of a selected group of citizens can be presented and accepted as the Voice of the People.

Because of its qualitative populism, Ur-Fascism must be *against "rotten" parliamentary governments*. Wherever a politician casts doubt on the legitimacy of a parliament because it no longer represents the Voice of the People, we can smell Ur-Fascism.

14. *Ur-Fascism speaks Newspeak.* Newspeak was invented by Orwell, in *Nineteen Eighty-Four,* as the official language of what he called Ingsoc, English Socialism. But elements of Ur-Fascism are common to different forms of dictatorship. All the Nazi or Fascist schoolbooks made use of an impoverished vocabulary, and an elementary syntax, in order to limit the instruments for complex and critical reasoning. But we must be ready to identify other kinds of Newspeak, even if they take the apparently innocent form of a popular talk show.

· · ·

Ur-Fascism is still around us, sometimes in plainclothes. It would be so much easier for us if there appeared on the world scene somebody saying, "I want to reopen Auschwitz, I want the Blackshirts to parade again in the Italian squares." Life is not that simple. Ur-Fascism can come back under the most innocent of disguises. Our duty is to uncover it and to point our finger at any of its new instances—every day, in every part of the world. Franklin Roosevelt's words of November 4, 1938, are worth recalling: "If American democracy ceases to move forward as a living force, seeking day and night by peaceful means to better the lot of our citizens, fascism will grow in strength in our land." Freedom and liberation are an unending task.

Contents

AMERICAN FASCISTS

CHAPTER ONE

Faith

Unlimited tolerance must lead to the disappearance of tolerance. If we extend unlimited tolerance even to those who are intolerant, if we are not prepared to defend a tolerant society against the onslaught of the intolerant, then the tolerant will be destroyed, and tolerance with them. In this formulation, I do not imply, for instance, that we should always suppress the utterance of intolerant philosophies; as long as we can counter them by rational argument and keep them in check by public opinion, suppression would certainly be most unwise. But we should claim the right to suppress them if necessary even by force; for it may easily turn out that they are not prepared to meet us on the level of rational argument, but begin by denouncing all argument; they may forbid their followers to listen to rational argument, because it is deceptive, and teach them to answer arguments by the use of their fists or pistols. We should therefore claim, in the name of tolerance, the right not to tolerate the intolerant. We should claim that any movement preaching intolerance places itself outside the law, and we should consider incitement to intolerance and persecution as criminal, in the same way as we should consider incitement to murder, or to kidnapping, or to the revival of the slave trade, as criminal.

—*Karl Popper,* The Open Society and Its Enemies[1]

I grew up in a small farming town in upstate New York where my life, and the life of my family, centered on the Presbyterian Church. I prayed and sang hymns every Sunday, went to Bible school, listened to my father preach the weekly sermon and attended seminary at Harvard Divinity School to be a preacher myself. America was a place where things could be better if we worked to make them better, and where our faith saved us from despair, self-righteousness and the dangerous belief that we knew the will of God or could carry it out. We were taught that those who claimed to speak for God, the self-appointed prophets who promised the Kingdom of God on earth, were dangerous. We had no ability to understand God's will. We did the best we could. We trusted and had faith in the mystery, the unknown before us. We made decisions—even decisions that on the outside looked unobjectionably moral—well aware of the numerous motives, some good and some bad, that went into every human act. In the end, we all stood in need of forgiveness. We were all tainted by sin. None were pure. The Bible was not the literal word of God. It was not a self-help manual that could predict the future. It did not tell us how to vote or allow us to divide the world into us and them, the righteous and the damned, the infidels and the blessed. It was a book written by a series of ancient writers, certainly fallible and at times at odds with each other, who asked the right questions and struggled with the mystery and transcendence of human existence. We took the Bible seriously and therefore could not take it literally.

There was no alcohol in the manse where I grew up. Indeed, my father railed against the Glass Bar, the one bar in town, and the drinking in the VFW Hall. We did not work on Sunday. I never heard my father swear. But coupled with this piety was a belief that as Christians we were called to fight for justice. My father took an early stand in the town in support of the civil-rights movement, a position that was highly unpopular in rural, white enclaves where Dr. Martin Luther King Jr. was one of the most hated men in America. A veteran of World War II, he opposed the Vietnam War, telling me when I was about 12 that if the war was still being waged when I was 18 and I was drafted, he would go to prison with me. To this day I carry in my head the rather gloomy image of sitting in a jail cell with my dad. Finally, because his youngest brother was gay, he understood the pain and isolation of being a gay man in America. He worked later in life in the gay-rights movement, calling for the ordination and marriage of gays. When he found that my college, Colgate University, had no gay and lesbian organization, he brought gay speakers to the campus. The meetings led gays and lesbians to confide in him that they felt uncomfortable coming out of the closet to start an open organization, a problem my father swiftly solved by taking me out to lunch and informing me that although I was not gay, I had to form the organization. When I went into the dining hall for breakfast, lunch and dinner, the checker behind the desk would take my card, mark off the appropriate box, and hand it back, muttering, "Faggot." This willingness to take a moral stand, to accept risk and ridicule, was, he showed me, the cost of the moral life.

The four Gospels, we understood, were filled with factual contradictions, two Gospels saying Jesus was baptized by John the Baptist, while Luke asserted that John was already in prison. Mark and John give little importance to the birth of Jesus, while Matthew and Luke give differing accounts. There are three separate and different versions of the 10 Commandments (Exodus 20, Exodus 34, and Deuteronomy 5). As for the question of God's true nature, there are many substantive contradictions. Is God a loving or a vengeful God? In some sections of the Bible, vicious acts of vengeance, including the genocidal extermination of opposing tribes and nations, appear to be blessed by God. God turns on the Egyptians and transforms the Nile into blood so the Egyptians will suffer from thirst—and then sends swarms of locusts and flies to torture them, along with hail, fire and thunder from the heavens to destroy all plants and trees. To liberate the children of Israel, God orders the firstborn in every Egyptian household killed so all will know "that the Lord makes a distinction between the Egyptians and Israel" (Exodus 11:7).[2] The killing does not cease until "there was not a house where one was not dead" (Exodus 12:30). Amid the carnage God orders Moses to loot all the clothing, jewelry, gold and silver from the Egyptian homes (Exodus 12:35–36). God looks at the devastation and says,

"I have made sport of the Egyptians" (Exodus 10:2). While the Exodus story fueled the hopes and dreams of oppressed Jews, and later African Americans in the bondage of slavery, it also has been used to foster religious chauvinism.

A literal reading of the Bible means reinstitution of slavery coupled with the understanding that the slavemaster has the right to beat his slave without mercy since "the slave is his money" (Exodus 21:21). Children who strike or curse a parent are to be executed (Exodus 21:15, 17). Those who pay homage to another god "shall be utterly destroyed" (Exodus 22:20). Menstruating women are to be considered unclean, and all they touch while menstruating becomes unclean (Leviticus 15:19–32). The blind, the lame, those with mutilated faces, those who are hunchbacks or dwarfs and those with itching diseases or scabs or crushed testicles cannot become priests (Leviticus 21:17–21). Blasphemers shall be executed (Leviticus 24:16). And "if the spirit of jealousy" comes upon a man, the high priest can order the jealous man's wife to drink the "water of bitterness." If she dies, it is proof of her guilt; if she survives, of her innocence (Numbers 5:11–31). Women, throughout the Bible, are subservient to men, often without legal rights, and men are free to sell their daughters into sexual bondage (Exodus 21:7–11).

Hatred of Jews and other non-Christians pervades the Gospel of John (3:18–20). Jews, he wrote, are children of the devil, the father of lies (John 8:39–44). Jesus calls on his followers to love their enemies and to pray for their persecutors (Matthew 5:44), a radical concept in the days of the Roman Empire. He says we must never demean or insult our enemies. But then we read of Jesus calling his enemies "a brood of vipers" (Matthew 12:34).

The Book of Revelation, a crucial text for the radical Christian Right, appears to show Christ returning to earth at the head of an avenging army. It is one of the few places in the Bible where Christ is associated with violence. This bizarre book, omitted from some of the early canons and relegated to the back of the Bible by Martin

Luther, may have been a way, as scholars contend, for the early Christians to cope with Roman persecution and their dreams of final triumph and glory. The book, however, paints a picture of a bloody battle between the forces of good and evil, Christ and the Antichrist, God and Satan, and the torment and utter destruction of all who do not follow the faith. In this vision, only the faithful will be allowed to enter the gates of the New Jerusalem. All others will disappear, cast into the lake of fire (Revelation 20:14–15). The Warrior's defeat of the armies of the nations, a vast apocalyptic vision of war, ends with birds of prey invited to "gather for the great supper of God, to eat the flesh of kings, the flesh of captains, the flesh of mighty men, the flesh of horses and their riders, and the flesh of all men, both free and slave, both small and great" (Revelation 19:17–18). It is a story of God's ruthless, terrifying and violent power unleashed on nonbelievers:

> *The fourth angel poured his bowl on the sun, and it was allowed to scorch men with fire; men were scorched by the fierce heat, and they cursed the name of God, who had power over these plagues, and they did not repent and give him glory. The fifth angel poured his bowl on the throne of the beast, and its kingdom was in darkness; men gnawed their tongues in anguish and cursed the God of heaven for their pain and sores, and did not repent of their deeds. (Revelation 16:8–11)*

There is enough hatred, bigotry and lust for violence in the pages of the Bible to satisfy anyone bent on justifying cruelty and violence. Religion, as Reinhold Niebuhr said, is a good thing for good people and a bad thing for bad people.[3] And the Bible has long been used in the wrong hands—such as antebellum slave owners in the American South who quoted from it to defend slavery—not to Christianize the culture, as those wielding it often claim, but to acculturate the Christian faith.

Many of the suppositions of the biblical writers, who understood little about the working of the cosmos or the human body, are so fanciful, and the accounts so wild, that even biblical literalists reject them. God is not, as many writers of the Bible believed, peering down at us through little peepholes in the sky called stars. These evangelicals and fundamentalists are, as the Reverend William Sloane Coffin wrote, not biblical literalists, as they claim, but "selective literalists," choosing the bits and pieces of the Bible that conform to their ideology and ignoring, distorting or inventing the rest.[4] And the selective literalists cannot have it both ways. Either the Bible is literally true and all of its edicts must be obeyed, or it must be read in another way.

Mainstream Christians can also cherry-pick the Bible to create a Jesus and God who are always loving and compassionate. Such Christians often fail to acknowledge that there are hateful passages in the Bible that give sacred authority to the rage, self-aggrandizement and intolerance of the Christian Right. Church leaders must denounce the biblical passages that champion apocalyptic violence and hateful political creeds. They must do so in the light of other biblical passages that teach a compassion and tolerance, often exemplified in the life of Christ, which stands opposed to bigotry and violence. Until this happens, until the Christian churches wade into the debate, these biblical passages will be used by bigots and despots to give sacred authority to their calls to subjugate or eradicate the enemies of God. This literature in the biblical canon keeps alive the virus of hatred, whether dormant or active, and the possibility of apocalyptic terror in the name of God. And the steady refusal by churches to challenge the canonical authority of these passages means these churches share some of the blame. "Unless the churches, Protestant and Catholic alike, come together on this, they will continue to make it legitimate to believe in the end as a time when there will be no non-Christians or infidels," theologian Richard Fenn wrote. "Silent complicity with apocalyptic rhetoric soon becomes collusion with plans for religiously inspired genocide."[5]

As long as scripture, blessed and accepted by the church, teaches that at the end of time there will be a Day of Wrath and Christians will control the shattered remnants of a world cleansed through violence and war, as long as it teaches that all nonbelievers will be tormented, destroyed and banished to hell, it will be hard to thwart the message of radical apocalyptic preachers or assuage the fears of the Islamic world that Christians are calling for its annihilation. Those who embrace this dark conclusion to life can find it endorsed in scripture, whether it is tucked into the back pew rack of a liberal Unitarian church in Boston or a megachurch in Florida. The mainstream Protestant and Catholic churches, declining in numbers and influence, cannot hope to combat the hysteria and excitement roused by these prophets of doom until they repudiate the apocalyptic writings in scripture.

The writers of Genesis, as the Reverend William Sloane Coffin has pointed out, who wrote about the creation of the world in seven days, knew nothing about the process of creation.[6] They believed the earth was flat with water above and below it. They wrote that God created light on the first day and the sun on the fourth day. Genesis was not written to explain the process of creation, of which these writers knew nothing. It was written to help explain the purpose of creation. It was written to help us grasp a spiritual truth, not a scientific or historical fact. And this purpose, this spiritual truth, is something the writers did know about. These biblical writers, at their best, understood our divided natures. They knew our internal conflicts and battles; how we could love our brother and yet hate him; the oppressive power of parents, even the best of parents; the impulses that drive us to commit violations against others; the yearning to lead a life of meaning; our fear of mortality; our struggles to deal with our uncertainty, our loneliness, our greed, our lust, our ambition, our desires to be God, as well as our moments of nobility, compassion and courage. They knew these emotions and feelings were entangled. They understood our weaknesses and strengths. They understood how we are often not the people we want to be or know we should be, how hard it is for us to articulate all this, and how life and creation can be as glorious and beautiful as it can be mysterious, evil and cruel. This is why Genesis is worth reading, indeed why the Bible stands as one of the great ethical and moral documents of our age. The biblical writers have helped shape and define Western civilization. Not to know the Bible is, in some ways, to be illiterate, to neglect the very roots of philosophy, art, literature, poetry and music. It is to fall into a dangerous provincialism, as myopic and narrow as that embraced by those who say everything in the Bible is literally true and we do not need any other kind of intellectual or scientific inquiry. Doubt and belief are not, as biblical literalists claim, incompatible. Those who act without any doubt are frightening.

"There lives more faith in honest doubt," the poet Alfred Tennyson noted, "believe me, than in half the creeds." [7]

This was my faith. It is a pretty good summary of my faith today. God is inscrutable, mysterious and unknowable. We do not understand what life is about, what it means, why we are here and what will happen to us after our brief sojourn on the planet ends. We are saved, in the end, by faith—faith that life is not meaningless and random, that there is a purpose to human existence, and that in the midst of this morally neutral universe the tiny, seemingly insignificant acts of compassion and blind human kindness, especially to those labeled our enemies and strangers, sustain the divine spark, which is love. We are not fully human if we live alone. These small acts of compassion—for they can never be organized and institutionalized as can hate—have a power that lives after us. Human kindness is deeply subversive to totalitarian creeds, which seek to thwart all compassion toward those deemed unworthy of moral consideration, those branded as internal or external enemies. These acts recognize and affirm the humanity of others, others who may be condemned as agents of Satan. Those who sacrifice for others, especially at great cost, who place com-

passion and tolerance above ideology and creeds, a
absolutes, especially moral absolutes, stand as constant w
in our lives to this love, even long after they are gone. In
gospels this is called resurrection.

Faith presupposes that we cannot know. We can never know.
Those who claim to know what life means play God. These false
prophets—the Pat Robertsons, the Jerry Falwells and the James
Dobsons—clutching the cross and the Bible, offer, like Mephis-
topheles, to lead us back to a mythical paradise and an impossible, unachievable happiness and security, at once seductive and
empowering. They ask us to hand over moral choice and responsibility to them. They will tell us they know what is right and
wrong in the eyes of God. They tell us how to act, how to live, and
in this process they elevate themselves above us. They remove the
anxiety of moral choice, the fundamental anxiety of human existence. This is part of their attraction. They give us the rules by
which we live. But once we hand over this anxiety and accept
their authority, we become enslaved and they become our idols.
And idols, as the Bible never ceases to tell us, destroy us.

I have seen enough of the world over the past two decades—
for although I graduated from seminary I was not ordained, and
instead worked in Latin America, Africa, the Middle East and the
Balkans as a foreign correspondent—to grasp that men and
women of great moral probity and courage arise in all cultures, all
nations and all religions to challenge the oppressor and fight for
the oppressed. I also saw how the dominant religions of these nations were often twisted and distorted by totalitarian movements,
turned into civic religions in which the goals of the movement or
the state became the goals of the divine. The wars I covered were
often fought in the name of one God or another. Armed groups,
from Hamas in the West Bank and Gaza Strip to the Serbian na-
tionalists in the former Yugoslavia, were fueled by apocalyptic visions that sanctified terrorism or genocide. They mocked the
faiths they purported to defend.

religions have no monopoly on
         as not chosen Americans as a peo-
        s of Christians are as flawed and im-
       liefs. But both the best of American
      f Christianity embody important values,
      sion, tolerance and belief in justice and
      nation where all have a voice in how we live
      erned. We have never fully adhered to these
valu   bbably never will—but our health as a country
is determi   our steadfastness in striving to attain them. And
there are times when taking a moral stance, perhaps the highest
form of patriotism, means facing down the community, even the
nation. Our loyalty to our community and our nation, Reinhold
Niebuhr wrote, "is therefore morally tolerable only if it includes
values wider than those of the community."[8]

These values, democratic and Christian, are being dismantled,
often with stealth, by a radical Christian movement, known as dominionism, which seeks to cloak itself in the mantle of the Christian faith and American patriotism. Dominionism takes its name
from Genesis 1:26–31, in which God gives human beings "dominion" over all creation. This movement, small in number but influential, departs from traditional evangelicalism. Dominionists now
control at least six national television networks, each reaching
tens of millions of homes, and virtually all of the nation's more
than 2,000 religious radio stations, as well as denominations such
as the Southern Baptist Convention. Dominionism seeks to redefine traditional democratic and Christian terms and concepts to fit
an ideology that calls on the radical church to take political power.
It shares many prominent features with classical fascist movements, at least as it is defined by the scholar Robert O. Paxton,
who sees fascism as "a form of political behavior marked by ob-
sessive preoccupation with community decline, humiliation, or
victimhood and by compensatory cultures of unity, energy, and
purity, in which a mass-based party of committed nationalist mil-

itants, working in uneasy but effective collaboration with traditional elites, abandons democratic liberties and pursues with re-
demptive violence and without ethical or legal restraints goals of
internal cleansing and external expansion."[9]

Dominionism, born out of a theology known as Christian reconstructionism, seeks to politicize faith. It has, like all fascist
movements, a belief in magic along with leadership adoration and
a strident call for moral and physical supremacy of a master race,
in this case American Christians. It also has, like fascist movements, an ill-defined and shifting set of beliefs, some of which
contradict one another. Paxton argues that the best way to understand authentic fascist movements, which he says exist in all societies, including democracies, is to focus not on what they say but
on how they act, for, as he writes, some of the ideas that underlie
fascist movements "remain unstated and implicit in fascist public
language," and "many of them belong more to the realm of visceral feelings than to the realm of reasoned propositions."[10]

"Fascism is . . . a kind of colonization," the Reverend Davidson Loehr noted. "A simple definition of 'colonization' is that it
takes people's stories away, and assigns them supportive roles in
stories that empower others at their expense."[11] The dominionist
movement, like all totalitarian movements, seeks to appropriate
not only our religious and patriotic language but also our stories,
to deny the validity of stories other than their own, to deny that
there are other acceptable ways of living and being. There becomes, in their rhetoric, only one way to be a Christian and only
one way to be an American.

Dominionism is a theocratic sect with its roots in a radical
Calvinism. It looks to the theocracy John Calvin implanted in
Geneva, Switzerland, in the 1500s as its political model. It teaches
that American Christians have been mandated by God to make
America a Christian state. A decades-long refusal by most Ameri-
can fundamentalists to engage in politics at all following the 1925
Scopes trial has been replaced by a call for Christian "dominion"

over the nation and eventually over the earth itself. Dominionism preaches that Jesus has called on Christians to build the kingdom of God in the here and now, whereas previously it was thought that we would have to wait for it. America becomes, in this militant biblicism, an agent of God, and all political and intellectual opponents of America's Christian leaders are viewed, quite simply, as agents of Satan. Under Christian dominion, America will be no longer a sinful and fallen nation but one in which the 10 Commandments form the basis of our legal system, creationism and "Christian values" form the basis of our educational system, and the media and the government proclaim the Good News to one and all. Labor unions, civil-rights laws and public schools will be abolished. Women will be removed from the workforce to stay at home, and all those deemed insufficiently Christian will be denied citizenship. Aside from its proselytizing mandate, the federal government will be reduced to the protection of property rights and "homeland" security. Some dominionists (not all of whom accept the label, at least not publicly) would further require all citizens to pay "tithes" to church organizations empowered by the government to run our social-welfare agencies and all schools. The only legitimate voices in this state will be Christian. All others will be silenced.

The racist and brutal intolerance of the intellectual godfathers of today's Christian Reconstructionism is a chilling reminder of the movement's lust for repression. *The Institutes of Biblical Law* by R. J. Rushdoony, written in 1973, is the most important book for the dominionist movement. Rushdoony calls for a Christian society that is harsh, unforgiving and violent. His work draws heavily on the calls for a repressive theocratic society laid out by Calvin in *Institutes of the Christian Religion*, first published in 1536 and one of the most important works of the Protestant Reformation. Christians are, Rushdoony argues, the new chosen people of God and are called to do what Adam and Eve failed to do: create a godly, Christian state. The Jews, who neglected to fulfill God's com-

mands in the Hebrew scriptures, have, in this belief system, for-
feited their place as God's chosen people and have been replaced
by Christians. The death penalty is to be imposed not only for of-
fenses such as rape, kidnapping and murder, but also for adultery,
blasphemy, homosexuality, astrology, incest, striking a parent, in-
corrigible juvenile delinquency, and, in the case of women, "un-
chastity before marriage." The world is to be subdued and ruled
by a Christian United States. Rushdoony dismissed the widely accepted estimate of 6 million Jews murdered in the Holocaust as
an inflated figure, and his theories on race often echo those found
in Nazi eugenics, in which there are higher and lower forms of
human beings. Those considered by the Christian state to be immoral and incapable of reform are to be exterminated.[12]

Rushdoony was deeply antagonistic toward the federal government. He believed the federal government should concern itself
with little more than national defense. Education and social welfare should be handed over to the churches. Biblical law must replace the secular legal code. This ideology, made more palatable
for the mainstream by later disciples such as Francis Schaeffer and
Pat Robertson, remains at the heart of the movement. Many of its
tenets are being enacted through the Office of Faith-Based and
Community Initiatives, currently channeling billions in federal
funds to groups such as National Right to Life and Pat Robertson's Operation Blessing, as well as to innumerable Christian
charities and organizations that do everything from running drug
and pregnancy clinics to promoting sexual abstinence-only programs in schools.[13]

While traditional fundamentalism shares many of the darker
traits of the new movement—such as a blind obedience to a male
hierarchy that often claims to speak for God, intolerance toward
nonbelievers, and disdain for rational, intellectual inquiry—it has
never attempted to impose its belief system on the rest of the nation. And it has not tried to transform government, as well as all
other secular institutions, into an extension of the church. The new

radical fundamentalisms amount to a huge and disastrous muta-
tion. Dominionists and their wealthy, right-wing sponsors speak in
terms and phrases that are familiar and comforting to most Americans, but they no longer use words to mean what they meant in the
past. They engage in a slow process of "logocide," the killing of
words. The old definitions of words are replaced by new ones. Code
words of the old belief system are deconstructed and assigned dia-
metrically opposed meanings. Words such as "truth," "wisdom,"
"death," "liberty," "life," and "love" no longer mean what they
mean in the secular world. "Life" and "death" mean life in Christ or
death to Christ, and are used to signal belief or unbelief in the risen
Lord. "Wisdom" has little to do with human wisdom but refers to
the level of commitment and obedience to the system of belief.
"Liberty" is not about freedom, but the "liberty" found when one
accepts Jesus Christ and is liberated from the world to obey Him.
But perhaps the most pernicious distortion comes with the word
"love," the word used to lure into the movement many who seek a
warm, loving community to counter their isolation and alienation.
"Love" is distorted to mean an unquestioned obedience to those
who claim to speak for God in return for the promise of everlasting
life. The blind, human love, the acceptance of the other, is attacked
as an inferior love, dangerous and untrustworthy.[14]

"The goal *must* be God's law-order in which alone is true liberty," wrote Rushdoony in *Institutes of Biblical Law:*

> *Whenever freedom is made into the absolute, the result is not free-*
> *dom but anarchism. Freedom must be under law or it is not free-*
> *dom. . . . Only a law-order which holds to the primacy of God's*
> *law can bring forth true freedom, freedom for justice, truth, and*
> *godly life.*
>
> *Freedom as an absolute is simply an assertion of man's "right"*
> *to be his own god; this means a radical denial of God's law-order.*
> *"Freedom" thus is another name for the claim by man to divinity*
> *and autonomy. It means that man becomes his own absolute. The*

word "freedom" is thus a pretext used by humanists of every variety . . . to disguise man's claim to be his own absolute. . . . If men have unrestricted free speech and free press, then there is no freedom for truth, in that no standard is permitted whereby the promulgation or publication of a lie can be judged and punished.[15]

As the process gains momentum—with some justices on the Supreme Court such as Antonin Scalia steeped in this ideology—America starts to speak a new language. There is a slow and inexorable hijacking of religious and political terminology. Terms such as "liberty" and "freedom" no longer mean what they meant in the past. Those in the movement speak of "liberty," but they do not speak about the traditional concepts of American liberty—the liberty to express divergent opinions, to respect other ways of believing and being, the liberty of individuals to seek and pursue their own goals and forms of happiness. When used by the Christian Right, the term "liberty" means the liberty that comes with accepting a very narrowly conceived Christ and the binary worldview that acceptance promotes.

America's Providential History, by Mark A. Beliles and Stephen K. McDowell, published in 1989, is the standard textbook on American history used in many Christian schools. It is also a staple of the home-schooling movement. In this book, authors Beliles and McDowell define the term "liberty" as fealty to "the Spirit of the Lord." The work of "liberty" is an ongoing process, one mounted by Christians, to free a society from the slavery imposed by "secular humanists." This process frees, or eradicates, different moral codes and belief systems, to introduce a single, uniform and unquestioned "Christian" orientation. Liberty, in a linguistic twist worthy of George Orwell, means theocratic tyranny:

The Bible reveals that "where the Spirit of the Lord is, there is liberty" (2 Corinthians 3:17). . . . When the Spirit of the Lord comes into a nation, that nation is liberated. The degree to which

the Spirit of the Lord is infused into a society (through its people,
laws and institutions) is the degree to which that society will ex-
perience liberty in every realm (civil, religious, economic, etc.).[16]

The Global Recordings Network, a missionary group striving to
bring "the Name of Jesus" to "every tribe and tongue and nation,"[17] gives close attention to the meaning of "liberty" in their
teachings. A tape of a missionary lesson plays: "I want to make
you understand this word 'liberty.' It is written in God's book:
'Where the Spirit of the Lord is, there is liberty.' Some say there is
not enough liberty in this land, but if that is true, it is because
there is not enough of the Spirit of the Lord. What do you think
yourselves? Do people do as God commands them? Do they love
each other? Do they help each other? Do they speak the truth? Do
they flee from fornication and adultery? You know there are those
who steal, who lie, who kill, and who worship things that are not
God. These things are not of the Spirit of God, but of the spirit of
Satan. Then how can there be true liberty?"[18]

The "infusion" of "the Spirit of the Lord" into society includes
its infusion into society's legal system. Liberty is defined as the
extent to which America obeys Christian law. When America is a
Christian nation, liberty becomes, in this view, liberation from
Satan. This slow, gradual and often imperceptible strangulation of
thought—the corruption of democratic concepts and ideas—
infects the society until the new, totalitarian vision is articulated
by the old vocabulary. This cannibalization of language occurs
subtly and stealthily. The ghoulish process leaves those leading
the movement mouthing platitudes little different from the bromides spoken by those who sincerely champion the open, democratic state.

These tactics, familiar and effective, have often been used by
movements that assault democracies. This seemingly innocent
hijacking of language mollifies opponents, the mainstream and
supporters within the movement who fail to grasp the radical

agenda. It gives believers a sense of continuity and tradition. Radical logocides paint themselves as the defenders of an idealized and more virtuous past. Most revolutionary movements, from those in Latin America to those shaped by Islamic militancy in the Middle East, root their radical ideas in what they claim are older, purer traditions.

While the radical Christian movement's leaders pay lip service to traditional justice, they call among their own for a legal system that promotes what they define as "Christian principles." The movement thus is able to preserve the appearance of law and respect for democracy even as its leaders condemn all opponents— dismissed as "atheists," "nonbelievers" or "secular humanists"— to moral and legal oblivion. Justice, under this process of logocide, is perverted to carry out injustice and becomes a mirage of law and order. The moral calculus no longer revolves around the concept of universal human rights. Its center is the well-being, protection and promotion of "Bible-believing Christians." Logocide slowly and stealthily removes whole segments of society from the moral map. As Joseph Goebbels wrote: "The best propaganda is that which, as it were, works invisibly, penetrates the whole of life without the public having any knowledge of the propagandistic initiative." [19]

Victor Klemperer, who was dismissed from his post as a professor of Romance languages at the University of Dresden in 1935 because of his Jewish ancestry, wrote what may have been the first literary critique of National Socialism. He noted that the Nazis also "changed the values, the frequency of words, [and] made them into common property, words that had previously been used by individuals or tiny troupes. They confiscated words for the party, saturated words and phrases and sentence forms with their poison. They made language serve their terrible system. They conquered words and made them into their strongest advertising tools [*Werebemittel*], at once the most public and the most secret." [20]

And while all this took place, he points out, most Germans never noticed.

"The language and symbols of an authentic American fascism would, of course, have little to do with the original European models," Robert O. Paxton wrote in *Anatomy of Fascism:*

> *They would have to be as familiar and reassuring to loyal Americans as the language and symbols of the original fascisms were familiar and reassuring to many Italians and Germans, as Orwell suggested. Hitler and Mussolini, after all, had not tried to seem exotic to their fellow citizens. No swastikas in an American fascism, but Stars and Stripes (or Stars and Bars) and Christian crosses. No fascist salute, but mass recitations of the Pledge of Allegiance. These symbols contain no whiff of fascism in themselves, of course, but an American fascism would transform them into obligatory litmus tests for detecting the internal enemy.*[21]

There are at least 70 million evangelicals in the United States—about 25 percent of the population—attending more than 200,000 evangelical churches. Polls indicate that about 40 percent of respondents believe in the Bible as the "actual word of God" and that it is "to be taken literally, word for word." Applied to the country's total population, this proportion would place the number of believers at about 100 million. These polls also suggest that about 84 percent of Americans accept that Jesus is the son of God; 80 percent of respondents say that they believe they will stand before God on the Day of Judgment. The same percentage of respondents say God works miracles, and half say they think angels exist. Almost a third of all respondents say they believe in the Rapture.[22]

American fundamentalists and evangelicals, however, are sharply divided between strict fundamentalists—those who refuse to grant legitimacy to alternative views of the Christian tradition—and the many evangelicals who concede that there are other legitimate ways to worship and serve Christ. Evangelicals, while they often embrace fundamentalist doctrine, do not always share the intolerance of the radical fundamentalists. While a majority of Christian Americans embrace a literal interpretation of the Bible, only a tiny minority—among them the Christian dominionists—are comfortable with this darker vision of an intolerant, theocratic America. Unfortunately, it is this minority that is taking over the machinery of U.S. state and religious institutions.

In a 2004 study, the political scientist John Green identifies those he calls "traditional evangelicals." This group, which Green estimates at 12.6 percent of the population, comes "closest to the 'religious right' widely discussed in the media." It is overwhelmingly Republican. It is openly hostile to democratic pluralism, and it champions totalitarian policies, such as denying homosexuals the same rights as other Americans and amending the Constitution to make America a "Christian nation." Green's "traditional evangelicals" can probably be called true dominionists. There are signs that this militant core may be smaller than even Green suggests, dipping to around 7 percent of the population in other polls, such as those conducted by George Barna.[23] But the potency of this radical movement far exceeds its numbers. Radical social movements, as Crane Brinton wrote in *The Anatomy of Revolution*, are almost always tiny, although they use the tools of modern propaganda to create the illusion of a mass following. As Brinton noted, "the impressive demonstrations the camera has recorded in Germany, Italy, Russia and China ought not to deceive the careful student of politics. Neither Communist, Nazi, nor Fascist victory over the moderates was achieved by the participation of the many; all were achieved by small, disciplined, principled, fanatical bodies."[24] These radicals, Brinton went on, "combine, in varying degrees, very high ideals and a complete contempt for the inhibitions and principles which serve most other men as ideals." They are, he said, "practical men unfettered by common sense, Machiavellians in the service of the Beautiful and the Good."[25] And once they are in power, "there is no more finicky regard for the liberties of the individual or for the forms of legality. The extremists, after clamoring for liberty and toleration while they were in opposition, turn very authoritarian when they reach power." [26]

Traditional evangelicals, those who come out of Billy Graham's mold, are not necessarily comfortable with the direction taken by the dominionists. And the multitude of churches, denominations and groups that do lend their support in varying degrees to this new movement are diverse and often antagonistic. While right-wing Catholics have joined forces with the movement, many of the movement's Protestant leaders, including D. James Kennedy, disdainfully label the Catholic Church a "cult." [27] These variances are held in check by the shared drive for political control, but the disputes simmer beneath the surface, threatening to tear apart the fragile coalitions. And those few evangelicals who challenge the dominionist drive for power are ruthlessly thrust aside, as the purges of the old guard within the Southern Baptist Convention three decades ago illustrate.

It is difficult to write in broad sweeps about this mass movement and detail these conflicts, since there are innumerable differences not only among groups but among believers. In the megachurches, there are worshippers and preachers who focus exclusively on the gospel of prosperity—centered on the belief that God wants Christians to be rich and successful—and who have little interest in politics. There are strict fundamentalists who view charismatics—those who speak in tongues—as Satan worshippers. There are small clusters of left-wing evangelicals, such as Jim Wallis's Sojourner movement and Ron Sider's Evangelicals for Social Action, who believe the Bible to be the literal word of God but embrace social activism and left-wing politics. There are evangelicals who focus more on what they can do in their communities as Christians than on what God's army can do to change the course of American history. And there are old-style evangelists, such as Luis Palau, who still tell Christians to keep their hands clean of politics, get right with Jesus and focus on spiritual and moral renewal.

But within this mass of divergent, fractious and varied groups is this core group of powerful Christian dominionists who have latched on to the despair, isolation, disconnectedness and fear that drives many people into these churches. Christian dominionist leaders have harnessed these discontents to further a frightening political agenda. If they do not have the active support of all in the evangelical churches, they often have their sympathy. They can count on the passive support of huge numbers of Christians, even if many of these Christians may not fully share dominionism's fierce utopian vision, fanaticism or ruthlessness. The appeal of the movement lies in the high ideals its radicals preach, the promise of a moral, Christian nation, the promise of a renewal. Its darker aims—seen in calls for widespread repression of nonbelievers; frequent use of the death penalty; illegalization of abortion, even in case of rape and incest; and the dismantling of public education—will, if achieved, alienate many who support them. But this combination of a disciplined, well-financed radical core and tens of millions of Americans who, discontent and anxious, yearn for a vague, revitalized "Christian nation," is a potent new force in American politics. Dominionists wait only for a fiscal, social or political crisis, a moment of upheaval in the form of an economic meltdown or another terrorist strike on American soil, to move to reconfigure the political system. Such a crisis could unleash a public clamor for drastic new national security measures and draconian reforms to safeguard the nation. Widespread discontent and fear, stoked and manipulated by dominionists and their sympathizers, could be used by these radicals to sweep aside the objections of beleaguered moderates in Congress and the courts, those clinging to a bankrupt and discredited liberalism, to establish an American theocracy, a Christian fascism.

The movement has sanctified a ruthless unfettered capitalism. In an essay in *Harper's* magazine titled "The Spirit of Disobedience: An Invitation to Resistance," Curtis White argued that "it is capitalism that now most defines our national character, not

Christianity or the Enlightenment." Although the values of capitalism are antithetical to Christ's vision and the Enlightenment ethic of Kant, the gospel of prosperity—which preaches that Jesus wants us all to be rich and powerful and the government to get out of the way—has formulated a belief system that delights corporate America. Corporations such as Tyson Foods—which has placed 128 part-time chaplains, nearly all evangelicals or fundamentalists, in 78 plants across the country—along with Purdue, Wal-Mart, and Sam's Wholesale, to name a few, are huge financial backers of the movement.

White concludes that "ours is a culture in which death has taken refuge in a legality that is supported by both reasonable liberals and Christian conservatives." This "legality" makes the systematic exploitation of human workers—paying less than living wages, while failing to provide adequate health care and retirement plans—simply a "part of our heritage of freedom." White goes on to excoriate our nationalist triumphalism and our unleashing of "the most fantastically destructive military power" the world has ever known in the course of "protecting and pursuing freedom." Among the resultant diseases of culture, he lists the "grotesque violence of video games and Hollywood movies," the "legality of abortions [which] at times covers over an attitude toward human life that subjects life to the low logic of efficiency and convenience," meaningless work, mindless consumerism, a distorted sense of time, housing developments where houses are "coffins" and neighborhoods are "shared cemeteries" and, "perhaps most destructively, the legality of property rights [which] condemns nature itself to annihilation even as we call it the freedom to pursue personal property."[28]

The power brokers in the radical Christian Right have already moved from the fringes of society to the executive branch, the House of Representatives, the Senate and the courts. The movement has seized control of the Republican Party. Christian fundamentalists now hold a majority of seats in 36 percent of all

Republican Party state committees, or 18 of 50 states, along with large minorities in the remaining states. Forty-five senators and 186 members of the House of Representatives earned approval ratings of 80 to 100 percent from the three most influential Christian Right advocacy groups: the Christian Coalition, Eagle Forum, and Family Resource Council.[29] Tom Coburn, elected in 2004 as senator from Oklahoma, called for a ban on abortion in his campaign, going so far as to call for the death penalty for doctors who carry out abortions once the ban went into place. Senator John Thune is a creationist. Jim DeMint, senator from South Carolina, wants to ban single mothers from teaching in schools.[30] The 2004 Election Day exit polls found that 23 percent of voters identified themselves as evangelical Christians; Bush won 78 percent of their vote. A plurality of voters said that the most important issue in the campaign had been "moral values."[31]

The Bush administration has steadily diverted billions of dollars of taxpayer money from secular and governmental social-service organizations to faith-based organizations, bankrolling churches and organizations that seek to dismantle American democracy and create a theocratic state.[32] The role of education and social-welfare agencies is being supplanted by these churches, nearly all of them evangelical, and the wall between church and state is being disassembled. These groups can and usually do discriminate by refusing to hire gays and lesbians, people of other faiths and those who do not embrace their strict version of Christianity. Christian clinics that treat addictions or do pregnancy counseling (usually with the aim of preventing abortion) do not have to hire trained counselors or therapists. The only requirement of a new hire is usually that he or she be a "Bible-believing Christian." In fiscal year 2003, faith-based organizations received 8.1 percent of the competitive social-service grant budget.[33] In fiscal year 2004, faith-based organizations received $2.005 billion in funding—10.3 percent of federal competitive service grants.[34, 35] The federal government awarded more than $2.15 billion in competitive social-service grants to faith-based organizations in fiscal year 2005, 11 percent of all federal competitive service grants.[36] Faith-based organizations are consistently winning a larger portion of federal social-service funding, a trend that has tremendous social and political consequences if it continues. The Bush administration has spent more than $1 billion on chastity programs alone. Thirty percent of American schools with sex-education programs teach abstinence only. Not only is there little accountability, not only are these organizations allowed to practice discriminatory hiring practices, but also, as research shows, while abstinence-only programs can sometimes get teenagers to delay sex, they also leave young men and women unprepared for sexual relations, resulting in higher rates of teenage pregnancy and sexually transmitted diseases.

It is perhaps telling that our closest allies in the United Nations on issues dealing with reproductive rights, one of the few issues where we cooperate with other nations, are Islamic states such as Iran. But then the Christian Right and radical Islamists, although locked in a holy war, increasingly mirror each other. They share the same obsessions. They do not tolerate other forms of belief or disbelief. They are at war with artistic and cultural expression. They seek to silence the media. They call for the subjugation of women. They promote severe sexual repression, and they seek to express themselves through violence.

Members of the Christian Right who have been elected to powerful political offices have worked in several instances to exclude opponents and manipulate vote counts. The current Republican candidate for governor of Ohio, Kenneth Blackwell, a stalwart of the Christian Right, was the secretary of state for Ohio as well as the co-chair of the state's Committee to Re-Elect George Bush during the last presidential election. Blackwell, as secretary of state, oversaw the administering of the 2004 presidential elections in Ohio. He handled all complaints of irregularities. He attempted to get the state to hand over all election polling to Diebold Election Systems, a subsidiary of Diebold Incorporated, a firm that makes electronic voting machines and has close ties with the Bush administration. By the time of the elections he had managed to ensure that Diebold ran the machines in 35 counties. In an August 14, 2003, fund-raising letter, Walden O'Dell, CEO of Diebold, told Republicans that he was "committed to helping Ohio deliver its electoral votes to the president next year."[37] O'Dell and other Diebold executives and board members are supporters of and donors to the Republican Party.[38]

Blackwell, an African American, oversaw a voting system in which African Americans, who vote primarily Democratic in national elections, found polling stations in their districts, especially in heavily Democratic areas such as Cleveland, grossly understaffed. There were in these polling stations long lines with delays that sometimes lasted as long as 10 hours, sending many potential voters home in frustration. Aggressive poll monitors questioned and often disqualified new voters because of what the monitors claimed was improper registration. Blackwell banned photographers and reporters from polling places, making irregularities and harassment harder to document. The Diebold machines recorded record high turnouts—124 percent in one of the precincts—where Bush won overwhelming victories and low voter turnout in districts that went for Democratic Senator John Kerry.[39] Kerry campaign workers reported numerous irregularities, including the discovery of a machine that diverted votes from Kerry to Bush. Ray Beckerman, part of the Kerry campaign, said that he found that touch-screen voting machines in Youngstown were registering "George W. Bush" when people pressed "John F. Kerry" during the entire day. Although he reported the glitch shortly after the polls opened, it was not fixed. All reports of irregularities, including complaints about precincts where votes were counted without the presence of election monitors, passed through Blackwell's office.[40] Nothing was ever done. Indeed, Blackwell went on after the elections to issue to county boards of elections a demand that voter registration forms be printed on "white, uncoated paper of not less than 80-pound text weight," a heavy card-like stock. This allowed his office to disqualify registrations because the paper was not thick enough.[41] The ruling has, his critics say, jeopardized the right of tens of thousands of would-be voters to participate in the next elections. As the Christian Right gains control of state offices throughout the country, it is being tarred by opponents with similar accusations.

Followers in the movement are locked within closed systems of information and indoctrination that cater to their hates and prejudices. Tens of millions of Americans rely exclusively on Christian broadcasters for their news, health, entertainment and devotional programs. These followers have been organized into disciplined and powerful voting blocs. They attend churches that during election time are little more than local headquarters for the Republican Party and during the rest of the year demand nearly all of their social, religious and recreational time. These believers are encased in a hermetic world. There is no questioning or dissent. There are anywhere from 1.1 million to 2.1 million children, nearly all evangelicals, now being home-schooled.[42] These children are not challenged with ideas or research that conflict with their biblical worldview. Evolution is not taught. God created the world in six days. America, they are told, was founded as a Christian nation and secular humanists are working to destroy the Christian nation. These young men and women are often funneled into Christian colleges and universities, such as Jerry Falwell's Liberty University, Pat Robertson's Regent University, and a host of other schools such as Patrick Henry University. They are taught, in short, to obey. They are discouraged from critical analysis, questioning and independent thought. And they believe, by the time they are done, a host of myths designed to destroy the open, pluralist society.

Most of America's fundamentalist and evangelical churches are led by pastors who peddle this non-reality-based belief system, one that embraces magic, the fiction of a "Christian nation" in need of revitalization, and dark, terrifying apocalyptic visions. They preach about the coming world war, drawing their visions from the Book of Daniel and the Book of Revelation. They preach that at the end of history Christians will dominate the earth and that all nonbelievers, including those who are not sufficiently Christian, will be cast into torment and outer darkness. They call for the destruction of whole cultures, nations and religions, those they have defined as the enemies of God.

As American history and the fundamentalist movement itself have changed, so have the objects of fundamentalist hatred. Believers were told a few decades ago that communists were behind the civil-rights movement, the antiwar movement and liberal groups such as the ACLU. They were racist and intolerant of African Americans, Jews and Catholics. Now the battle against communism has been reconfigured. The seat of Satan is no longer in the Kremlin. It has been assumed by individuals and institutions promoting a rival religion called "secular humanism." The obsession with the evils of secular humanism would be laughable if it were not such an effective scare tactic. The only organized movement of secular humanists who call themselves by that name is the American Humanist Association (AHA), which has about 5,000 members and whose credo was published in the 1933 *Humanist Manifesto I* and the 1973 *Humanist Manifesto II*. Its *Humanist Magazine* has a minuscule circulation. In terms of influence, as Barbara Parker and Christy Macy wrote, "these humanists rank with militant vegetarians and agrarian anarchists, and were about as well known—until the Religious Right set out to make them famous."[43] But it is not important who is fingered as Satan's agent, as long as the wild conspiracy theories and paranoia are stoked by an array of duplicitous, phantom enemies that lurk behind the scenes of public school boards or the media. As the movement reaches out to the African American churches and right-wing Catholics, it has exchanged old hatreds for new ones, preferring now to demonize gays, liberals, immigrants, Muslims and others as forces beholden to the Antichrist while painting themselves as the heirs of the civil-rights movement. The movement is fueled by the fear of powerful external and internal enemies whose duplicity and cunning is constantly at work. These phantom enemies serve to keep believers afraid and in a heightened state of alert, ready to support repressive measures against all who do not embrace the movement. But this tactic has required the airbrushing out of past racist creeds—an effort that, sometime after 1970, saw Jerry Falwell recall all copies of his earlier sermons warning against integration and the evils of the black race. The only sermon left in print from the 1960s is called "Ministers and Marchers." In the sermon Falwell angrily denounces preachers who engage in politics, specifically those who support the civil-rights movement. The effort to erase the past, to distort truth and reinvent himself as a past supporter of civil rights, is a frightening example of how, if a lie is broadcast long enough and loud enough, it becomes true. Distortions and lies permeate the movement, which fends off criticism by encasing its followers in closed information systems and wrapping itself in Christian vestments and the American flag.

The movement is marked not only by its obsessions with conspiracy theories, magic, sexual repression, paranoia and death, but also by its infatuation with apocalyptic violence and military force. On its outer fringes are collections of odd messianic warriors, those ready to fight and die for Christ. These include American Veterans in Domestic Defense, a Texas group that transported former Alabama Supreme Court justice Roy Moore's 2.6-ton 10 Commandment monument by truck around the country. Moore, who graduated from the U.S. military academy at West Point, lost his job as chief justice of the Alabama Supreme Court after he defied a judge's order to remove his monument from the Montgomery judicial building. He and his monument instantly became celebrities for those preaching that Christians were under siege, that there was an organized effort to persecute all who upheld God's law. These carefully cultivated feelings of persecution foster a permanent state of crisis, a deep paranoia and fear, and they make it easier to call for violence—always, of course, as a form of self-defense. It turns all outside the movement into enemies: even those who appear benign, the believer is warned, seek to destroy Christians. There are an array of obscure, shadowy paramilitary groups, such as Christian Identity, the members of which, emboldened by the rhetoric of the movement, believe they will one day fight a religious war. Military leaders who stoke this belief in a holy war are lionized. After leading American troops into battle against a Somalian warlord, General William Boykin announced: "I knew my God was bigger than his. I knew that my God was a real God and his God was an idol." General Boykin belongs to a small group called the Faith Force Multiplier, whose members apply military principles to evangelism in a manifesto summoning warriors "to the spiritual warfare for souls." Boykin, rather than being reprimanded for his inflammatory rhetoric, was promoted to the position of deputy undersecretary of defense for intelligence. He believes America is engaged in a holy war as a "Christian nation" battling Satan and that America's Muslim adversaries will be defeated "only if we come against them in the name of Jesus."[44]

The Christian Right is deeply involved in the building of America's first modern mercenary army. Erik Prince is the secretive, mega-millionaire, right-wing Christian founder of Blackwater, the private security firm that has built a formidable mercenary force in Iraq. He champions his company as a patriotic extension of the U.S. military. His employees, in an act as cynical as it is dishonest, take an oath of loyalty to the Constitution. There are an estimated 20,000 to 30,000 armed security contractors working in Iraq, although there are no official figures and some estimates run much higher. Security contractors are not counted as part of the coalition forces. When the number of private mercenary fighters is added to other civilian military "contractors" who carry out logistical support activities such as food preparation and transport, the number rises to about 126,000.

"We got 126,000 contractors over there, some of them making more than the secretary of defense," said House defense appropriations subcommittee Chairman John Murtha (D., Pa.). "How in the hell do you justify that?"

The creation of this mercenary force, empowered by the apocalyptic rhetoric of the Christian Right, is giving rise to a Praetorian Guard. The Praetorian Guard in ancient Rome was a paramilitary force that defied legal constraints, made violence part of the political discourse, and eventually plunged the Empire into tyranny and despotism. Despotic movements need paramilitary forces that operate outside the law, forces that sow fear among potential opponents and silence those branded as traitors. Mercenary forces like Blackwater in Iraq already operate beyond civilian and military law. They are protected by a 2004 edict passed by American occupation authorities in Iraq that immunizes all civilian contractors in Iraq from prosecution.

American taxpayers have so far handed a staggering $4 billion to "armed security" companies in Iraq, according to House Oversight and Government Reform Committee Chairman Rep. Henry Waxman (D., Calif.). Tens of billions more have been paid to companies that provide logistical support. Rep. Jan Schakowsky (D., Ill.) of the House Intelligence Committee estimates that 40 cents of every dollar spent on the occupation has gone to war contractors. It is unlikely that any of these corporations will push for an early withdrawal. The occupation is too lucrative.

Blackwater, barely a decade old, has migrated from Iraq to set up operations in the United States and nine other countries. It trains Afghan security forces and has established a base a few miles from the Iranian border. The huge contracts from the Iraqi war—including $750 million from the State Department since 2004—have allowed Blackwater to amass a fleet of more than 20 aircraft, including helicopter gunships. Blackwater has also constructed the world's largest private military facility—a 7,000-acre compound near the Great Dismal Swamp of North Carolina—and opened a facility in Illinois ("Blackwater North"). Despite local opposition, it is moving ahead with plans to build another huge training base near San Diego. The company has also formed a private intelligence branch called "Total Intelligence."

Prince and his allies have built a mercenary army, paid for with government money, which operates without constitutional constraint. Blackwater fighters, heavily armed and wearing their trademark black uniforms, were contracted by the government at a cost of $ 240,000 a day to patrol the streets of New Orleans after Hurricane Katrina. They moved about the city in vehicles without license plates. This may be a grim taste of our future.

The term "contractor" deflects attention from the ominous rise of a mercenary army. Paramilitary forces have no place in a democratic state. These forces, protected and assisted by fellow ideologues in the police and military, could ruthlessly abolish what is left of our eroding democracy. War, with the huge profits it hands to corporations, and to right-wing interests that back the Christian Right, could become a permanent condition. And the thugs with automatic weapons, black uniforms and wraparound sunglasses who appeared on the streets in New Orleans could appear on our streets.

"Unlike police officers they are not trained in protecting constitutional rights," said Michael Ratner, the president of the Center for Constitutional Rights. "And unlike police officers or the military they have no system of accountability whether within their organization or outside it. These kind of paramilitary groups bring to mind Nazi Party brownshirts, functioning as an extrajudicial enforcement mechanism that can and does operate outside the law. The use of these paramilitary groups is an extremely dangerous threat to our rights."

The politicization of the military, the fostering of the belief that violence must be used to further a particular ideology rather than defend a democracy, was on display when Air Force and Army generals and colonels, filmed in uniform at the Pentagon, appeared in a promotional video distributed by the Christian Embassy, a radical Washington—based organization dedicated to building a "Christian America." Radical Christians now hold roughly 50 percent of chaplaincy appointments in the armed services and service academies, and increasingly use their positions to openly proselytize cadets and denigrate other religious faiths.

Dan Cooper, an undersecretary of veterans affairs, says in the Christian Embassy video that his weekly prayer sessions are "more important than doing the job." Major General Jack Catton says that his being an adviser to the Joint Chiefs of Staff is a "wonderful opportunity" to evangelize men and women setting defense policy. "My first priority is my faith," he says. "I think it's a huge impact. . . . You have many men and women who are seeking God's counsel and wisdom as they advise the chairman [of the Joint Chiefs] and the secretary of defense."

The group hosts weekly Bible sessions with senior officers, by its own count some 40 generals, and weekly prayer breakfasts each Wednesday from 7 to 7:50 a.m. in the executive dining room as well as numerous outreach events to, in the words of the organization, "share and sharpen one another in their quest to bridge the gap between faith and work."

Colonel Ralph Benson, a Pentagon chaplain, says in the video: "Christian Embassy is a blessing to the Washington area, a blessing to our capital; it's a blessing to our country. They are interceding on behalf of people all over the United States, talking to ambassadors, talking to people in the Congress, in the Senate, talking to people in the Pentagon, and being able to share the message of Jesus Christ in a very, very important time in our world [when we are] winning a worldwide war on terrorism. What more do we need than Christian people leading us and guiding us, so, they're needed in this hour."

Visions of a holy war at once terrify and delight followers.

Such visions peddle a bizarre spiritual Darwinism. True Christians will rise to heaven and be saved, and all lesser faiths and nonbelievers will be viciously destroyed by an angry God in an orgy of horrific, apocalyptic violence. The yearning for this final battle runs through the movement like an electric current. Christian Right firebrands employ the language of war, speak in the metaphors of battle, and paint graphic and chilling scenes of the violence and mayhem that will envelop the earth. War is the final aesthetic of the movement.

"Now, this revolution is not for the temperate," the Ohio pastor Rod Parsley shouted out to a crowd when I heard him speak in Washington in March of 2006. "This revolution—that's what it is—is not for the timid and the weak, but for the brave and strong, who step over the line out of their comfort zone and truly decide to become disciples of Christ. I'm talking about red-blooded men and women who don't have to be right, recognized, rewarded or regarded. . . . So my admonishment to you this morning is this. Sound the alarm. A spiritual invasion is taking place. The secular media never likes it when I say this, so let me say it twice," he says to laughter. "Man your battle stations! Ready your weapons! They say this rhetoric is so inciting. I came to incite a riot. I came to effect a divine disturbance in the heart and soul of the church. Man your battle stations. Ready your weapons. Lock and load!"

BattleCry, a Christian fundamentalist youth movement that has attracted as many as 25,000 people to Christian rock concerts in San Francisco, Philadelphia and Detroit, uses elaborate light shows, Hummers, ranks of Navy SEALs and the imagery and rhetoric of battle to pound home its message. Ron Luce, who runs it, exhorts the young Christians to defeat the secular forces around them. "This is war," he has said. "And Jesus invites us to get into the action, telling us that the violent—the 'forceful' ones—will lay hold of the kingdom." The rock band Delirious, which played in the Philadelphia gathering, pounded out a song with the words: "We're an army of God and we're ready to die. . . . Let's paint this

big ol' town red. . . . We see nothing but the blood of Jesus. . . ."
The lyrics were projected on large screens so some 17,000 partici-
pants could sing along. The crowd in the Wachovia sports stadium
shouted in unison: "We are warriors!" [45]

The use of elaborate spectacle to channel and shape the passions of mass followers is a staple of totalitarian movements. It
gives to young adherents the raw material for their interior lives,
for love and hate, joy and sorrow, excitement and belonging. It imparts the illusion of personal empowerment. It creates comradeship
and solidarity, possible only as long as those within the movement
do not defy the collective emotions of the crowd and willingly de-
vote themselves to the communal objective, in this case creating a
Christian America and defeating those who stand in the way. It
gives meaning and purpose to life, turning a mundane existence
into an epic battle against forces of darkness, forces out to crush all
that is good and pure in America. And it is very hard for the voices
of moderation to compete, for these spectacles work to shut down
individual conscience and reflection. They give to adherents a permissiveness, a rhetorical license to engage in acts of violence that
are normally taboo in a democratic society. It becomes permissible
to hate. The crowds are wrapped in the seductive language of violence, which soon enough leads to acts of real violence.

Apocalyptic visions inspire genocidal killers who glorify violence as the mechanism that will lead to the end of history. Such
visions nourished the butchers who led the Inquisition and the
Crusades, as well as the conquistadores who swept through the
Americas hastily converting en masse native populations and then
exterminating them. The Puritans, who hoped to create a theocratic state, believed that Satan ruled the wilderness surrounding
their settlements. They believed that God had called them to cast
Satan out of this wilderness to create a promised land. That divine
command sanctioned the removal or slaughter of Native Americans. This hubris fed the deadly doctrine of Manifest Destiny.
Similar apocalyptic visions of a world cleansed through violence

and extermination nourished the Nazis, the Stalinists who consigned tens of thousands of Ukrainians to starvation and death, the torturers in the clandestine prisons in Argentina during the Dirty War, and the Serbian thugs with heavy machine guns and wraparound sunglasses who stood over the bodies of Muslims they had slain in the smoking ruins of Bosnian villages.

The ecstatic belief in the cleansing power of apocalyptic violence does not recognize the right of the victims to self-preservation or self-defense. It does not admit them into a moral universe where they have a criminal's right to be punished and rehabilitated. They are seen instead through this poisonous lens as pollutants, viruses, mutations that must be eradicated to halt further infection and degeneration within society and usher in utopia. This sacred violence—whether it arises from the Bible, Serbian nationalism, the dream of a classless society, or the goal of a world where all "subhumans" are eradicated—allows its perpetrators and henchmen to avoid moral responsibility for their crimes. The brutality they carry out is sanctified, an expression of not human volition but divine wrath. The victims, in a final irony, are considered responsible for their suffering and destruction. They are to blame because, in the eyes of the dominionists, they have defied God.

Those who promise to cleanse the world through sacred violence, to relieve anxiety over moral pollution by building mounds of corpses, always appeal to our noblest sentiments, our highest virtues, our capacity for self-sacrifice and our utopian visions of a purified life. It is this coupling of fantastic hope and profound despair—dreams of peace and light and reigns of terror, self-sacrifice and mass murder—that frees the consciences of those who call for and carry out the eradication of fellow human beings in the name of God.

Societies that embrace apocalyptic visions and seek through sacred violence to implement them commit collective suicide. When Jerry Falwell and Pat Robertson, as they do, sanction preemptive nuclear strikes against those they condemn as the enemies of God, they fuel the passions of terrorists driven by the same vision of a world cleansed and purified through apocalyptic violence. They lead us closer and closer toward our own annihilation, in the delusion that once the dogs of war, even nuclear war, are unleashed, God will protect Christians; that hundreds of millions will die, but because Christians have been blessed they alone will rise in triumph from the ash heap. Those who seek to do us harm will soon have in their hands cruder versions of the apocalyptic weapons we possess: dirty bombs and chemical or biological agents. Those who fervently wish for, indeed, seek to hasten the apocalypse and the end of time, who believe they will be lifted up into the sky by a returning Jesus, force us all to kneel before the god of death.

If this mass movement succeeds, it will do so not simply because of its ruthlessness and mendacity, its callous manipulation of the people it lures into its arms, many of whom live on the margins of American society. It will succeed because of the moral failure of those, including Christians, who understand the intent of the radicals yet fail to confront them, those who treat this mass movement as if it were another legitimate player in an open society. The leading American institutions tasked with defending tolerance and liberty—from the mainstream churches to the great research universities, to the Democratic Party and the media—have failed the country. This is the awful paradox of tolerance. There arise moments when those who would destroy the tolerance that makes an open society possible should no longer be tolerated. They must be held accountable by institutions that maintain the free exchange of ideas and liberty. The radical Christian Right must be forced to include other points of view to counter their hate talk in their own broadcasts, watched by tens of millions of Americans. They must be denied the right to demonize whole segments of American society, saying they are manipulated by Satan and worthy only of conversion or eradication. They must be made to treat their opponents with respect and acknowledge the right of a fair hearing even as they exercise their own freedom to disagree with their opponents. Passivity in the face of the rise of the Christian Right threatens the democratic state. And the movement has targeted the last remaining obstacles to its systems of indoctrination, mounting a fierce campaign to defeat hate-crime legislation, fearing the courts could apply it to them as they spew hate talk over the radio, television and Internet. Despotic movements harness the power of modern communications to keep their followers locked in closed systems. If this long, steady poisoning of civil discourse within these closed information systems is not challenged, if this movement continues to teach neighbor to hate neighbor, if its followers remain convinced that cataclysmic violence offers a solution to their own ills and the ills of the world, civil society in America will collapse.

"Hope has two beautiful daughters," Augustine wrote. "Their names are anger and courage; anger at the way things are, and courage to see that they do not remain the way they are." [46]

Anger, when directed against movements that would abuse the weak, preach bigotry and injustice, trample the poor, crush dissent and impose a religious tyranny, is a blessing. Read the biblical prophets in First and Second Isaiah, Jeremiah, Micah and Amos. Liberal institutions, seeing tolerance as the highest virtue, tolerate the intolerant. They swallow the hate talk that calls for the destruction of nonbelievers. Mainstream believers have often come to the comfortable conclusion that any form of announced religiosity is acceptable, that heretics do not exist.

The mainstream churches stumble along, congregations often mumbling creeds they no longer believe, trying to peddle a fuzzy, feel-good theology that can distort and ignore the darker visions in the Bible as egregiously as the Christian Right does. The Christian Right understands the ills of American society even as it exploits these ills to plunge us into tyranny. Its leaders grasp the endemic hollowness, timidity and hypocrisy of the liberal churches. The Christian Right attacks "cultural relativism," the creed that there is no absolute good and that all value systems have equal merit—

even as it benefits, in a final irony, from the passivity of people who tolerate it in the name of cultural relativism.

The most potent opposition to the movement may come from within the evangelical tradition. The radical fundamentalist movement must fear these Christians, who have remained loyal to the core values of the Gospel, who delineate between right and wrong, who are willing to be vilified and attacked in the name of a higher good and who have the courage to fight back. Most liberals, the movement has figured out, will stand complacently to be sheared like sheep, attempting to open dialogues and reaching out to those who spit venom in their faces.

Radical Christian dominionists have no religious legitimacy. They are manipulating Christianity, and millions of sincere believers, to build a frightening political mass movement with many similarities with other mass movements, from fascism to communism to the ethnic nationalist parties in the former Yugoslavia. It shares with these movements an inability to cope with ambiguity, doubt and uncertainty. It creates its own "truth." It embraces a world of miracles and signs and removes followers from a rational, reality-based world. It condemns self-criticism and debate as apostasy. It places a premium on action and finds its final aesthetic in war and apocalyptic violence.

The pain, the dislocation, alienation, suffering and despair that led millions of Americans into the movement are real. Many Americans are striking back at a culture they blame for the debacle of their lives. The democratic traditions and the values of the Enlightenment, they believe, have betrayed them. They speak of numbness, an inability to feel pain or joy or love, a vast emptiness, a frightening loneliness and loss of control. The rational, liberal world of personal freedoms and choice lured many of these people into one snake pit after another. And liberal democratic society, for most, stood by passively as their communities, families and lives splintered and self-destructed.

These believers have abandoned, in this despair, their trust and belief in the world of science, law and rationality. They eschew personal choice and freedom. They have replaced the world that has failed them with a new, glorious world filled with prophets and mystical signs. They believe in a creator who performs miracles for them, speaks directly to them and guides their lives, as well as the destiny of America. They are utopians who have found rigid, clearly defined moral edicts, rights and wrongs, to guide them in life and in politics. And they are terrified of losing this new, mystical world of signs, wonders and moral certitude, of returning to the old world of despair. They see criticism of their belief system, whether from scientists or judges, as vicious attempts by Satan to lure them back into the morass. The split in America, rather than simply economic, is between those who embrace reason, who function in the real world of cause and effect, and those who, numbed by isolation and despair, now seek meaning in a mythical world of intuition, a world that is no longer reality-based, a world of magic.

Those in the movement now fight, fueled by the rage of the dispossessed, to crush and silence the reality-based world. The dominionist movement is the response of people trapped in a deformed, fragmented and disoriented culture that has become callous and unforgiving, a culture that has too often failed to provide the belonging, care and purpose that make life bearable, a culture that, as many in the movement like to say, has become "a culture of death." The new utopians are not always wrong in their critique of American society. But what they have set out to create is far, far worse than what we endure. What is happening in America is revolutionary. A group of religious utopians, with the sympathy and support of tens of millions of Americans, are slowly dismantling democratic institutions to establish a religious tyranny, the springboard to an American fascism.

CHAPTER TWO

The Culture of Despair

They attacked liberalism because it seemed to them the principal premise of modern society; everything they dreaded seemed to spring from it: the bourgeois life, Manchesterism, materialism, parliament and the parties, the lack of political leadership. Even more, they sensed in liberalism the source of all their inner sufferings. Theirs was a resentment of loneliness; their one desire was for a new faith, a new community of believers, a world with fixed standards and no doubts, a new national religion that would bind all Germans together. All this, liberalism denied. Hence, they hated liberalism, blamed it for making outcasts of them, for uprooting them from their imaginary past, and from their faith.

—*Fritz Stern*, The Politics of Cultural Despair:
A Study in the Rise of the Germanic Ideology[1]

S tories of rage are first stories of despair.

Jeniece Learned stands amid a crowd of earnest-looking men and women, many with small gold crosses in the lapels of their jackets or around their necks, in a hotel lobby in Valley Forge, Pennsylvania. She has an easy smile and a thick mane of black, shoulder-length hair. She is carrying a booklet called *Ringing in a Culture of Life*. The booklet has the schedule of the two-day event she is attending organized by the Pennsylvania Pro-Life Federation. The event, says the booklet, is "dedicated to the 46 million children who have died from legal abortions since 1973 and the mothers and fathers who mourn their loss."

Learned, who drove five hours from a town outside of Youngstown, Ohio, was raised Jewish. She wears a gold Star of

David around her neck with a Christian cross inset in the middle of the design. She stood up in one of the morning sessions, attended by about 300 people, most of them women, when the speaker, Alveda King, niece of Dr. Martin Luther King Jr., asked if there were any "postabortive" women present. Learned runs a small pregnancy counseling clinic called Pregnancy Services of Western Pennsylvania in Sharon, where she tries to talk young girls and women, most of them poor, out of abortions. She speaks in local public schools, promoting sexual abstinence rather than birth control as the only acceptable form of contraception. And in the fight against abortion and in her conversion, she has found a structure, purpose and meaning that previously eluded her.

Her life, before she was saved, was chaotic and painful. Her childhood was stolen from her. She says she was sexually abused by a family member. Her father left her mother when Learned was 12. She says her mother periodically woke her and her younger sister and two younger brothers in the middle of the night to flee landlords who wanted back rent. The children were bundled into the car and driven in darkness to a strange apartment in another town. Her mother worked nights and weekends as a bartender. Learned, the oldest, often had to run the home.

"There was a lot of fighting," she says. "I remember my dad hitting my mom one time and him going to jail. I don't have a lot of memories, mind you, before eighth grade because of the sexual abuse. When my dad divorced my mom, he divorced us, too."

Learned said she repressed and contained her emotions. She remembers sitting bewildered at a meal with the family member who had molested her the night before and wondering why he treated her with ice-cold disdain. Her younger sister, who was sexually abused by another member of the family, eventually committed suicide as an adult, something Learned also considered. Suicide seemed, as she grew into adulthood, a release, the only road out of the hell of her existence.

"My grandfather committed suicide, close family members tried suicide," she says. "In my family, there was no hope. The only way to solve problems when they got bad was to end your life.

"My family put the 'dys' in 'function,'" she adds. "I had relatives switching husbands and wives with other couples. I am so thankful that God moved me 3,000 miles away. I am so thankful He pulled me out of that. Because I am so glad my children . . . you know, when I was pregnant with my daughter, I said, 'God, just break the chains . . . just break the chains.' And He has. My children have no idea about the dysfunction I lived through. I really truly believe that Satan got a hold of my family early on. I feel like Satan had this huge grip."

The instability and abuse, the constant moving, saw her retreat into herself. By the time she graduated she had attended three high schools. She was an angry young woman. At 15 she became pregnant. She had an abortion, using the name of her school bus driver to get into the clinic.

"Between being sexually abused, my parents being divorced, my mom being gone all the time, my brothers giving my mom such a hard time, my mother was always in a bad mood," she says. "I was criticized and put down a lot. I was never good enough. Things were never good enough. The only time I got love was when my mom was taking me to these photo shoots and beauty pageants, and really pushing modeling. And the only time I got love from my mom is when I would win beauty pageants."

Learned moved out of the house before she was 18, drifted and ended up in Beverly Hills, working nights in a strip club wearing a leotard and French corset. At one point she was homeless and called a family member for a place to stay. On the ride over, driving her 1968 Volkswagen Beetle, she thought of veering it over the edge of the raised highway. On the second night at the house, the family member came into her room and tried to molest her. She fled to a friend's apartment. It was not long after that she married her husband Rod and found Jesus, but the trauma of her past continued to plague her.

"I started having some major sexual dysfunctions," she says. "A lot of flashbacks were coming back. A lot of memories that I did not remember were coming back. I was really struggling. And here I am newly married. I didn't want any part of it. There would be times when Rod and I would try to be intimate and I would just fall apart. And he didn't know what to do."

She was taking classes at Pacific Christian College when she and Rod were living in Orange County. During a chapel service an antiabortion group, Living Alternative, showed a film called *The Silent Scream*.

"You see in this movie this baby backing up trying to get away from this suction tube," she says. "And its mouth is open, and it is like this baby is screaming. I flipped out. It was at that moment that God just took this veil that I had over my eyes for the last eight years. I couldn't breathe. I was hyperventilating. I ran outside. One of the girls followed me from Living Alternative. And she said, 'Did you commit your life to Christ?' And I said, 'I did.' And she said, 'Did you ask for your forgiveness of sins?' And I said, 'I did.' And she goes, 'Does that mean all your sins, or does that mean some of them?' And I said, 'I guess it means all of them.' So she said, 'Basically, you are thinking God hasn't forgiven you for your abortion because that is a worse sin than any of your other sins that you have done.'"

The film brought her into the fight to make abortion illegal. Her activism became atonement for her own abortion. She struggled with depression after she gave birth to Rachel. When she came home from the hospital she was unable to care for her infant. She thought she saw an eight-year-old boy standing next to her bed. It was, she is sure, the image of the son she had murdered.

"I started crying and asking God over and over again to forgive me," she says. "I had murdered His child. I asked Him to forgive me over and over again. It was just incredible. I was possessed.

On the fourth day I remember hearing God's voice: 'I have your baby, now get up!' It was the most incredibly freeing and peaceful moment. I got up and I showered and I ate. I just knew it was God's voice."

The combination of abuse, shame and guilt, as well as the depression and despair, marked a period of her life that she wants to forget. The certitude of her new life is a comfort. It is a life of moral absolutes. It is a battle against a culture she despises. Its rigidity—its sanctification of hatred for those who would "murder" the unborn or contaminate America with the godless creed of secular humanism—brings with it feelings of righteousness and virtue. Her faith gives her an emotional grounding and a vent for her anger. Embracing the Christian community means destroying competing communities. The power of her yearning for inclusion, for those who surrender to Jesus, is matched by the power of her destructive fury. She is fighting for something good and against something evil, and it is an evil she knows intimately.

The stories many in this movement tell are stories of failure—personal, communal and sometimes economic. They are stories of public and private institutions that are increasingly distant and irrelevant, stories of loneliness and abuse. Isolation, the plague of the modern industrial society, has torn apart networks of extended families and communities. It has empowered this new movement of dreamers, who bombard the airwaves with an idealistic and religious utopianism that promises, through apocalyptic purification, to eradicate the old, sinful world and fill the resulting emptiness with a new world where time stops and all problems are solved. The movement promises to followers what many never had: a stable home and family, a loving community, fixed moral standards, financial and personal success and an abolition of uncertainty and doubt. It offers a religious vision that will make fragmented, lost individuals whole. It provides moral clarity. It also promises to exterminate, in one final, apocalyptic battle, the forces many of these people blame for their despair. Learned, through her faith, put her life back together. And she waits, like many believers, for a day when the forces that nearly destroyed her life are vanquished and rendered impotent.

Learned lives in the nation's rust belt. The flight of manufacturing jobs has turned most of the old steel mill towns around her into wastelands of poverty and urban decay. The days when steelworkers could make middle-class salaries are a distant and cherished memory. She lives amid America's vast and growing class of dispossessed, tens of millions of working poor, 30 million of whom make less than $8.70 an hour, the official poverty level for a family of four. Most economists contend that it takes at least twice this rate of pay to provide basic necessities to a family. These low-wage jobs, which come without benefits or job security, have meant billions in profits for the corporations that no longer feel the pressure or the need to take care of their workers. Learned and her neighbors have watched helplessly as jobs are automated or outsourced. After 1970, when manufacturers closed huge plants and moved them abroad, the real earning power of wages for men, who once could bring in enough income for their households, stopped rising. Economics professors Peter Gottschalk of Boston College and Sheldon Danziger of the University of Michigan found that about half of those whose family income ranked in the bottom 20 percent in 1968 were in the same group in 1991. Of those who moved up, nearly three-quarters still remained below the median income.[2]

The loss of manufacturing jobs has dealt a body blow to the American middle class. Manufacturing jobs accounted for 53 percent of the economy in 1965; by 1988, they accounted for 39 percent. By 2004 they accounted for 9 percent. This is the first time since the industrial revolution that less than 10 percent of the American workforce is employed in manufacturing.[3] There has been a loss of nearly 3 million manufacturing jobs nationwide since mid-2000.[4] The forced retreat by workers into the service sector, into jobs that pay little more than the minimum wage, has left many households desperate. Laborers in the steel mills and manufacturing plants once made an average of $51,000 annually. Those who have moved into the service sector now make $16,000 in the leisure and hospitality sector, $33,000 in health care, or $39,000 in construction. In 2004, average employee compensation in the United States fell for the first time in 14 years.[5] Between 2000 and 2004, Ohio lost a quarter of a million jobs. Cleveland became the nation's poorest big city, and young people are fleeing the state in massive numbers to find work.

The bleakness of life in Ohio exposes the myth peddled by the Christian Right about the American heartland: that here alone are family values and piety cherished, nurtured and protected. The so-called red states, which vote Republican and have large evangelical populations, have higher rates of murder, illegitimacy and teenage births than the so-called blue states, which vote Democrat and have kept the evangelicals at bay. The lowest divorce rates tend to be found in blue states as well as in the Northeast and upper Midwest. The state with the lowest divorce rate is Massachusetts, a state singled out by televangelists because of its liberal politicians and legalization of same-sex marriage. In 2003, Massachusetts had a divorce rate of 5.7 divorces per 1,000 married people, compared with 10.8 in Kentucky, 11.1 in Mississippi and 12.7 in Arkansas.[6]

Couples in former manufacturing states such as Ohio have to find two jobs to survive. The economic catastrophe has been accompanied by the erosion in federal and state assistance programs, the cutting of funds to elementary and secondary education, the reduction in assistance to women through the Women, Infants and Children Supplemental Nutrition Program, along with reductions in programs such as Head Start and federal programs to assist low-income families, elderly people, and people with disabilities who once turned to the government for rental assistance.[7] Federal abandonment of the destitute came at a time when these communities most needed support. As the years passed and the future began to look as bleak as the present, this despair morphed into rage. Learned has watched families unravel under the pressure. Domestic violence, alcoholism and drug abuse run like plagues through the depressed pockets around her community. And Ohio, seething, has more white nationalist groups than any state in the Midwest (73), according to the Center for New Community in Chicago.[8]

It is hard to argue that Learned, or any other convert, is typical. The movement cuts across class and economic lines. Not all who fall into despair turn to the Christian Right. Learned focuses her life on the fight against abortion rather than on campaigns to elect Christian candidates. She is not particularly political. But she knows intimately the despair that is the fuel of the movement. While this despair manifests itself in many ways and produces many varied reactions and belief systems, it shares a common feeling of loss, of abandonment, of deep pessimism about the future. When despair is this profound, the desperate begin to seek miracles. It is easier, indeed understandable, to look for hope and comfort in the mystical hand of God. It is easier to believe that destiny has been preordained and that the faithful will be blessed, even if they have to go through hard times. Christian conservatism has allowed Learned to redirect her anger, an anger many around her share, at those who have failed to heed the word of God. She believes, like 36 percent of all respondents according to a Gallup poll, that the world is soon coming to an end.[9] She has read and accepts as prophetic the 12-volume *Left Behind* series of apocalyptic Christian novels by Timothy LaHaye and Jerry B. Jenkins that has sold more than 60 million copies. The manufacturing and industrial world around her has already seen its apocalypse. The hulks of old plants loom, giant rusted dinosaurs along the roadside. The labor and pain and sacrifice of a lifetime of toil have left workers bereft, impoverished and living in urban squalor and neglect. The world has crashed and burned for them. Another apocalypse, one that will lift Christians out of this morass, seems a welcome relief.

The ecstatic expectation of the Rapture, in which the elect are raised up into heaven while the damned suffer unspeakable torments below, creates, for the despairing, a dramatic and miraculous reversal of roles. This belief comforts those thrust aside in America, and in an age of greater and greater inequality, allows people to privatize their morality. They are told that people who suffer are responsible for their suffering; they must not be right with God. These believers can ignore their own social responsibility for inadequate inner-city schools, for the 18 percent of American children who don't get enough to eat each day, for the homeless, for the mentally ill. They accept the curtailing of federal assistance programs and turn inward, assisting only those within their exclusive Christian community and damning the world outside.[10] This social concern is replaced by tiny, more manageable acts of personal charity, such as giving food packages to a family in the church or teaching young girls about abstinence. Learned, like many in the movement, has little time for those who depend on the state. Goodness has become, in the new creed of the Christian Right, a question of judgment and carries with it condemnation. The movement allows marginalized people the pleasure of denouncing others, of condemning those they fear becoming. The condemnations give them the illusion of distance, as if by denouncing the indigent they are protected from becoming indigent. But this road also leads to a disastrous disengagement with the larger, more complicated systems and imbalances that fuel poverty and injustice.

"I think welfare has played a huge role," Learned says when asked about what contributed to the sickness of American society. "I know that I am speaking just for my own area, but these men are not taking responsibility for their children. They live with their welfare moms until the welfare moms get sick of them. They spit them out to some other welfare mom. And these guys don't work! They don't work. They live off the welfare money of these girls. They create babies all over the place. It is sickening! It is ab-

4 Taxi to the dark side documentary.

solutely sickening that we are not making these men take respon-sibility for their babies. And what sickens me is these guys are driving around in these incredible cars, and you know they are dealing drugs!"

But while the movement depends on the dislocation and rage of millions of working-class Americans, it is not defined solely by economic boundaries. The common denominator is despair, a de-spair creeping into a threatened middle class, where jobs are also being outsourced and company layoffs are throwing older workers out of jobs. There may be more despair in places like Youngstown, but it exists in communities across the nation, including those of the middle and upper classes, where people feel isolated and adrift. In interview after interview, those in the movement spoke of desires for suicide before finding Jesus. Even if the feelings were fleeting and never acted upon, they indicate how terrible life had become before conversion. Despair is the most powerful force driving people into the movement.

June Hunt is the daughter of Texas billionaire H. L. Hunt, one of his 15 children by three different mothers. Her father, a staunch conservative who hated President John F. Kennedy, was a bigamist and con artist. He abused her mother and was remote, often terrifying. The terror, the fear and the instability of her childhood mirrored that of Learned. And as with Learned it was this shame, abuse, loss of control, and guilt that drove her to em-brace religious utopianism.

"I grew up in a home where immorality abounded," she told an audience of Christian broadcasters in Anaheim, California, where she spoke for the first time in public about her past. "I grew up in a dysfunctional family, before there was knowledge of the word 'dysfunctional.' And it was not fun. There was fear, walking on eggshells. There was disarray, there was disruption and dissension. During my teenage years, my father was an enormous success in the business world, but an enormous failure in our family world. We were all eggshell walkers, at least around him.

"And let me try to explain. Until I was 12 years old, I grew up with a different name, a different last name. My name was June Wright. My father became romantically involved with my mother although he was twice her age. He was a married man with six children. My mother's father, meaning my grandfather, whom I never knew, died when she was three years old. And I believe she was trying to fill the father-void when he came along. And he was persuasive. And we were a covert family on the side, with four children, me being one. Actually, I will say this: truthfully, I discovered my father had a third family with four children in another city, another major city. We were the 'Wright' family. W-R-I-G-H-T. I was told it was because my parents did what they thought was right. My mother was deceived, and later, she lived with horrendous guilt and shame. And I, as I share this with you, I can remember her taking us to church, and her craving to go inside, but she felt too guilty, and so she couldn't walk into the doors of church. Shame poured out of every pore of her being. And she loved the Lord, and she felt trapped. She didn't know what to do. She certainly didn't have the skills to deal with my father; at least she didn't know how to handle the situation. And I saw the agony on her face, and many times she would just go to a church, during the week, and just stay there for hours and just pray.

"I prayed, I wasn't even a Christian at the time, but I prayed, 'Oh God, give my mother a friend.' You see, mother was afraid to have a friend, because she thought no one would accept her, that she would be rejected, and she didn't want to bring shame on a friend. Eventually, the first Mrs. Hunt died, and my father married my mother, and I became June Hunt. It was very difficult to explain this because my name already on the birth certificate was June Hunt. Ruth June Hunt. You'd think this would make things so much better, but it didn't. Dad was totally possessive of Mother. She was a beautiful, gracious, and kind woman, but she was his trophy whom he showed off nightly to his dinner guests. We kids were forbidden to speak at dinner; children were to be seen not heard, unless there was a conversation that would be of interest to everyone, and nothing was ever of interest to him.

"I truly hated him," she tells the gathering. "I remember being 14 years old. I had a friend who had a father who was a lawyer. I asked him one evening, 'I have a friend who wants to know what would happen to a 14-year-old boy who commits murder.' He answered, 'Well, the 14-year-old is a minor, so he probably would be released at age 18.' That's all I needed to know. A few weeks later, I approached my mother with a proposition. I said, 'Mom, I figured out a way, how I can kill dad. There won't be much of a repercussion because I am just a minor.' I was dead serious. What I appreciate, is my mother did not chide me, she did not laugh at me. Instead, with heart she said, 'Honey, I appreciate what you're trying to do, but that really won't be necessary.' It's not that I actually wanted to commit murder, I just wanted the pain to stop.

"I know what it's like also to look for love in all the wrong places, anything for security, anything for comfort," she says. "I clearly know what it's like to feel desperate for hope in the night. I had a nighttime of my life that lasted a number of years. The Book of Proverbs [Proverbs 14:12 and 16:25] says, there's a way that seems right, but in the end it leads to death. Clearly, I was headed the wrong way."

Those propelled into the movement, like Learned and Hunt, seek forgiveness for what they have thought or said, for what they have done, often for how they have lived. They seek meaning out of meaninglessness, worth out of lives that felt worthless. They seek firm, moral absolutes after being unable to distinguish between right and wrong. They seek safety, the safety that comes with a utopian vision that tells them they are protected, loved, guided and blessed. They seek a world where good people, which they have become, have good things happen to them and bad people are tossed aside to be destroyed. Converts seek a world where they will never again have to return to the lives they led, never again wonder if it might be better to end their lives, never again be tempted by the dark impulses that beset them. They embrace a collective madness to crush their personal madness.

This despair does not always rise out of severe want, the kind of want that plagues much of the developing world, or out of the immediate threat of war, but rather is the product of the disconnectedness and loss of direction that comes with living in vast, soulless landscapes filled with strip malls and highways, where centers of existence and meaning have been obliterated. It is a response to a national malaise. This despair has created, perhaps more than any other force, the opening for these utopian visionaries.

CHAPTER THREE

Conversion

Thus there is such a thing as human absorption. It appears in all the forms of conversion wherever the superior power of one person is consciously or unconsciously misused to influence profoundly and draw into his spell another individual or a whole community. Here one soul operates directly upon another soul. The weak have been overcome by the strong, the resistance of the weak has broken down under the influence of another person. He has been overpowered. . . .

—*Dietrich Bonhoeffer*, Life Together[1]

D r. D. James Kennedy, tanned and dapper in a dark brown suit with a white handkerchief in his breast pocket and meticulously combed silver hair, stands to the side of the podium and shares with us the most important tool in winning converts to Christ: becoming a friend. The seminar I am attending is being held in a hall of the Coral Ridge Presbyterian Church complex at Coral Ridge, Florida. Three spindly, white spires, all topped with crosses, tower above the cut-rate shopping centers and convenience stores stretched along North Federal Highway in Fort Lauderdale. The five-day seminar is designed to train us to teach Evangelism Explosion. The program was begun by Kennedy in 1967 and is designed to train evangelists in the tactics and methods used to save souls for Christ.

"I would always go in first, introduce myself, Jim Kennedy," he begins. "I'm checking the lay of the land, and I will look around the living room and see if there's something there that I can comment about. Frequently, there will be a large picture somewhere and where did they put it, this picture? Why would they put it over the fireplace? Significant."

"In Fort Lauderdale you don't find too many fireplaces," he adds, smiling, "but there's some kind of central focus. Maybe . . . golf trophies . . . I'm over here looking at these golf trophies . . . painting . . . I say, 'Beautiful painting. Did you paint that?' The first rule about looking at trophies: don't touch them . . . 'Did you win all those trophies?' So we have a little conversation about golf, but I know enough about golf to have this conversation. Now what have I done? I'm making a friend.

"Compliment them on whatever you can," Kennedy says. "Discuss what they do. You're going to find out what are their hobbies, maybe right there in the living room. Then you're going to ask them about what they do, where they're from, how long they've been there . . . something to discuss with them . . . In doing this, you have made a friend."

We sit with our green marbled Evangelism Explosion workbooks open to the chapter titled "Making Friends." We are being taught how to get prospective converts to open up and feel at ease. The manual suggests asking questions such as: "Tell me something about yourself."[2] We are instructed to listen attentively, since "people usually are most interested in what they themselves have to say."[3] Evangelists should "look the prospect in the eye, move your head up and down, echo what he says by repeating his words and voice inflection. Be sensitive to his felt needs and respond appropriately. Remember and use his name often in the conversation." And, it adds, "Pay a sincere compliment."[4]

Kennedy warns us not to carry a large Bible, but to keep a small one hidden in our pockets: "Don't show your gun until you're ready to shoot it."

Metaphors of war and sex saturate the lectures and the readings. Kennedy says that the primary task of Christians is to recruit "soldiers in the army of Jesus Christ who are absent without official leave (AWOL)."[5] He speaks of himself and other pastors as generals or admirals and of evangelists as soldiers. And he warns that it is Satan who convinces believers not to take part in the battle.

What is [Satan's] idea? It is this: that wars are very dangerous, complicated operations, and ordinary persons could get hurt needlessly; therefore, they should go home and let the generals and admirals fight wars . . . in the church this, in essence, is exactly what Satan has done![6]

Sexual metaphors are also sprinkled into the bellicosity of the conversion message. A "functionally mature, responsible, reproducing Christian"[7] should be producing others like himself. Christians who receive the gospel for themselves but do not convert others "are like immoral seducers." "The seducer," Kennedy writes, "is satisfied merely to exploit and then tell of his exploits rather than entering into a meaningful marriage commitment."[8] Kennedy recalls the difficulties he had one night during which he was unable to "consummate the witness"[9] with a new disciple's wife.

Conversion is a form of sexual warfare, a form of seduction and finally a form of physical conquest.

You must "seek to identify with your prospect. If that person would talk about the fact that they were lonely and you had a lonely experience, man, you want to tie into that, you jump onto that . . . get all over that with your testimony . . . because they're going to identify with you," Kennedy says.

The tactics of conversion come with layers of deception, including, we soon learn, false friendships and cooked testimonies, the promise that the evangelists are giving the "free gift" of eternal life and that what they preach is the inerrant word of God and cannot be questioned. Conversion is supposed to banish the deepest dreads, fears and anxieties of human existence, including the fear of death. This is the central message we are told to impart to potential believers. But along with this message comes a disorienting mixture of love and fear, of promises of a warm embrace by a kind and gentle God that yearns to direct and guide the life of the convert toward success, wealth and happiness, and also of an angry, wrathful God who must punish nonbelievers, those who are not saved, tossing them into outer darkness and eternal suffering. The message swings the faces of this Janus-like God back and forth, one terrifying and one loving, in dizzying confusion. The emotions of love and fear pulsate through the message. God will love and protect those who come to Him. God will torment and reject those who do not come to Him. It becomes a bewildering mantra.

Conversion, at first, is euphoric. It is about new friends, loving and accepting friends; about the final conquering of human anxieties, fears and addictions; about attainment of wealth, power, success and happiness through God. For those who have known despair, it feels like a new life, a new beginning. The new church friends call them, invite them to dinner, have time to listen to their troubles and answer their questions. Kennedy tells us that we must keep in touch in the days after conversion. He encourages us to keep detailed files on those we proselytize. We must be sure new converts are never left standing alone at church. We must care when no one else seems to care. The new converts are assigned a "discipler" or prayer partner, a new friend who is wiser than they are in the ways of the Lord and able to instruct them in their new life.

The intense interest by a group of three or four evangelists in a potential convert, the flattery and feigned affection, the rapt attention to those being recruited and the flurry of "sincere" compliments are forms of "love-bombing," the same technique employed by cults, such as the Unification Church or Moonies, to attract prospects. It was a well-developed tactic of the Russian and Chinese communist parties, which share many of the communal and repressive characteristics of the Christian Right. This intense showering of affection on an individual, as psychiatrist Margaret Thaler Singer described in her 1996 book *Cults in Our Midst,* is often very effective:

> As soon as any interest is shown by the recruits, they may be love-bombed by the recruiter or other cult members. This process of

feigning friendship and interest in the recruit was initially associ-
ated with one of the early youth cults, but soon it was taken up by
a number of groups as part of their program for luring people in.
Love-bombing is a coordinated effort, usually under the direction
of leadership, that involves long-term members flooding recruits
and newer members with flattery, verbal seduction, affectionate
but usually nonsexual touching, and lots of attention to their
every remark. Love-bombing—or the offer of instant companion-
ship—is a deceptive ploy accounting for many successful recruit-
ment drives.[10]

The new convert is drawn gradually into a host of church activities by his or her new friends, leaving little time for outside so-
cializing. But the warmth and embrace soon brings new rules.
When you violate the rules you sin, you flirt with rebellion, with
becoming a "backslider," someone who was converted but has
fallen and is once again on the wrong side of God. And as the
new converts are increasingly invested in the church community, as they cut ties with their old community, it is harder to
dismiss the demands of the "discipler" and church leaders.
"Backsliding" is a sin. Doubt is a sin. Questioning is a sin. The
only proper relationship is submission to those above you, the
abandonment of critical thought and the mouthing of religious
jargon that is morally charged and instantly identifies believers
as part of the same, hermetic community. The psychiatrist
Robert Jay Lifton describes this heavily loaded language, the
words and phrases that allow believers to speak in code, as
"thought-terminating clichés."[11] "Jesus is my personal Lord and
Savior" or "The wages of sin are death" are used, in this instance, to end all discussion.

Rules are incorporated slowly and deliberately into the
convert's belief system. These include obedience to church leaders; the teaching of an exclusive, spiritual elitism that demo-
nizes all other ways of being and believing; and a persecution

complex that keeps followers mobilized and distrustful of outsiders. The rules create a system of total submission to church
doctrine. They discourage independent thought and action. And
the result is the destruction of old communities and old friendships. Believers are soon enclosed in the church community.
They are taught to value personal experience over reason, and to
reject reason. For those who defy the system, who walk away,
there is a collective banishment. The exit process is humiliating,
and those who leave are condemned as "backsliders" no longer
favored by God.

There is a gradual establishment of new standards for every
aspect of life. Those who choose spouses must choose Christian
spouses. Families and friends are divided into groups of "saved"
and "unsaved." The movement, while it purports to be about families, is the great divider of families, friends and communities. It
competes with the family for loyalty. It seeks to place itself above
the family, either drawing all family members into its embrace or
pushing aside those who resist conversion. There are frequent
prayers during the seminar for relatives who are unsaved, who remain beyond the control of the movement. Many of these prayers,
including one by a grandmother in my prayer group for her unsaved grandchildren, are emotional, and it is not unusual to see
saved Christians weeping over the possible damnation of those
they love.

This control, while destructive to personal initiative and independence, does keep believers from wandering back into the messy
situations they fled. The new ideology gives the believers a cause, a
sense of purpose, meaning, feelings of superiority, and a way to
justify and sanctify their hatreds. For many, the rewards of cleaning up their lives, repairing their damaged self-esteem, and joining
an elite and blessed group are worth the cost of submission. They
know how to define and identify themselves. They do not have to
make moral choices. They are made for them. They submerge their
individual personas into the single persona of the Christian crowd.

Their hope lies not in the real world, but in this new world of miracles. For many, the conformity, the flight away from themselves, the dismissal of facts and logic for magic, the destruction (even with its latent totalitarianism) of personal autonomy amount to a welcome and joyous relief. The flight into the arms of the Christian Right, into blind acceptance of a holy cause, compensates for converts' despair and lack of faith in themselves. And the more corrupted and soiled they feel, the more profound the despair, the more militant they become, shouting, organizing and agitating to create a pure and sanctified Christian nation, believing that this purity will offset their own shame and guilt. Many yearn to be deceived and directed. It makes life easier to bear.

The most susceptible people, we are told in the seminar, are those in crisis: people in the midst of a divorce; those who have lost a job or are grieving for the death of a close friend or relative; those suffering addictions they cannot control, illness, or the trauma of emotional or physical abuse. We are encouraged to target the vulnerable. In *The Varieties of Religious Experience*, William James wrote that those who experienced dramatic conversions might have been born with a "melancholy disposition," a chronically "divided" mind—or else, he suspected, they had drunk "too deep of the cup of bitterness."[12] It is easier to bring about a conversion when the person being proselytized is in crisis. Indeed, the goal of the conversion is to generate a sense of crisis by stressing that all who are unsaved are lost and in desperate need of help.

When he speaks, Kennedy exudes the oily charm of a traveling salesman. He is meticulous about his appearance: never a hair out of place, his face tanned to a leathery brown and his suits finely cut. He talks in a low, sonorous voice, one he uses every Sunday when, decked out in his robe and academic hood, he stands behind his massive mahogany pulpit at the start of the service and announces, "This is the day the Lord has made; let us rejoice and be glad in it," at which point the thunderous organ erupts in pulsations that rock the church. He is a rigid fundamentalist, determined to defend and prove the truths of the Bible through what he sees as intellectual, rational and scientific argument. His sermons can often be pedantic, filled with windy discussions about what he says are historical or scientific facts that illustrate the inerrant truth of the Bible. He is one of America's most public and vocal dominionists.

Kennedy was born in 1930 in Augusta, Georgia, and raised in a neighborhood on the South Side of Chicago by a glassware-salesman father, rarely at home, and an abusive, alcoholic mother. It was not a happy childhood. Kennedy moved with his parents to Jacksonville, Florida, while he was in high school and by his own admission spent most of his time surfing and water-skiing. In his early 20s, he taught the fox-trot at an Arthur Murray Dance School in Tampa. He met his wife, Anne, there in 1952. But the official literature reads, "It all began on a Sunday morning in 1953, when he [Kennedy] was startled awake by a preacher's stern question on his clock radio: 'Suppose you were to die today and stand before God, and He were to ask you, "What right do you have to enter into My heaven?"—What would you say?'" [13]

Kennedy explains he was unsure of his answer. He says he went to a bookstore and bought The Greatest Story Ever Told, the 1949 novel by Fulton Oursler that chronicles the life of Christ. Kennedy had little experience with religion. He did not attend church regularly. The book, he says, opened his eyes to God, and he enrolled in seminary. He, unlike some of his charismatic or evangelical counterparts, did real academic work. He studied at Columbia Theological Seminary and the Chicago Graduate School of Theology, and received a PhD from New York University.

He began modestly with a small church, affiliated with the Presbyterian Church in America, which split with the mainline Presbyterian Church over what the schismatic sect branded its liberal theology. It had fewer than 100 members. But Fort Lauderdale proved to be fertile ground for the young preacher, with families moving in droves into sprawling new developments. The population influx helped swell his congregation, although the church literature portrays its growth as the result of successful proselytizing. He slowly built a massive multimedia empire. Kennedy's weekly broadcasts of *The Coral Ridge Hour* can be seen on more than 600 television stations and four cable networks and heard on the Armed Forces Network. It is the third most widely syndicated Christian program in the nation, reaching more than 3.5 million people. His radio show, *Truths That Transform,* is on more than 744 stations, six days a week.[14] He runs a lobbying group in Washington called the Center for Reclaiming America, as well as the Center for Christian Statesmanship, which evangelizes those who work in Congress. He hosts monthly luncheons, for members of Congress and their staffs, which feature conservative speakers. Kennedy believes that "the Christian view of morality and life is the one that should prevail in America."[15] He is fond of quoting John Jay, the Chief Justice of the first U.S. Supreme Court, who said that "God in His providence has given to us a Christian nation, and it behooves us as Christians to prefer and select Christians to rule over us." Kennedy argues that this "was the Christian perspective of most of the founders in the beginning of this country."[16]

"Our job is to reclaim America for Christ, whatever the cost," Kennedy has said. "As the vice regents of God, we are to exercise godly dominion and influence over our neighborhoods, our schools, our government, our literature and arts, our sports arenas, our entertainment media, our news media, our scientific endeavors—in short, over every aspect and institution of human society."[17]

Kennedy is opposed to abortion, homosexuality and the study of evolution. He rails against the values of the Enlightenment. He says that theories of evolution were the basis for Nazism, communism and fascism and that "these are the views of men that have resulted in millions and millions of people dying."[18]

He once told a reporter he'd never had a gay friend, adding, "I believe one was working at the dance studio [where he worked in his 20s], but I couldn't tell for sure. They are very good at blend-ing in."[19] Still, despite having no personal interaction with gay people (he says only ex-gays are members at his church), Kennedy formed Worthy Creations Ministry, a branch of Exodus International, in 1998. Worthy Creations preaches that homosex-uality is a sickness that can be healed.[20]

The cultural decline in America is the result, he says, of stray-ing from Christian values. *In The Gates of Hell Shall Not Prevail: The Attack on Christianity and What You Need to Know to Combat It*, a book Kennedy wrote in 1996, he writes that although the United States was once a "Christian nation," that is no longer the case because today "the hostile barrage from atheists, agnostics and other secular humanists has begun to take a serious toll on that heritage. In recent years, they have built up their forces and even increased their assault upon all our Christian institutions, and they have been enormously successful in taking over the 'public square.' Public education, the media, the government, the courts, and even the church in many places, now belong to them."[21]

The goal is not simply conversion but also eventual recruit-ment into a political movement to create a Christian nation. But this process is riddled with lies and deception. In the seminar, evangelists are told to pretend at first that they are taking a sur-vey of religious belief to get people to talk and that proselytizers should hide their Bibles so their targets do not know they are being proselytized, and should ignore "No Soliciting" signs, since what they are giving people is "a free gift."

Kennedy begins to talk about the godless character of liberal churches. He dismisses the members of these churches as "nomi-nal Christians." Referring to a potential convert whom he calls Scott, Kennedy tells us that since Scott had previously attended Grace Baptist Church, the word "grace" being a popular term within the Christian Right, he was probably a real Christian.

"Suppose we've got a lot of liberal churches in this area, and if you just named a church in this area that you go to, probably 90 to

10, I could tell whether or not you're a Christian," he says. "And how could I do that? Simply because these liberal churches don't preach the Gospel. I can tell you a big liberal church in this area where you can stand outside the church, Sunday morning after service, and say, 'Excuse me, sir, I'm lost, I wonder if you can tell me how to get to heaven.' And I would venture to say that 98 percent could not tell you, and that's because the pastor is a liberal and he doesn't believe in heaven. He doesn't believe in salvation; he probably doesn't believe in sin. Certainly doesn't believe in hell.

"There are millions of people in this country who attend church regularly," Kennedy tells us, "trying to live a good life and follow God's teachings, and yet somehow—now underline this next phrase—the church has failed to communicate to them how they can know for sure that they have eternal life and they're going to heaven."

At the Evangelism Explosion workshop we must write and rewrite our personal testimonies and practice delivering them in front of our assigned prayer partners, who critique them according to the manual. The testimony is an illustration to the nonbeliever that the converted are absolutely certain of eternal life and have been freed from all human anxieties. The testimony, we are told by the instructor, must state explicitly that the fear of death has been banished forever. We must describe moments in our lives when death appeared certain and we felt at peace and certain of eternal life. The testimony has to stress and repeat this total certitude of our belief in eternal life and freedom from fear. We turn our testimonies in for correction by the instructors to make sure our essays have not deviated from the two approved outlines of conversion, and we rewrite them when they come back with "errors" marked in red.

Freedom from fear, especially the fear of death, is what is being sold. It is a lie, as everyone who works to write and rewrite their testimonies has to know on some level. But few people would have the firmness of mind to admit this in front of other believers. Such an admission would be interpreted as a lack of faith. Yet creation of this internal conflict is also part of the process, for it fosters a dread of being found out, a morbid guilt that we are not as good or as Christian as those around us. The process, from its inception, is not only dishonest but cruel. The dissonance between individual sensibility and the group does not go away with conversion or blind obedience or submission. Belief systems that preach a utopian and unachievable ideal drive this angst underground, forcing the convert to measure him- or herself against an impossible ideal. This system ensures continuous feelings of inadequacy, self-doubt, guilt and self-loathing. That many converts feel deep remorse for past actions, for mistakes and cruelties, for the despair that has gripped their lives, only makes them more insecure.

The proper form for a conversion testimony is detailed for us in the Evangelism Explosion workbook:

Stage 1: What I was before. "Select one life concept such as loneliness, strife, guilt, fear of death, emptiness, rejection, insecurity, depression. Then include it (only one life concept per testimony) in an opening statement, saying, 'Before I received eternal life, my life was filled with a paralyzing fear of death.' Next, move from the general statement to a specific illustration out of your own life experiences. Give concrete details to make your illustration come alive." [22]

Stage 2: How I received eternal life. "At this point, you may want to say something like, 'Not many months later, a friend shared with me the most wonderful news I'd ever heard—that God had provided eternal life for me and what the conditions were to receive that life. As a result, many things changed in my life.'" [23]

Stage 3: What eternal life has meant to me. "At this point, you may want to share the life concept in reverse. If you selected fear of death as your life concept, you will now want to speak of courage in the face of death. If you chose the concept of guilt, you may now want to speak of forgiveness. The reverse of depression is hope; of emptiness, purpose; of rebellion, obedience, etc. Then you will want to illustrate the reverse life concept with another illustration from your experience. For instance, you may want to say, 'The fear of death is now gone, and in its place is courage when facing death situations or thoughts about death.'"[24]

"As you prepare your testimony," Kennedy says, "realize that you are fashioning an evangelical tool, so that you will be a more proficient witness."

There are two possible types of conversion experiences, the class is told: a childhood conversion and an adult conversion. Those who have experienced childhood conversions are told by the instructors not to state in the testimony that they were converted as a child. It will hurt their credibility with adults.

A childhood conversion testimony starts with the sentence "I'm glad I have eternal life because it's given me the certainty of knowing where I'm going when I die. And because of this, I have no fear of death."

The instructor gives us an example of an effective childhood conversion testimony:

"'Not long ago we were driving north on Interstate 57 during an ice storm that put a sheet of glazed ice on the highway. . . . We were easily easing along at 25 miles per hour, looking for a place to get off the highway to find shelter for the night, and as we were driving we came alongside a semitrailer truck.' They're painting a picture here. 'The wind was blowing very hard, and the trailer truck became like a sailboat, catching the wind.' Got this picture? 'Whoa. The truck was gradually being pushed across the center line, and steadily toward the car. There was nowhere to go. We couldn't go to the right because we'd run into the truck; we couldn't go to the left because we would eventually end up in a ditch with the truck on top of us. And as we waited to see the outcome, our tragic injury seemed certain. My whole life came before me, and yet God gave me complete peace in my heart, knowing that even in light of this almost certain tragedy, I knew for certain that if I were to die, I'd go to heaven. What a joy and a difference that made as I faced that danger. And it's the same today. I know that if I were to die right now, I'd go to be with God in heaven.'

"See?" the instructor goes on. "He captured your attention with a story, and that's what we're wanting you to build into your story, because all of you have that. I teach my trainers that they should be able to write a testimony like that. As they're listening in the introduction, the Lord will capture them with something in their own story with which they can build a testimony."

The adult conversion testimony, however, is different, although it too focuses on overcoming the fear of death. A stocky instructor recounts it for us:

"'Before I received eternal life, I had a fear of death and dying.' Same concept: the thought of death terrified me. 'I had no idea what lay beyond death's door for me. When I was in college I was living in a small home alone. One night, a terrible storm arose with wind gusts over 50 miles per hour. Kind of like Wilma down here; she was packing some heavy winds. The wind was so strong that the rain was pouring horizontally across the ground, our little mobile home was rocking on its concrete block foundation, and a bolt of lightning struck a tall oak tree right next to me. I was frightened, and I set up near to the sofa, fearful that I was going to die. Not many months later, a friend shared with me something very wonderful, and I received eternal life. Many things changed in my life. And now that I have eternal life, the fear of death and dying is gone. Not long after I received eternal life, we were driving north on Interstate 57 during an ice storm that put a sheet of glazed ice on the highway.' . . . Same illustration, only in the life of a person who's accepted Christ, you know?

And what happened before and then what happened after. 'As we waited to see the outcome, death or tragic injury seemed certain, and my whole life came before me.'"

The class has their workbooks open to the chapter "Sharing Your Testimony."

"Now here's *not* how to give a testimony," an instructor says. "'I received blessing when I became a Christian! I received deliverance through the Sinners' Prayer! I was unsaved and needed to be saved! My conversion happened when I put my faith in Jesus Christ, my savior, who died for the sins of those who trust Him. Praise the Lord! Hallelujah! Amen! I received salvation when I believed the Gospel and was washed in the blood of the Lamb, and I was born again when the Holy Spirit spoke to me at the altar of God. I lost all my friends and I lost my job, but God has looked after me ever since, and praise His name! The trials and tests are unbearable, and I just hope I can hold out until the end, and then maybe I'll be able to go to heaven!'

"You know," he says, "really, all of those things are true. All of those things are true of what happens in our lives. 'The blood of the Lamb,' that's a great, great phrase. 'The Gospel,' 'washed in the blood of the Lamb,' 'born again when the Holy Spirit spoke to me at the altar of God.' What's wrong with those statements? Way too *churchy*. Now you think how lost people think, and they don't think that way. They don't understand that. That is a jargon, and they just don't have any clue. . . . We use phrases like that and toss them back and forth, and a lost person thinks we've dropped off another planet. So what we want you to do, we want you to go into your prayer groups and we want you to talk them through your story."

The class of 60 evangelism students, many of them pastors, breaks up into preassigned prayer groups to practice their personal testimonies again.

We are told to always emphasize the positive and to find common interests, experiences, or viewpoints that will allow "your prospect," as the potential converts are called in our manual, to identify with us. We are told to pepper our talk with uplifting thoughts, such as the comfort we have of going to bed every night and knowing that if we do not wake in the morning we will be in paradise with God. We are instructed to paint detailed pictures of terrible personal tragedies that have been solved by God. As an example, the manual quotes a parent saying that they had "a Christian son killed in Vietnam" but they are at peace with the loss because the parent knows that, since the son was a Christian, he has eternal life, and the parent will be reunited with him in heaven. Our testimonies and conversions must be sprinkled with words like "love," "peace," "faithfulness," "hope," "purpose," and "obedience." But the core of the message, the point we must impart to the potential convert, is that conversion has obliterated our fear of death, not only for ourselves, but the fear we have of losing those we love. This is what is being sold. And we, as the salespeople, are meant to stand as proof that humankind's deepest fear, the fear of nonbeing, the fear of death, can be banished from life.

Two women from the church walk up in front of the group to role-play the conversion process. One sits in one of two green leather chairs on a raised platform. The other stands and pretends to knock on an imaginary door. The woman in the chair gets up to greet her visitor and welcomes her inside. They sit. The evangelist exchanges a few banalities about how nice the house looks and compliments her hostess on her taste in home furnishings. She "makes a friend." She then gives her personal testimony. After the testimony, in quick succession, she asks the two questions that have to be asked early of every potential convert. The class has been cautioned that "when two people are present, begin by asking the person who seems least likely to have the correct answer." The goal is to elicit incorrect answers, answers that allow the evangelist to push home the message that time is running out, sin is accumulating. The gift of eternal life waits to be taken, but without salvation everyone is damned to eternal punishment.

"'Have you come to the place in your spiritual life where you know for certain that if you were to die today you would go to heaven, or is that something you would say you're still working on?'" the evangelist says, repeating verbatim the first question.

"I would say I am still working on it," the other woman answers.

The evangelist launches into the second question.

"Suppose you were to die today and stand before God and He were to say to you, 'Why should I let you into My heaven?' What would you say?"

Her mock recruit fumbles, talks about having lived a good life.

The evangelist repeats the answer, because, as the instructor has told the group, "this will help preclude the prospect saying at the end of the Gospel presentation, 'I've always believed in Jesus Christ and trusted Him alone for salvation.'"

This is an important moment, we are told, because the conversion process depends on potential converts saying they are not sure they will be granted eternal life and they have not placed their total trust and faith in Jesus Christ for salvation.

"When you answered that first question, I thought I had some good news for you," the evangelist says, lifting the sentence verbatim from the manual. "But after hearing your answer to this second question, I know that I have the greatest news you have ever heard."

The workbook, lying open in front of the onlookers, instructs the evangelist to say this sentence with "great enthusiasm," since, the workbook adds, this "precludes a hostile reaction." [25]

Heaven, the potential convert is told after the questions are asked, is "unearned, undeserved, and unmerited. It's free." But it can come only through a commitment to Jesus Christ.

And then the discussion in the conversion process turns to sin. The evangelists are told to disabuse converts of the notion that sin is limited to robbery, murder, adultery or other specific acts. We are informed that sin "is anything that doesn't please

God or is a transgression of His law." [26] Sin, the convert is to be told, is "the fatal malignancy which infects the soul of the entire human race." [27] The convert is to be told that there is no escape from sin and that even the most righteous commit innumerable sinful acts.

This definition of sin is a subtle and pernicious twist to the traditional Christian concept of sin. As defined by Paul in his letters, sin is a state of being, a split between our conscious will and our real will, between us and something strange and alien within us. Sin is not, as Kennedy claims, a scorecard of rights and wrongs. For Paul, as well as many theologians such as Paul Tillich, there is no action, no matter how moral and good, which is totally pure or moral, totally free from sin. Sin is, rather, a way of describing our estrangement from others and ourselves, from what Tillich calls "the ground of our being." [28] It is estrangement from the origin and aim of life. When we carry out acts that further this estrangement, when we violate our relationships with others and with ourselves, we sin. But Kennedy paints sin as something quantifiable, as if there were a digital counter that recorded one sin after another and stored the information in some heavenly bank account.

An instructor turns to a church member and illustrates how to speak about sin to a potential convert:

"Suppose I could get to the point where only ten times a day or five times, or let's say three times a day, maybe one attitude [of] sin—jealousy or anger or bigotry—maybe one thing . . . slips from my mouth that's hateful," he says. "And maybe I miss doing something that I know I should do, like help my neighbor when they're having a special need. What do you suppose would happen if I got that good? Man, I'd practically be a walking angel! But do you realize that at the end of the year I [would] have a thousand violations against God's law? And if I live to be, well I'm 59 right now, so I'd have 59,000 violations against God's law. What would happen if I died right now, or not died right now but stood before a judge right now with 59,000 traffic violations? Think what would happen. He'd say, 'This is a habitual offender; let's get him off the road.' And he'd basically take my license and I wouldn't be able to drive. Well, imagine standing before the judge of the universe with 60 or 70 *thousand* violations against God's law. And that's at the very best, that's at the very best! But what we're really trying to say with this is, you know, not only does a little add up to a lot, but our sin problem is serious. And then you can move right in."

At that point the pairs form again to practice delivering the message about sin.

After the practice session, the instructor asks: "Why do we put the three-sins-a-day illustration in there?" Several people call out answers.

"A little bit of sin turns into a lot of sin," he says. "All right. It's that multiplication again."

The point the evangelists are instructed to make is that eternal life cannot be achieved through good deeds or even a good life. It is impossible to earn your way into heaven. We must accept that we have sinned, will always commit sins, and ask to be born again so Jesus will take our sins upon Him. Once this is done we can learn to live a new way, a way that, while not totally free of sin, allows us to live a life approved by God, a life in which, with the help of the church, we learn to reject sinful acts. The believer can learn to condemn and avoid sinful acts—acts defined for him or her by church leaders as anything that doesn't please God or is a transgression of His law. The leaders determine these acts, rousing the believer against what they label as sins, such as abortion or homosexuality. The emphasis, once the conversion is made, is on acts, acts that please or displease God. The believer can delineate these acts only with the aid of church leaders. There is a calculated destruction of individual conscience. All must submit to the will of those godly men who define the communal good. Sin, in short, is anything the leaders do not like.

"Because He is a just judge, He must punish our sins; His law declares that our sins must be punished and that He 'will by no means clear the guilty.' There is no doubt about this!" the instructor tells us.

The potential convert is to be told, finally, that Jesus came to earth and died "to pay the penalty for our sins and to purchase a place in heaven for us" and that "to receive eternal life you must transfer your trust from yourself to Jesus Christ alone for eternal life."[29] The convert is asked whether he or she is willing "to turn from what you have been doing that is not pleasing to Him and follow Him as He reveals His will to you in His Word."

The evangelist and convert bow their heads and pray, with the convert repeating each line after the evangelist.

"Lord Jesus, I want You to come in and take over my life right now. I am a sinner. I have been trusting in myself and my own good works. But now I place my trust in You. I accept You as my own personal Savior. I believe You died for me. I receive You as Lord and Master of my life. Help me to turn from my sins and to follow You. I accept the free gift of eternal life. I am not worthy of it, but I thank You for it. Amen."

When this prayer is over the believers are told, "Welcome to the family of God." They are told to read a chapter a day in the Gospel of John and that they will be visited again in a week to talk about the Bible. They are encouraged to pray because God "promised to hear and answer our prayers." They are told to find "a good Bible-believing church and become a part of it." They are told to join a Christian fellowship group. And they are told to witness to their families. With this, the process of deconstructing an individual and building a submissive follower is begun.

The goal is more than building the church; it is building a Christian America. Kennedy talks often about the recruitment of legions of new believers to the political as well as the religious arena. He claims to have brought in millions through Evangelism Explosion.

Kennedy insists that America was founded as a "Christian nation." The denial of the Christian roots of the nation, he says, is a "great deception [that] has been used to destroy much of the religious freedom and liberty this country has enjoyed since its inception."[30] And Kennedy's crusade is well funded and well organized. He is backed with grants, often for millions of dollars, from conservative trusts such as the Orville D. and Ruth A. Merillat Foundation and the Richard and Helen DeVos Foundation, which has over the years given nearly $6 million to his church organizations.[31] The drive to bring in new souls is also an open drive to broaden the political base of the movement and impose a theocracy.

The prayer partners are told to separate into clusters. Those in the room take turns practicing their testimonies in front of their group of three or four, with the other members critiquing the performance. The final version of each participant's written testimony is to be turned in the next day. My prayer group has three other people, including one of the few African Americans, a thoughtful man who grew up in the church and was converted as a child; a middle-aged man who overcame drug and alcohol abuse as an adult through his conversion; and a grandmother, who said that as a child she had a morbid fear of death that was overcome only when she was saved and assured of eternal life. I pair off with the grandmother, who is chatty and friendly. We read our testimonies, trying to get them exactly right.

A woman from the church tells us how to share the Gospel with a person who suffers from dementia or Alzheimer's disease. She heads teams that go into 24-hour nursing homes and assisted-living facilities.

"These precious people are basically confined to these types of facilities," she says. "Now they say by the year 2025, there will be two seniors for every teenager on the face of this earth. And with multiplication and with people living longer, in the United States they say pretty soon there will be about 50 million people that are alive [who] will end up spending their final years in some type of facility. So this is an untapped resource.

"They're always there," she tells the group. "And so we get to go back and we get to see Miss Mary, week after week after week, and share with her.

"The other thing that we're dealing with is different forms of dementia," she adds. "The most common form is Alzheimer's. So for most of us—and I mean, I forget things easily—we have to go back and repeat ourselves. But that's OK. Maybe the first week we'll just get through an introduction and maybe share our testimony, maybe the two questions. The next week we'll go back, we'll pick up with Miss Mary, maybe we'll have to refresh her memory.

"One thing that we get a lot with the elderly," she says, "they are so works-oriented because of the culture in which they were raised and having gone through the Depression. So we really have to talk about eternal life as a free gift. That has to be emphasized over and over and over."

Disruptions, reluctance to accept the message, open hostility and interruptions during the evangelization process are always blamed on Satan, part of what is described to us as "spiritual warfare."

"The devil is so obvious," an instructor says. "I mean, he's so easy to figure out."

The instructor recounts the story of a house visit. The evangelists were sitting in the living room of a woman who asked the team to convert her unsaved husband. At the moment the evangelists were about to get him to accept Christ, the phone rang.

"It was an old-fashioned message machine where you could hear the person," the instructor says. Through the loudspeaker on the machine, the group heard a child call out, "Daddy, Daddy, I know you're in there."

The group sat and listened to the plea of the child. Finally the father said, "'Excuse me,' and he walked over and just clicked it back off," the instructor tells us. "He came back over, and my trainees at the time were just praying so hard, great drops of blood . . . that that guy could receive Christ. We got ahead of the distractions."

CHAPTER FOUR

The Cult of Masculinity

The monumentalism of fascism would seem to be a safety mechanism against the bewildering multiplicity of the living. The more lifeless, regimented, and monumental reality appears to be, the more secure the men feel. The danger is being alive itself.

—*Klaus Theweleit*, Male Fantasies[1]

Roberta Pughe was in second grade when her family moved to Fort Lauderdale. The family attended the church run by the Reverend D. James Kennedy on Commercial Boulevard. She grew up, along with the congregation, which eventually moved to a sprawling white building on Federal Highway.

By the time she was a teenager she was doing part-time modeling, taking tennis lessons from Chris Evert's father and studying classical piano. She was an honors student and captain of the cheerleading team at Stranahan Public High School. When Pughe was 13, her mother was diagnosed with polycystic kidneys, a condition in which multiple cysts in the kidneys deplete their function. This moment of panic, of looming mortality, changed the household. Although she would learn to cope with the illness and survive for many years, her mother believed that her life was about to end.

"It was somewhere in there that she told me that she was going to die," Pughe says. "Her two kidneys were functioning as one. So she was going through her own depression and had a born-again experience."

Her mother, who had once attended Kennedy's church as a Sunday ritual, threw herself into the activities of the congregation. She led coffeehouses and home Bible studies. She took part in healing services, and pastors from the church came to the home and did a hands-on healing with oil in an effort to thwart her disease.

Roberta and her brothers fought their parents' efforts to pull them into the church. They made fun of the teenagers who attended Westminster Academy, the church-run high school. Roberta, who retreated to the third balcony during Sunday services, passing notes to her friends, paid little attention to the sermons preached by Kennedy before a congregation that had swelled to 10,000 people.

"Then one day, Nicki came along, who was a 25-year-old stud," she says. "He was very, very good-looking, with brown eyes, brown hair, a mustache and he rode a motorcycle. I went after him. He was my ticket to God. He started taking me to Bible studies. I started attending Bible studies two weeks before my sixteenth birthday and had a born-again experience."

The embrace of the new community, the sense that she had found an extended family, was at first exciting and appealing. But it also soon brought with it radical changes. She was told to adopt a more "Christian" lifestyle. Funk and pop music, her non-believing friends, the part-time modeling jobs and even the secular high school were, she was told, thwarting her attempts to be a Christian. She destroyed her Motown and Michael Jackson records. She gave up modeling. She transferred to Westminster Academy, Coral Ridge's Christian school. She walked out on her old community.

"I was doing TV shoots, was in magazines," she says. "I was doing lots of stuff that now was sinful. All of it stopped. I started going to the Greenhouse Christian fellowship at the church four nights a week, where we did Bible study."

Pughe turned her back on the world of nonbelievers. She struggled to obey. She suppressed her periodic waves of anger and frustration at the abrupt, painful and difficult changes imposed upon her, believing she had no right to question the demands of the church's male hierarchy. She feared the judgment and disapproval of her new community. She feared that she would displease God. She kept down her longings for freedom and escape from the claustrophobic community. She was told to blame these feelings on Satan. She wanted to be "a good Christian woman." The infusion of Christian jargon and clichés into her vocabulary, the inability to speak with others who might have validated her doubts and anxieties, left her unable to articulate or confront her feelings of dislocation. No longer sure what she felt or believed, she worked harder to obey.

Pughe soon believed that God would punish her if she failed to carry out the demands of the men who spoke for God, those who now defined right and wrong. And the more she struggled with her inner turmoil, seeking to please God, which meant pleasing the male hierarchy that now dominated her life, the worse she felt. All these anxieties, however, remained unnamed, unrecognized.

She began working at the GangWay Ministries for youth at the church and was involved in Kennedy's Evangelism Explosion program, designed to teach people how to spread the Gospel in 20 minutes. The continuous dialectical training, much of it numbing in its boredom and repetitiveness, made it hard to articulate her doubt. Her life was filled with church meetings, new lessons to be learned and lectures. Solitude and reflection, along with thought itself, became difficult. Her head was spinning with slogans, clichés and religious jargon that gave believers the illusion of knowledge.

I meet her late in the afternoon in her office in New Jersey, where she now is a family therapist. "It is a fear-based model," she says. "The idea is to make people afraid and to then proceed to share the Gospel. I began training ministers from around the world. We were training ministers [on] how to train their youth to go out and proselytize. We used to go cold turkey onto the beaches. We used to go to shopping malls. There was a pamphlet with questions, and you had to ask all of them. You would go up to people cold, and you'd always start with the two questions.

"'So would you like to accept Jesus Christ as your Lord and Savior right now?' we would ask," she remembers. "We can pray the prayer."

She went to Calvin College in Michigan, a Christian school, when she graduated from Westminster Academy. It was the only college to which she applied. During her senior year she decided to go to seminary, although she could not be ordained because she was a woman. Her father announced, however, that he would not pay for seminary. He told her it was time for her to get married and start a family. This, he assured her, would make her happy.

"In my senior year, I remember hearing on the radio an advertisement for the Miss Greater Grand Rapids Scholarship Pageant, which was a part of the Miss Michigan Pageant, which was a part of the Miss America Scholarship Pageant," she says, "and I could win $2,500 in scholarship fees, which would cover my first semester of seminary. I entered the contest. I threw together a bathing suit, high heels, and I think I played 'Für Elise.' I pulled something out of my bag of tricks and I won."

She started competing for the Miss Michigan contest. She practiced three hours a day on the upright piano at Calvin Seminary. Many of her professors were cheering her on, telling her that, like the biblical figure Esther, she had been called to such a time as this. She was going to use the platform of the Miss America scholarship pageant, she told herself, to spread the Gospel. Her victory seemed ordained by God.

"This was a legitimate way a woman could have a pulpit," she says. "I bought all this. I was still quite asleep. This is what is so scary. I was anesthetized. I was programmed to believe all this. It was reinforced by my family and the church. There was this double authority that came from God. The male authorities in my life spoke for God. God spoke through my father, who was very authoritative and who held the power, as did the twelve male pastors in the church. All the leaders in my life were male. On

Sunday in the sermons God spoke to us as a male. I had nothing to plug into other than what these men told me, and they were all telling me the same thing.

"My female truth was not diminished, it was completely silenced," she remembers. "It was obliterated. I had a mother, who was not a questioning female, who had also been socialized to be obedient. The good woman, they tell you, is the obedient woman. I did not have any model of a woman who owned her own feminine truth."

She looks back on the time as one filled with fear, fear of not conforming, of disapproval in the eyes of the men who spoke for God, of falling out of God's favor, of not living up to Christian standards and incurring God's wrath and punishment.

"I was not conscious of this fear," she says, "and fear has a lot of power when it is not named. I didn't even know I was afraid. I was not allowed to be afraid. The message that is communicated is there is nothing to be afraid of. When you hear someone say this, then that is when you should be most afraid."

She entered the contest, now certain that God had chosen her to be Miss America and spread the Gospel.

"I met Cheryl Pruett, who had been the previous reigning Miss America," she says. "She too was an evangelical, born-again and from the South. She was just as convinced that God was raising Christian women to take the platform."

The state pageant was at Muskegon. She spent a week being paraded around before local groups, smearing Vaseline on her lips and keeping a smile pasted on her face. She lost ten pounds during the week before the pageant and did not have time to take in her gown, which now hung on her. When she mounted the stage, many of the professors from the seminary had come to watch.

"There I am in my bathing suit and my four-inch heels and, you know, professing God, you have three minutes to say who you are in an evening gown," she says. "I said something about God and my mission for God. So I was playing the piano, at that point I had played Rachmaninoff's Prelude in G Minor. I suddenly went blank. I thought, 'What are you doing here?' It was a moment of clarity as I sat there on that stage. I didn't win. I was in the top ten, but that blank moment during the prelude lost me points. I was devastated."

She left the seminary. She joined the staff for youth ministries at Coral Ridge, where she was the only woman. But even as she evangelized to others, she struggled with anger and betrayal. She felt God had called her to the beauty pageants and then abandoned her.

"How could God lead me down this path and promise me this? And then not come through?" she remembers asking herself. "I blamed God for failing to make my secret fantasies come true. I never acknowledged, of course, that these were secret fantasies, that what I wanted was fame and fortune. I wasn't allowed to name these fantasies, not even to myself. I was going to buy my dad a Jag, because that was his favorite car, and he would never have bought it for himself. I was going to be proud on some level that I had attained this powerful position, when in my denomination, women couldn't even preach from a pulpit. So I had done it. You know, it was a big 'Fuck you!' Now you're telling me I can't? Watch me do it. But watch me do it within your confines, watch me do it within the restraints you put on me. But I was not aware of the expense to myself."

She drifted slowly away from the church, marrying, moving to Boston, raising two boys, finishing a two-year seminary degree and studying to become a licensed marriage and family therapist. During those years she slowly deconstructed her life and what had been done to her, until she quietly left the evangelical church, believing it had stunted her as a woman and forced her into a system based on submission.

The hypermasculinity of radical Christian conservatism, which crushes the independence and self-expression of women, is a way for men in the movement to compensate for the curtailing of their

82 AMERICAN FASCISTS

own independence, their abject obedience to church authorities and the calls for sexual restraint. It is also a way to cope with fear. Those who lead these churches fear, perhaps most deeply, their own internal contradictions. They make war on the internal contradictions in others. Those who are not subdued, who do not bow before the church authorities, are seen as contaminants. Believers are driven into a primitive state, a prenatal existence, a return to the womb and a life of submission. The assault on freedom, human equality and reason, however, also engenders feelings of omnipotence. Death and decay seem to be overcome. All are empowered by God, promised a utopian paradise and immortality. The movement feeds off of power and powerlessness, off of subjugation and control. It induces mass delusion. And the crowd, stripped of personal initiative, soon projects its dreams and aspirations for power through the leader. The surrender of personal power allows believers to indulge in fantasies about becoming instruments of a limitless, divine power. As the spiritual vacuum grows, as fear increases, violence in the name of God becomes not only seductive but imperative. The movement, to compensate for the loss of personal power and submission, fosters a warrior cult and feeds its hapless followers a steady diet of battles, wars and apocalyptic violence.

Images of Jesus often show Him with thick muscles, clutching a sword. Christian men are portrayed as powerful warriors. The language of the movement is filled with metaphors about the use of excessive force and violence against God's enemies. Christ's stoic endurance of the brutal whippings in Mel Gibson's movie *The Passion of the Christ* reflects the brutal, masculine world of this ideology, a world that knows little of tenderness, personal freedom, ambiguity, nurturing and even pleasure. Jerry Falwell, in a *New Yorker* interview, said Christ was not a gentle-looking, willowy man: "Christ was a man with muscles," he insisted.[2] Falwell and Gibson see real men, godly men, as powerful, able to endure physical pain and suffering without complaint. Jesus, like God, has to be a real man, a man who dominates through force.

Hypermasculinity becomes a way to compensate, especially since the unspoken truth is that Christian men are required to have a personal, loving relationship with a male deity and surrender their will to a male-dominated authoritarian church. Submission to church authority, after all, is a potent form of emasculation. It entails a surrendering of conscience and personal control and deadens emotions and feelings. Glorified acts of force and violence against outsiders, against nonbelievers, compensate for this unquestioning submission. The domination men are encouraged to practice in the home over women and children becomes a reflection of the domination they are taught to endure outside of the home.

There runs through the fundamentalist belief system a deep dread of ambiguity, disorder and chaos. Accordingly, the cult of masculinity keeps all ambiguity, especially sexual ambiguity, in check. It fosters a world of binary opposites: God and man, saved and unsaved, the church and the world, Christianity and secular humanism, male and female. These tidy pairings keep life from slipping back into a complicated nightmare. Reality, thus defined, is made predictable and understandable, something deeply comforting to believers who have had trouble coping with the messiness of human existence. There is, in this "Christian" worldview, clearly demarcated order and disorder. Behaviors that do not conform—such as homosexuality—are forms of disorder, tools of Satan, and must be abolished. A world that can be predicted and understood, a world that has clear boundaries, can be made rational. It can be managed and controlled. The petrified, binary world of fixed, immutable roles is a world where people, many of them damaged by bouts with failure, despair and their own ambiguities, can bury their chaotic and fragmented personalities and live with the illusion that they are now strong, whole and protected. Those who do not fit, who are not subservient to dominant Christian males, must be proselytized, converted and "cured" (if they are gay or lesbian) through quack therapy. If they remain recalcitrant they must be silenced. The decline of America is described as the result of the decline of male prowess. This decline has led to weakness and moral decay. It has resulted in a bewildering human and social complexity that, often seen as feminine, is the work of Satan. By submitting to the Christian leader, and to a powerful male God who will destroy those who misbehave, followers avoid dealing with life. The movement seeks, above all, to banish mystery, the very essence of faith. Not only is the binary world knowable and predictable, but finally God is knowable and predictable.

Fundamentalism, Karen McCarthy Brown wrote, "is the religion of those at once seduced and betrayed by the promise that we human beings can comprehend and control our world. Bitterly disappointed by the politics of rationalized bureaucracies, the limitations of science, and the perversions of industrialization, fundamentalists seek to reject the modern world, while nevertheless holding onto these habits of mind: clarity, certitude, and control." [3]

Since life has a way of not respecting these artificial lines, since ambiguity, inconsistency and irrationality are part of human existence, the only way believers can push forward is to pretend that these troubling aspects of our internal and external reality do not exist. They create a parallel reality, one that allows them to escape from the reality-based world into a world of their own creation. "Unconscious motives, deep longings, and fears are denied," Brown wrote, "and responsibility for them is abandoned, as fundamentalism makes a pretense of being all about cut-and-dried truth and clear and recognizable feelings." [4]

Popular Christian conservative leader and talk-show host James Dobson has built his career on perpetuating these stereotypes. Born to evangelist parents, Dobson grew up in Louisiana, Oklahoma and Texas. He says he was born again when he was three at one of his father's church services. He attended Pasadena College and received a PhD in child development from the University of Southern California, where he went on to teach. [5] His first book, *Dare to Discipline,* encouraged parents to spank their children with "sufficient magnitude to cause the child to cry genuinely."[6] It has sold more than 3.5 million copies since its release in 1970. He has built a massive empire based on his advice to families as a Christian therapist. He is heard on *Focus on the Family,* a program broadcast on more than 3,000 radio stations; runs a grassroots organization with chapters in 36 states; and runs his operation out of an 81-acre campus in Colorado Springs, Colorado, a campus that has its own zip code. He employs 1,300 people, sends out four million pieces of mail each month, and is heard in 116 countries. His estimated listening audience is more than 200 million worldwide, and in the United States he appears on 80 television stations each day. He is antichoice, supports abstinence-only sex education exclusively and is fiercely antigay.[7] He calls for prayer in public schools, but only if led by students, since teachers might encourage Christian students "to pray to Allah, Buddha or the goddess Sophia."[8] He has backed political candidates who call for the execution of abortion providers, defines stem-cell research as "state-funded cannibalism" and urges Christian parents to pull their children out of the public school system.[9] On his Family.org Web site he discusses "the countless physiological and emotional differences between the sexes." The article "Gender Gap?" on the Web site lists the physical distinctions between man and woman, including strength, size, red blood cell count and metabolism. For a woman, Dobson writes, love is her most important experience: love gives woman her "zest"; it makes up her "life-blood"; it is her primary "psychological need." Love holds less meaning in a man's life than a woman's—though a man can appreciate love, he does not "need" it.[10]

"Genesis tells us that the Creator made two sexes, not one, and that He designed each gender for a specific purpose," Dobson goes on. And these differences mean different roles: they mean the man is the master and the woman must obey.

One masculine need comes to mind that wives should not fail to heed. It reflects what men want most in their homes. A survey was taken a few years ago to determine what men care about most and what they hope their wives will understand. The results were surprising. . . . What [men] wanted most was tranquillity at home. Competition is so fierce in the workplace today, and the stresses of pleasing a boss and surviving professionally are so severe, that the home needs to be a haven to which a man can return. It is a smart woman who tries to make her home what her husband needs it to be.

Dobson says that to achieve this tranquillity wives have to be submissive. He instructs the husband in how he "should handle his wife's submission" and goes on in Family.org to insist that "submission is a *choice* we make. It's something each one of us must decide to do. And this decision happens first in the heart. If we don't *decide in our hearts* that we are going to willingly submit to whomever it is we need to be submitting to, then we are not truly submitting." Of course, the choice not to submit to the male head of the household, Dobson makes clear, is a violation of God's law.

The hierarchy fears romantic love. Love, especially eroticism, in its most passionate, romantic form, threatens the iron control of the church leader. In Freudian terms, romantic love allows the id, or the "it," to be unleashed in a drive to satisfy uncontrollable passions. Restraint and self-control over these desires and passions are disarmed by romantic love. At the height of romantic love our fractious internal world suddenly appears whole. Men no longer rule women and women do not rule men. Male and female are ruled by the need to be affirmed by the other, by the lover. It is a moment of magical well-being, at least until passions cool and libido is tamed. Freud feared the intoxicating effects of romantic love, which he called "the overestimation of the erotic object," for the same reason he feared religion and totalitarian movements. Freud cautioned against any emotion or movement that promised to unify the psyche behind a collective cause. The assault against romantic love within the radical Christian conservative movement is an assault by the male hierarchy against its most potent competitor.

"Freud had no compunction in calling the relationship that crowds forge with an absolute leader an erotic one," wrote Mark Edmundson:

> *(In this he was seconded by Hitler, who suggested that in his speeches he made love to the German masses.) What happens when members of the crowd are 'hypnotized' (that is the word Freud uses) by [a] tyrant? The tyrant takes the place of the over-I, and for a variety of reasons he stays there. What he offers to individuals is a new, psychological dispensation. Where the individual superego is inconsistent and often inaccessible because it is unconscious, the collective superego, the leader, is clear and absolute in his values. By promulgating one code—one fundamental way of being—he wipes away the differences between different people, with different codes and different values, which are a source of anxiety to the psyche.*[11]

An absolute leader, called in Freudian terms the collective superego, is morally permissive. This is part of the leader's attraction. Murder may be wrong, but the murder of infidel Iraqis or Islamic terrorists—or the genocidal slaughter of nonbelievers by an angry Christ at the end of time—is celebrated. This moral permissiveness is exciting and seductive and empowers followers to carry out acts of violence, often with a clean conscience. Those nonbelievers who are hurt or killed are at fault for turning their backs on God. Blind adherence to an absolute leader, especially one who permits violence, hands followers a license to unleash hidden, prohibited lusts and passions usually kept locked within the human heart. It permits followers to kill in the name of God.

"Freud believed that the inner tensions that we experience are by and large necessary tensions," Edmundson wrote, "not because they are so enjoyable in themselves—they are not—but because the alternatives to them are so much worse. For Freud, a healthy psyche is not always a psyche that feels good."[12]

These male church leaders, as Susan Friend Harding observed in *The Book of Jerry Falwell*, speak almost exclusively in their public pronouncements to other men. They implicitly privilege men in their rhetoric. She recounts a story of Falwell joking in 1986 at Temple Baptist Church about surrendering unconditionally to his wife, Macel. Falwell said he let Macel get what she wanted. This was a decision he made. As an aside he quipped that, while he had not thought of divorce, he had thought of murder a few times.

"The anger and the threat of force here were ironic," Harding wrote, "but still served as little reminders of men's ostensible physical authority, their 'power-in-reserve'":

> More unambiguously, this flash of rhetorical violence revealed to whom the entire joke about his marriage was addressed. It was addressed to men. In this way it not only upheld public male authority, it enacted it. Indeed, the whole sermon, the entire Moral Majority jeremiad, and fundamentalism in general were addressed to men. The joke, the sermon, the jeremiad, and fundamentalism were essentially men's movements, public speech rites that enacted male authority. Not that they were "for men only" but that they, their rhetorics, were addressed primarily, or rather directly, to men. Women were meant to overhear them.[13]

"These men suffered a loss of their own masculinity," Roberta Pughe says, "so they have taken on this extreme form of masculine power, the power to oppress and to dominate. On the extreme end of the masculine continuum, it is the oppressive force that kills, that destroys. There is no room for anything else.

Everything else is a threat. The feminine is a threat. Children are a threat. Homosexuality is a threat because it embraces a feminine, nurturing side between men. All power has to be concentrated at the top and be destructive."

And she concedes that she still fights the fears instilled in her by the church.

"Here I am, a woman, 46 years old, seasoned and trained in my field, and I still am terrified to speak what I believe," she says. "It gets clogged right here in my throat. I tremble at the thought of speaking my own thoughts when I go back to them, into their circles. They see me as a heretic, a backslider, and say I am not a Christian any longer. They say I have lost my way. So there's nothing, from their point of view, that I have to offer.

"The goal of the movement is to create a theocracy, but they must dominate women first to keep the system in place," Pughe says, the late afternoon light spilling into the windows of her office. "They want to have one nation under God, based on their view of God and their interpretation of the rules that this peculiar God puts in place. They are doing this underground. They have huge networks. They are deeply connected, and they're connecting with people who have lots of money and lots of power, and these people are very smart and savvy. They know how to put forward a public front that hides the private agenda. They have found a niche to be heard, to provide something. They run home Bible studies. They offer people a sense of belonging and connection. They know the family's falling apart. The divorce rate is high. Families are in flux. Roles are in flux. Men and women are trying to figure out what we're doing together. And the church is filling the niche, providing the extended family. There is no extended family, so the church is providing it for these people. Their ticket to power is family values. That's the hook. People are hungry for that. But with this church family comes the imposition of an extreme male power structure. First, they use this power structure to control the family, then the church, and finally the nation."

The use of control and force is also designed to raise obedient, unquestioning and fearful children, children who as adults will not be tempted to challenge powerful male figures. These children are conditioned to rely on external authority for moral choice. They obey out of fear and often repeat this pattern of fearful obedience as adults. Refusal to submit to authority is heresy. Raised in a home and a school where he or she is taught to see the world as one where the possibility of attack and danger lurks behind every crevice, the child learns to distrust outsiders. The benign and trivial take on satanic proportions. There is no safety. Satan is always present. The pathology of fear, ingrained in the child, plays itself out in the constant search for phantom enemies who seek the destruction of the adult believer. These elusive and protean enemies, always there to lure the believer toward self-destruction, must be defeated to establish a world, ushered in by Christ's return, where no one will be able to do them harm, where the irrational is abolished and the binary lines of right and wrong are enforced by a Christian government. Only then will the believers be safe.

One of the tools used to keep believers obedient is the "prophecy" of the Rapture. One day, without warning, the saved will be lifted into heaven and the unsaved left behind to suffer a seven-year period of torment and chaos known as the Tribulation. This event will, believers are told, suddenly and unexpectedly tear apart families. Those who are not good Christians will lose their mothers and fathers or their children. The big-budget films *Apocalypse, Revelation, Tribulation* and *Left Behind,* based on the *Left Behind* series by LaHaye and Jenkins, have popularized these fears, the films employing Hollywood stars such as Gary Busey, Margot Kidder and Corbin Bernsen. The films show parents left behind as their infants have been raptured into heaven, screaming "My babies, my babies!" Abandoned teddy bears and diapers litter empty airplane seats. Children come home to find their parents gone. The world descends into anarchy, with trains, planes and cars, now without engineers, pilots or drivers, crashing in deadly fireballs. In an instant, the United States, with as much as half its population lifted into heaven, is reduced to the status of a developing country, dominated now by an ascendant Europe that carries out the will of Satan through the Antichrist.

This conditioning of children to fear nonconformity and blindly obey ensures continued obedience as adults. The difficult task of learning how to make moral choices, how to accept personal responsibility, how to deal with the chaos of human life is handed over to God-like authority figures. The process makes possible a perpetuation of childhood. It allows the adult to bask in the warm glow and magic of divine protection. It masks from them and from others the array of human weaknesses, including our deepest dreads, our fear of irrelevance and death, our vulnerability and uncertainty. It also makes it difficult, if not impossible, to build mature, loving relationships, for the believer is told it is all about them, about their needs, their desires, and above all, their protection and advancement. Relationships, even within families, splinter and fracture. Those who adopt the belief system, who find in the dictates of the church and its male leaders a binary world of right and wrong, build an exclusive and intolerant comradeship that subtly or overtly shuns and condemns the "unsaved." People are no longer judged by their intrinsic qualities, by their actions or capacity for self-sacrifice and compassion, but by the rigidity of their obedience. This defines the good and the bad, the Christian and the infidel. And this obedience is a blunt and effective weapon against the possibility of a love that could overpower the dictates of the hierarchy. In many ways it is love the leaders fear most, for it is love that unleashes passions and bonds that defy the carefully constructed edifices that keep followers trapped and enclosed. And while they speak often about love, as they do about family, it is the cohesive bonds created by family and love they war against.

Joost A. M. Meerloo, the author of *The Rape of the Mind: The Psychology of Thought Control, Menticide, and Brainwashing*, wrote:

> *Living requires mutuality of giving and taking. Above all, to live is to love. And many people are afraid to take the responsibility of loving; of having an emotional investment in their fellow beings. They want only to be loved and to be protected; they are afraid of being hurt and rejected.*
>
> *It is important for us to realize that emphasis on conformity and the fear of spontaneous living can have an effect almost as devastating as the totalitarian's deliberate assault on the mind. . . . Trained into conformity the child may well grow up into an adult who welcomes with relief the authoritarian demands of a totalitarian leader. It is the welcome repetition of an old pattern that can be followed without investment of a new emotional energy.*[14]

All those who do not subscribe to this male fantasy, or who were born female or gay, must be pressured to conform. By disempowering women, by returning them to their "proper" place as a subservient partner in the male-dominated home, the movement creates the larger paradigm of the Christian state. The men's movement Promise Keepers, which at its height a decade ago drew tens of thousands of men into football stadiums, called on men to "take back" their role as the head of the household. The movement used the verse from Ephesians that calls on wives to "be subject to your husbands, as to the Lord" (Ephesians 5:22) to give the stance biblical authority.[15] Women were not allowed to attend the events, although some could volunteer at concession stands outside. The founder of the group, former Colorado football coach Bill McCartney, called the movement's battle against abortion the "Second Civil War" and lambasted gays and lesbians as "stark raving mad." He dismissed gays and lesbians as "a group of people who don't reproduce, yet want to be compared to people who do reproduce, and that lifestyle doesn't entitle anyone to special rights."[16] The organization mounted campaigns such as "Real Men Matter," in which men were instructed to recover their maleness in a "morally bankrupt, godless society." The goal of the movement, strongly supported by Dobson, was designed to help men regain their place in society. And while Promise Keepers as an organization is on the wane, the agenda it promoted is firmly embedded in the masculinity cult of the Christian Right.

In the megachurches, the pastor, nearly always male, is obeyed by the congregation. It is the pastor who interprets the word of God. This pattern is established on a smaller scale in the home. The male leader governs through a divine mandate, a mandate that cannot be challenged since it comes from God. And these leaders speak often about taking their cues directly from God. These concentric male fiefdoms, radiating out from the home, do not permit revolt, discussion or dissent. And once women buy into this message, one that supposedly protects their families, makes their boys into men, their husbands into protectors and themselves into godly Christian women, they cede personal, political and economic power. Those who are weak or different, those who do not conform to the rigid stereotype, those who have other ways of being, must be forced by the stern father to conform and obey. If they do not bend, they will be destroyed by God.

The consequence of this disempowering of women was poignantly captured when Dobson interviewed Karen Santorum, wife of Pennsylvania Senator Rick Santorum, on October 17, 2005, in the studios of the Family Research Council for his radio program. Karen Santorum home-schools her children, the principal role for women with children, according to Dobson and many others in the movement.

"Have you ever looked out at the women who are in these exciting careers and making money and advancing in the corporate world, and so on? Have you ever looked at that and said, 'Did I do the right thing?'" Dobson asked.

"I really believe that the devil really tries to work on mothers at home," she told Dobson. "We all know he's the master of lies, and he will do everything he can to try to make mothers at home feel that way, like we're so inadequate, we're not fulfilled. And through my prayer life and just my relationship with Jesus, I feel without a doubt this [being a housewife] is the most important thing I can do. It is what God wants for me; it's what He wants for my family. So I have in the early days—I did once in a while—Rick would be leaving to go to some nice event in a tuxedo, and I'd be on the floor cleaning up milk. I'd be like, 'What's wrong with this picture?' And I feel so blessed and honored to be home, and I know that my presence in their life will make a difference."[17]

The televangelists Benny Hinn and Pat Robertson rule their fiefdoms as despotic potentates. They travel on private jets, have huge personal fortunes and descend on the faithful in limousines and surrounded by a small retinue of burly bodyguards. These tiny kingdoms, awash in the leadership cult, mirror on a smaller scale the America they seek to create. There is no questioning. Followers surrender their personal and political power, in much the same way women and children surrender their power to the male at home. The divinely anointed male leader rules a flock of obedient and submissive sheep. All must hand over their freedom. All must cease to think independently.

The earnestness on the part of believers often gives the mass movement its air of honesty, sincerity and decency. Believers are not brainwashed. They are not mindless automatons. They are convinced that what they are doing is godly, moral and good. They work with the passion of the converted to bring this Christian goodness to everyone, even those who resist. They believe that what they promote is moral and beneficial. And just as they fear for their own souls, they fear for the souls of those around them who remain unsaved. This often well-intended earnestness, although employed for frightening ends, is a powerful engine within the movement. These idealists are willing to make great personal sacrifices for the cause of Christ. They justify the disempowerment and eradication of whole peoples, such as Muslims or those they castigate as secular humanists, as mandated by God. Nonbelievers have no place on the moral map. It is a small step from this toxic rhetoric and exclusive belief system to the disempowerment and eradication of nonbelievers, a step a frightened and enraged population could well demand during a period of prolonged instability or a national crisis.

The ruling elite of the movement, the James Dobsons and Pat Robertsons, are at the same time very distant from the masses. They assume a higher intelligence and understanding that give them a divine right to rule. These men are—writ large—the powerful, all-knowing father. Those they direct become as powerless, credulous and submissive as children.

Danuta Pfeiffer, who from 1983 to 1988 was the co-host on *The 700 Club* with Pat Robertson, sat with me and her husband one evening on the patio of her home outside of Eugene, Oregon. She reached heights, because of her celebrity status, usually reserved for men, although it was always clear she had a role subservient to Robertson's. She was the first person to be allowed to lead the mandatory half-hour chapel service held before lunch at the Christian Broadcasting Network, where *The 700 Club* is filmed. She was sent to speak at national Christian women's groups and later mixed audiences, numbering in the thousands, at several of the nation's largest megachurches.

She was also told, however, that being a single woman at the broadcasting network was inappropriate. She said she was "pressured" to get married and did, although the shaky union, not one she would have made on her own, soon fizzled and ended in divorce.

"An adviser at the network told me that marriage was the 'appearance of appropriateness,' and since I had been a single woman, traveling at times alone with the very married Pat Robertson, it was time to 'be appropriate,'" she said, a wood fire throwing up sparks from the fireplace on her patio. "I had been a 'baby Christian' for only two short years. I was just beginning to learn that Christians perceived an unwed woman [as] a source of temptation. This was a man's world. And I had to be anchored to a man in order to move freely around them."

Her reception at the gatherings she addressed was frightening. Crowds swarmed toward her, asking her to touch them and heal them. Her status was nothing compared with that of Robertson, she said, "who stands for his followers as the embodiment of God's conscience.

"They were seeking a message, a healing, hope, a little encouragement," she remembered. "They wanted a little piece of God. They thought I could give it to them. People wept when I prayed for them, touched them or hugged them. It was as if they were meeting a rock star."

She was increasingly disturbed by the power that had been thrust upon her and the emotions unleashed by those who begged her for guidance in every aspect of their lives. She understood how pliant these people had become and how cleverly they were being manipulated. The realization led her finally to leave the movement. Her experience was a window into how willingly followers handed over their consciences to these leaders, abandoned all moral responsibility for the word of those who had elevated themselves to the status of quasi-deities.

"They trusted us more than their family," she says. "They thought we had a clearer path to God because we were on television. They thought we were on television because God put us there. We were prophets to these people. We were seen as people who could walk on clouds and heal and pray. We were God's special messengers. Pat was seen as having the ear of God. He had words of knowledge that could identify their deepest fears and illnesses. We would identify people on the air by speaking about the color of their clothes or an illness they had. We would say, 'There is a woman with a blue blouse crying at this moment. She has bad hearing in one ear. She is being healed right now.' And viewers would claim these healings. They saw our presence on the show as a sign that we were anointed. They wanted to know how to live, how to operate on a daily basis, how to communicate with their family and friends, what jobs to get and how to interpret the world around them, even the daily news. They wanted every type of emotional, spiritual and physical information. We had this kind of authority over their lives. They abdicated their hopes and lives to us because we spoke for God."

CHAPTER FIVE

Persecution

JOE: . . . Does it make any difference? That I might be one thing deep within, no matter how wrong or ugly that thing is, so long as I have fought, with everything I have, to kill it. What do you want from me? What do you want from me, Harper? More than that? For God's sake, there's nothing left, I'm a shell. There's nothing left to kill.

As long as my behavior is what I know it has to be. Decent. Correct. That alone in the eyes of God.

—*Tony Kushner*, Angels in America[1]

Flakes of snow fall gently over the ponds, statues and lawns sloping down from the gold-domed Massachusetts State House. A cluster of several dozen young men and women walk along the edge of the Boston Common on Tremont Street. They chant, "Hate is curable and preventable!" "Jesus, cleanse this temple!" and "Conversion Therapy kills gay teens!" It is 7:30 in the morning. Many in the group carry rainbow-colored posters that say, "We're God's Children Too" and "God Loves Gays." Some peel away from the procession to dart into a Dunkin' Donuts. They emerge a few minutes later cradling a cup of coffee or hot chocolate.

When they reach the Tremont Temple Church, they form a half-circle outside the front doors. Boston police are standing out front to block people without registration papers from entering the building. The protesters have converged on the church to demonstrate against a Love Won Out conference, sponsored by Dobson's Focus on the Family, being held inside. Love Won Out officials, already nervous, have ordered lunch from Subway for the nearly 800 people attending their conference so no one will have to leave the church. Love Won Out volunteers meet everyone coming through the front doors.

"Are you registered?" a woman asks new arrivals politely.

If so, people are directed upstairs, where their bags are searched for tape recorders and cameras. Wrists are stamped and wrapped in bright orange-red bands. Only those wearing wristbands are allowed to file into the sanctuary. The church has long, dark, wooden pews. It is surrounded on three sides by a balcony and has towering stained-glass windows depicting biblical scenes.

The crowd takes several minutes to move through the swinging doors and settle into the pews. There are mothers and nervous teenage sons. Husbands and wives, their heads bent over the conference forms, circle on printed schedules the breakout sessions they plan to attend. Single men and women sit alone, thumbing through the conference notes. In a small media section at the back of the sanctuary, only a couple of seats are occupied. The event does not welcome the "secular" media, which it accuses of promoting an anti-Christian agenda. Love Won Out volunteers walk up and down the aisles looking for potential infiltrators or anyone holding a tape recorder or a camera. Those who attempt to tape or photograph the conference will be ejected.

Love Won Out was founded, its brochure says, to help families, men and women, and especially those plagued by what the movement calls "same-sex attraction," recover traditional male and female roles. The organization, led by many who identify themselves as "ex-gays," brands homosexuality as a disease and condemns it as a threat to the family, the health of the nation and Christianity. The movement's professed goal is to "cure" those who have "same-sex attraction." But it has also declared war against gays and lesbians who are unrepentant, those they brand as "militant" and who actively promote "the gay agenda." Although they speak the language of compassion toward those willing to be healed, they also say there should be no tolerance or acceptance of gays and lesbians who refuse to seek help. And America will soon pay a price, they warn, for permitting gays and lesbians to live openly in defiance of God.

The legalization of gay marriage in Massachusetts has helped mobilize the Christian Right, including many in the state who see the move as morally polluting their schools and communities. Christian activists in Massachusetts are frequent guests at Christian conferences, where they speak of their persecution by "homosexual radicals." This cultivated sense of persecution—cultivated by those doing the persecuting—allows the Christian Right to promote bigotry and attack any outcry as part of the war against the Christian faith. A group trying to curtail the civil rights of gays and lesbians portrays itself, in this rhetorical twist, as victims of an effort to curtail the civil rights of Christians. One of the most vocal is Tom Crouse, a pastor in Holland, Massachusetts, who hosts a show titled *Engaging Your World* broadcast on local Christian radio station WVNE-AM 760 in Worcester. He features antigay guests and has held a "Mr. Hetero" contest in Wooster. The contest included "ex-gays." Crouse says the contest was a way of promoting "God's design" in response to a "Mr. Gay 2005" competition held in San Diego. He refuses to use the word "gay" on his talk show, saying he uses the word only "in its proper context, which means 'happy.'"

"People will call in to my show and say, 'You're gay,' to me on the air, and I'll say, 'I'm gay, you're gay.'" He lashes out at "homosexual activists" who he says "are well financed, well organized, and small in numbers.

"They're rabid and they're active, and they have no problem telling you they're going to kill you," he has said, "no problem telling you they're going to burn you to death, no problem telling you anything, all in the name of tolerance.

"If you listen to how Jesus is proclaimed today, you'd think Jesus is some tie-dye-shirt-wearing, pot-smoking hippie. That's not who Jesus is. You know, Jesus was a man who spoke the truth. He said, 'You're of your father, the devil.' He walked away from those who could have stoned him and killed him. Jesus said, 'I am God, you are not. I am the living truth and the life. No one knows what God knows but me'—I say Jesus was the most intolerant person in the world. Jesus would not be accepted in many churches today."

Mike Haley, director of gender issues at Focus on the Family, and himself an "ex-gay," walks up and stands behind the pulpit in the Boston church. His collared shirt is pressed and tucked into his khaki pants. His sandy blond hair is combed neatly to the side. He welcomes the crowd to the first Love Won Out conference in Boston, the organization's 36th event since its founding in 1998. Trinity Temple, he reminds those in the sanctuary, has hosted every president since John F. Kennedy and now, Love Won Out. He raises his fist in the air as the crowd claps and says, "Amen." The successful staging of the event in Massachusetts, where same-sex marriages were first legalized, is, he assures the crowd, a victory for Christians.

Dr. Joseph Nicolosi, a clinical psychologist, is president of the National Association for Research and Therapy of Homosexuality, an organization known as NARTH. He says he has treated more than 1,000 men who came to him with "unwanted homosexuality." He has written three books on the subject, including his most recent, *A Parent's Guide to Preventing Homosexuality,* co-authored with his wife, Linda Ames Nicolosi.

Nicolosi says that all men are "born to be heterosexual." He calls heterosexual orientation that which corresponds to man's "true nature." Homosexuality, he says, "is a masculine inferiority." He speaks of "the gender identity phase" when the boy begins to realize that the world is divided into male and female. Children who cannot disconnect from their mothers and identify with their fathers, he explains, become homosexuals. He says the male child is biologically "trying to fulfill his natural masculine strivings. He is wired to be masculine. His body is designed for a woman." The job of the child is "to dis-identify with the mother and bond with the father."

The boy, he says, "begins to realize that he's like this father image that he never really paid attention to before. He becomes interested in the father. And if he reaches out to the father, and if the mother supports him in making this transition, and if the father is welcoming and encouraging, the boy will make the transition. He'll bond emotionally with his father, make that male identification, and that becomes the foundation of his sexual preference, what he finds sexually attractive."

But if the father is distant, detached, unavailable, in short a "negative figure in the boy's eye," the boy will reach out to the father and be hurt.

"He will be made to feel ashamed of his masculine ambition," Nicolosi says. "The father's nonresponsiveness will make him feel bad about that effort, and he will basically shut down. And he will be shamed for his masculine strivings, and basically what he says is, 'If you make me unimportant, I make you unimportant. If you're not interested in me, I'm not interested in you.' And you know, if you know any homosexual men, they do not have a good relationship with their fathers. Their fathers are just not that important in their lives, period."

Nicolosi warns against fathers who are "weak and unmasculine, and perhaps beaten down by the mother." He says that boys need a "strong, masculine father who is worthy of imitation, of modeling, worthy of disconnecting from the mother." He also cautions against an "overemotionally involved mother" who is a "dominant, strong personality."

He argues that mothers who do not cede authority to the father, who do not represent to the boy that dad is the leader of the family, contribute to their child's homosexuality. In proper development, he says, the nurturing of women becomes less important as the boy grows older. The rougher play of the father is required if the boy is to develop into a man.

"You know, the young father tossing the son up in the air and catching him," Nicolosi says. "And, you know, the father is laughing and the kid is petrified, you know? And the mother is watching this ritual and she has no idea, she's getting a heart attack watching this. But as the father is tossing the kid up and down, because the father is laughing, the son starts laughing. And a very important lesson has just been taught, one that men teach boys: danger can be fun. Even if the father drops the kid and cracks his head a little bit, at least he will be straight. A small price to pay, I tell ya."

And when males are brought up by masculine fathers, when they become fully developed men, they are, he says, "a little dull, you know what I mean? We don't see colors as vividly. Have you noticed? We don't seem to remember show tunes, I don't know why. Anyway, more importantly than 'Danger can be fun,' the boy is caught by the father, 'And I can trust dad.' And men with a homosexual problem do not trust other men."

Those who fail to achieve their masculinity, however, become mama's boys. They seek to please the mother. They are the kind of boys, he says, who leave for school with their hair in place and wearing neat, clean clothes and come home from school in the same, perfect condition.

"And you can see how in adulthood, the gay man desires to break that good little boy mold," Nicolosi says. "He is angry and wants to rebel. He's aggressive. He's shocking. He's offensive. He's provocative because he wants to break out of that good little boy mold that he was in. While all the other boys were being bad, he was sitting with mommy in the kitchen; now he wants to be bad. Have you ever seen a gay pride parade? That's exactly right. If you walk into a gay bar, it looks like a bunch of men who want to be bad little boys. You walk into a straight bar, and all these straight guys are sitting there, 'Yeah, yeah, yeah,' because they got it out of their system a long time ago. They're exhausted. Their wives exhausted them."

He throws out that gay men gravitate toward theater to "escape into fantasy" because "fantasy is a big part of the gay identity."

A woman in a pew leans toward her husband and whispers that this is a description of their son.

The cure for what he terms the "male gender deficit," for those who suffer from "same-sex attraction," is "reparative therapy." It can come about through a close connection with a strong, heterosexual man who is comfortable in his male role. When homosexuals "make an emotional connection with a straight man, their homosexuality disappears," he says. They no longer have trouble being assertive, and these "heterosexual men with a homosexual problem" are cured.

It is left to Mike Haley, who identifies himself as an ex-gay, to back up Nicolosi's assertions with personal testimony. He tells the group that his father was cold and distant, refusing to initiate him into the world of men, and taunted him because of his lack of athletic ability as "Michelle" or "my third daughter." He describes his close relationship as an 11-year-old boy with a man who eventually began to have sex with him.

Eventually Haley went to see a counselor who told him he was born gay. He frequented the gay bars and discos at Laguna Beach in California, not far from his home. He felt, he says, as if he had "come home." His lifestyle, however, conflicted with the views of his church. And his pastor, when he confessed, told him he had to reform. The conflict between his desires and what he thought was right in the eyes of God began to haunt him.

"So what do you think I did as a 17-year-old junior in high school that didn't want to be gay?" Haley says. "I read my Bible and I read my Bible and I read my Bible and I prayed and I prayed and I prayed. I remember kneeling next to my bed and saying, 'Lord, I'm not going to stop praying until I feel different,' only to fall asleep, waking up to feel just the same as I had when I had started to pray."

He finally turned his back on the church. He tells the group that at this juncture he believed Christianity was "a lie" and "hated Christians."

"I wanted to be moral within my homosexuality," he says. "I wanted to have that long-term monogamous relationship. But when I didn't find it in this city, I'd move to the next." He lived, he says, on the "gay treadmill."

"It's not a whole lot different than the treadmill that I see some heterosexual women buy in to," Haley says. "When they believe they have to be a certain size, look a certain way, dress a certain way, to be acceptable to the heterosexual male population. Well, you take that same phenomenon and put it into the gay community, and it seems overexaggerated. To be the accepted commodity, you need to look a certain way, act a certain way, drive a certain car, talk a certain way. So I was working out three to four hours a day, I was doing injectable steroids. I was bulimic because I wanted to eat, but I didn't want to gain weight because I had to have that perfect physique because that physique was what defined my value and my worth during my time and involvement in the gay community."

He says he became a gay activist in Dallas. He marched in Gay Pride parades.

And then one night Haley picked up a man at a gay gym, but as they progressed the man stopped and told Haley he could not have sex. Haley recalls him saying: "I'm sorry that I've led you on, but I'm a Christian, and I'm trying to walk away from this."

The two men spoke most of the night. Haley was introduced through the man to a counselor named Jeff Conrad, who promised to help cure him of his homosexuality. Haley started what he says was "a godly, Christian mentoring relationship."

"He sent me birthday cards: 'I don't even know if you're getting this card, but I want to let you know that I love you, that God loves you, that change is possible,'" Haley says. "I'd write him back the nastiest, ugly letters about his faith, about his God: 'Leave me alone, I was born this way.' He'd write me back: 'Mike, I want you to go to the library. I want you to find me a study that will prove to me that you were born gay. And if you can do that, then I will change the way that I believe.'"

Haley says he left his "homosexual lifestyle" in December 1989 after his sessions with Conrad. He omits the details of his "cure." He got married. He returned to the church and became a youth pastor. He started working for Dobson.

Dobson's attacks on gays are relentless and brutal. He likens the proponents of gay marriage to the Nazis.[2] He warns in his book *Marriage Under Fire* that sanctioning gay marriage is the first salvo by the gay movement to destroy the American family. "This is an issue America has got to wake up to," Dobson writes. "The homosexual agenda is a beast. It wants our kids. . . ."[3] And he goes on to ask, "How about group marriage? Or marriage between daddies and little girls? How about marriage between a man and his donkey?[4]

"Moms and dads, are you listening? This movement is THE greatest threat to your children," Dobson warns. "It is of particular danger to your wide-eyed boys, who have no idea what demoralization is planned for them."[5]

This conference is one of many Dobson and his associates mount throughout the country every year. Bill Maier, vice president and psychologist in residence for Focus on the Family, rises to speak. He attacks the legalization of gay marriage in Massachusetts, which he calls "the most radical social experiment ever proposed in our country that's redefining the institution of marriage." He defines the ruling as one made by "four rogue judges on the Supreme Judicial Court who basically forced their will on the people and the legislature of Massachusetts." The ruling, he says, is "a radical redefinition of the human family." At issue is "whether men and women are unique and different and whether the two genders complete each other in their differences. It's about whether mother and father are both essential in the process of healthy child development, and it's about whether there are compelling societal reasons to define marriage as one thing and not define it as something else.

"When we follow God's blueprint for how we're supposed to live, things usually work out the way they're supposed to," Maier says. "But when we defy God, when we live in ways that are contrary to God's design for us, we often reap a harvest of pain and suffering in our lives." He warns that "if we redefine marriage in one way, there is no logical reason for us to not redefine it in other ways," leading to the legalization of "polygamy or group marriage." This opens up the possibility, he says, of fathers marrying their daughters. "They say, 'Well, if marriage can be redefined to include two men or two women, what's to stop us from redefining it to allow marriage between a man and four women, or a group of six or seven adults and their various children?'"

The danger of same-sex marriage is that it "will also teach our children that the words 'male' and 'female' and 'mother' and 'father' are simply meaningless social constructs."

Melissa Fryrear, who says she used to be a lesbian, blames abusive parental relationships for "same-sex attraction."

"For those who have been abused by a male, oftentimes that tremendous rage, that hurt, can go underground, if you will, and it can begin to emerge later in life, perhaps in rejecting your female identity or the fact that you look like a woman," she says. "When I lived homosexually, I was very butch and very mannish. I still have some work to do"—a comment that elicits laughter—"but I've covered some bases, too. I looked mannish and I looked masculine because it was a liability to be a woman. Because it meant that I could be hurt, it meant that I could be victimized, and it was my suit of armor to keep me safe. So [it was a] rejection of that female identity. It can be a fleeing from men."

Many in the church take notes in the space provided in their conference booklets. Many cry softly when speakers mention giving up their lives to God and being cured of "same-sex attraction." And periodically, especially during the testimonies, there are shouts of "amen."

The speakers accuse gays of controlling television, radio and Hollywood. The gay movement, they say, is more politically active and powerful than other movements. Gays are attacked as diseased and part of the criminal class. But the bedrock of the attack is that homosexuality is against God's ordained natural order, that what gay men and women do is perverted and pathological. They are not only a threat to children, but a threat to Christians. Gays, those at tonight's conference are told, hate them and want to destroy them.

"Religion is treated as irrelevant or downright evil," Robert H. Knight writes in *The Homosexual Agenda in Schools,* distributed by Dobson's Family Research Council. "Homosexual books, magazines and newspapers are filled with bitter and often obscene denunciations of religion in general and Christianity in particular. One activist calls for the outlawing of churches that disapprove of homosexual conduct. Another carefully outlines an advertising campaign that equates Christian clergy with Nazis and Klansmen. Homosexual stage performers dress up in clerical garb and commit obscene acts. A gay-rights cartoonist depicts Christ having anal intercourse with His cross. These are not isolated examples from an otherwise gentle and loving literature. The attitude pervades the homosexual movement." [6]

Gays and lesbians within the church, seeking desperately to deny their sexuality and remain in the Christian collective, suffer severe depression and blows to their self-esteem. The U.S. Surgeon General's office has published data indicating those who are young and gay are two to three times more likely to commit suicide. [7] Those who are able to conform, no matter what the personal cost, will find acceptance. Those who remain militant, who stand up for another way of being, are condemned. The tactics that will finally remove them and their supporters from a future Christian America are left unmentioned, but the rhetoric makes it plain that there will not be a place for them. And these preachers warn that if America does not act soon to repress the lifestyles of gays and lesbians, God will punish the nation.

When Pat Robertson was asked by Jerry Falwell if God had allowed the attacks on September 11, both the question and its answer stoked this fear of divine wrath and apocalyptic judgment:

> *I believe that the protection, the covering of God that has been on this great land of ours for so many years, had lifted on September 11, and allowed this thing to happen. God apparently had good reasons for exposing the U.S.A. to such destruction, given the many sins that Americans have committed ever since the Roe versus Wade court case and the Supreme Court's decision to keep God out of the schools. In fact, American infidelity goes back to the 1920s and 1930s, to situational ethics and notions of cultural relativity, along with a flirtation with communism at the highest levels of government. The point is not just that Americans have been bad and forfeited their entitlements. It is that unless they reform themselves in a hurry, something far worse may happen to them.*[8]

Should another catastrophic attack occur, what will prevent these preachers from calling for the punishment, detention and quarantining of gays and lesbians—as well as abortionists, Muslims and other nonbelievers—to safeguard the nation? What will stanch the hate crimes and physical attacks against those deemed immoral by fearful and angry Christians, those condemned by these preachers as responsible for the nation's abandonment by God? How will the nation function rationally if homeland security depends on an elusive piety as interpreted by the Christian Right? And most ominously, the fringe groups of the Christian Right believe they have been mandated by God to carry out Christian terrorism, anointed to murder doctors who perform abortions and godless Muslims in Iraq. In a time of anxiety and chaos, of overwhelming fear and uncertainty, how many more will be prodded by this talk of divine vengeance to join the ranks of these Christian extremists?

The drive to ban same-sex marriages in the 2004 election was just one step in a campaign to strip gays and lesbians of civil rights. A 1996 federal law already defines marriage as a union occurring between a man and a woman. Currently 19 states have written prohibitions on same-sex marriage into their state constitutions. As of this writing the latest were passed in Kansas and Texas in 2005; 13 states adopted constitutional bans on gay marriage in 2004, while four had previous bans. At least seven states will hold statewide votes on same-sex marriage bans in 2006.[9] These referendums fan the fires of fear and hatred. Bans have to be passed, believers are told, so "activist judges" will not overturn the laws forbidding same-sex marriages. The Christian Right, with its constant need for scapegoats and satanic enemies to be defeated, use the state referendums to mobilize and energize followers, even as the most pressing social ills of the country are ignored.

Any relationships outside the rigid, traditional model of male and female threaten the hierarchical male power structure vital to the movement. Women who do not depend on men for their identity and their sexuality, who live outside a male power relationship, challenge the cult of masculinity, as do men who find tenderness and love with men as equals. The lifestyle of gays and lesbians is intolerable to the Christian Right because their existence is a threat to the movement's chain of command, one its leaders insist was ordained by God.

The Reverend Dr. Mel White, who produced films and worked with most of the prominent leaders within the Christian Right, came out as a gay man in 1993 in his installation as dean at the Universal Fellowship of Metropolitan Community Churches Cathedral of Hope church in Dallas. Like many gay men in the church, he struggled until late in life with his homosexuality, condemning himself for feelings and inclinations he could not control.

"Conservative Christians shaped the very core of my faith and passed on to me my love for Jesus, the Bible, and the church," White wrote in his autobiography, *Stranger at the Gate: To Be Gay and Christian in America*. "But all through those wonderful days of childhood and early adolescence, a heavy layer of clouds floated between me and the heavens. In spite of their many gifts to me, those same conservative Christians remained silent about the secret longings of my heart. And though I was surrounded by their loving presence, that same silence left me feeling increasingly isolated and lonely. In the days of my gay childhood, there was no one who even tried to help clear up my growing confusion, guilt, and fear." [10]

White's grandmother was a tent revival preacher, traveling around the country on trains to preach and set up storefront churches. When White was 12 years old, she told him that she had given up sex with her husband to "work for the Kingdom." "Jesus is coming soon," she told White. "Don't be distracted by anything." [11]

White was a model Christian youth. He worked to save the souls of his friends and classmates. He was the student body president at his high school.

"In those early years, I thought for certain that my secret longings were a sign that my Creator had abandoned me," White wrote. [12]

White would lie awake, "begging God to heal me, to take away the feelings I could not understand, to make me like the rest of them once and for all. It was a prayer I had prayed hundreds of times before. I prayed it in my junior high gym when we showered together and I was terrified by my involuntary physical response to the other naked boys. I prayed it at the beach when I lay with my fellow surfers in the sand and was aroused by their bodies. I prayed it when I was alone in my room at night, cutting out ads from bodybuilding magazines and hiding them under my bed." [13]

In high school, White began to date Lyla Lee Loehr, whom he had known since seventh grade. White took Loehr, for their first date, to a Youth for Christ rally. He knew he could never bring her home to his parents—she wasn't saved. But after a few weeks of spending time together at White's church, she accepted Christ into her life.

White struggled to conform to a "heterosexual lifestyle." His new girlfriend was the ticket out of sin.

"By then I had memorized the Old Testament lines from Leviticus that say a man who sleeps with another man is an abomination and should be killed," he wrote. "Although I thought that God still loved me, I wasn't certain how far God's love would go if I ever 'gave in' to my 'evil passions.'"[14]

White married Loehr and raised two children. He had a successful career in the church. He watched passively, however, as colleagues in the church struggled with homosexuality, suffered mental breakdowns or committed suicide. One such troubled man cut off his testicles.

When White's younger brother was struck and killed by a car while riding his bicycle, White wondered if this was a message from God.

"There were desperate, irrational times when I thought maybe God was punishing me for my homosexual thoughts by letting my brother die," he wrote.[15]

White, like many in the church, saw a series of Christian psychologists and psychiatrists. The first told him he needed to tell his wife. He did. Lyla agreed to help. White wanted to keep his family and career. He wanted to conquer his homosexuality.

"For the next years, I read and memorized biblical texts on faith. I fasted and prayed for healing. I believed that God had 'healed me' or was 'in the process of healing me.' But over the long haul, my sexual orientation didn't change. My natural attraction to other men never lessened. After months of trying, my psychiatrist implied that I wasn't really cooperating with the Spirit of God. After that, my guilt and fear just escalated."[16]

In 1977, White began his first relationship with another homosexual man. The relationship lasted for a year, but the secrecy caused emotional strain. At the same time, he began ghostwriting for Francis Schaeffer, Jerry Falwell, D. James Kennedy, Pat Robertson and other Christian Right leaders.

"I wasn't wise enough to anticipate where all this talk of 'cleansing the nation' might lead. I didn't foresee that one day those same religious media personalities and the political groups they would organize could become a dangerous threat to me, to my gay brothers and lesbian sisters, and to all persons who might disagree with their political, religious and social agenda for our country."[17]

He contemplated suicide while scuba diving in Hawaii and later atop a bridge. He saw more Christian counselors, and in despair slashed his wrists with a coat hanger as his wife screamed at him to stop. It was the end of their marriage. White met his partner, Gary Nixon, who sang in the church choir. He walked away from one world and into another. It became his mission to document the hate talk of his former employers and organize gay and lesbian Christians to denounce the bigotry of the Christian Right.

"This is a black and white world," White says. "It is between good and evil. It is not a natural political conflict where people of good will can disagree, and they're playing the political game beautifully. They pretend that it's a political game, whereas in fact it's a fight between God and Satan. They don't ever say that. So they have taken the political process, and used it fairly against us. They've won the Congress and the presidency, and they're about to win the courts because of their Congress and the president. They've won state houses across the country and precincts everywhere by the political process. So they have done what we didn't do. They have a system to throw democracy out the window.

"They want to end homosexuality in America," he says, ". . . one step at a time, first the federal marriage amendment, and then comes no adoption, no service in the military, the reinstatement of the sodomy laws and driving us back into our closets, or worse. They do not want to compromise, but they begin with compromise after compromise after compromise."

The advance, White says, is demoralizing the gay community, which he warns "is losing the will to fight.

"It's safer back in the closet anyway, and since we can pass, or the gay leaders can pass, the ones who wear suits and have good jobs and have plenty of money, they will go underground," he says. "It is the gay people out there in the hinterlands who have no options. They are being rejected by their families, discarded by their parents, kicked out of their jobs, harassed, outed and killed. The gay leaders don't have a clue about this suffering.

"There are no fountains or cafeterias or bus stations we can integrate," White says. "There are no symbols that we can attack. Marriage, the one great act of defiance, in San Francisco and Massachusetts showed to the country gay couples lined up to get married. This is something they didn't like. The faces looked normal. They had children. These pictures were killing the caricatures. That, for me, is one of the great things we've done, just go to get married no matter what.

"What frightens me most are gay people who don't understand what's happening and who are unwilling to take a stand," he says. "Once they take away our rights they're going to start wanting to register us because we're the ones who have the most sexually transmitted diseases. They're going to say, 'We want to register you so we can give you special medical attention.' Quarantine comes next, along with taking away our children, the children we've adopted. They will take away the partnership rights the corporations put in place, because they can put pressure on the corporations. My bleakest description is that we'll not only be driven back into our closets, but we'll have to leave the country. Right now, we have to leave the state of Virginia, because of the law that says we can't have any agreements, or any contracts, or any powers of attorney that represent marriage. So every gay person who has a business here lives in fear."

The attack against gays and lesbians seeks to paint homosexual behavior as a form of barbarity, one step above bestiality. Gays and lesbians, like other enemies of Christ, are not fully human; they are "unnatural." And in this assault there is often lurid fascination with the grittier details of homosexual encounters. Peter LaBarbera is the executive director of the Illinois Family Institute, based in Glen Ellyn, Illinois, and a speaker who uses this rhetoric to depict gays as depraved. He denies the possibility of loving, committed relationships between gays and lesbians. He brands the lifestyle as one of "extreme promiscuity," saying that "when homosexuals call it monogamy, it's not real monogamy." And sexual relations itself between gays and lesbians is, he insists, "gross, unnatural and dangerous behavior."

He warns about what he calls "the totalitarian impulse of a gay man." He viciously attacks National Gay and Lesbian Task Force director Matt Foreman, who has criticized ex-gay therapies and the role some members of the clergy play in pushing gay men to these ex-gay groups.

LaBarbera calls on the crowd to "stop backing up in the face of homosexual cultural aggression." It is time to fight, he insists. And then he hints ominously at what he would like to see happen, how he would like to see Christians battle in ways, perhaps outside the law, that are no longer "nice," how he would like to take this war to the streets.

"We need a good cop, bad cop strategy. . . ." he says. "We've been too nice. We need to have some people go over and do the tough things, like the other side does."

CHAPTER SIX

The War on Truth

Before they seize power and establish a world according to their doctrines, totalitarian movements conjure up a lying world of consistency which is more adequate to the needs of the human mind than reality itself; in which, through sheer imagination, uprooted masses can feel at home and are spared the never-ending shocks which real life and real experiences deal to human beings and their expectations. The force possessed by totalitarian propaganda—before the movements have the power to drop iron curtains to prevent anyone's disturbing, by the slightest reality, the gruesome quiet of an entirely imaginary world—lies in its ability to shut the masses off from the real world.

—*Hannah Arendt,* The Origins of Totalitarianism[1]

In the middle of the lobby of the 50,000-square-foot Creation Museum in Petersburg, Kentucky, tumbles a 20-foot water-fall. Two life-size figures of children with long, black hair and wearing buckskin clothes play in the stream a few feet from two towering *Tyrannosaurus rex* models that move and roar. The museum has a scale model of Noah's ark, which shows how dinosaurs fit into the three levels of the vessel, along with other species such as horses, giraffes, hippopotamuses, penguins and bears. It boasts an elaborate display of the Garden of Eden in which Adam and Eve, naked but strategically positioned not to show it, swim in a river as dinosaurs and giant lizards roam the banks. Before Adam and Eve were expelled from paradise, museum visitors are informed, all of the dinosaurs were peaceable plant eaters. The evidence, they are told, is found in Genesis 1:30, in which God gives "green herb" to every creature to eat. There were no predators. Only after Adam and Eve sinned and were cast out of paradise did the dinosaurs start to eat flesh. And Adam's sin is a key component of the belief system, for in the eyes of many creationists, in order for Jesus' death to be meaningful it had to atone for that sin.

The museum has a theater equipped with seats that shake and gadgets that spray mist at the audience as the story of God's six-day creation of the world unfolds on the screen and the sound system rocks the auditorium. There are 30-foot-high walls that represent the cliffs of the Grand Canyon, floors that resemble rocks embedded with fossils, and rooms where a "Christian" paleontologist counters the claims of an "evolutionist" paleontologist. It has the appearance of a real science museum, complete with a planetarium, a gift shop, and plaques on the wall with quotes from creationist "scientists" who have the title "Doctor" conspicuously before their names. It has charts, time lines, and graphs with facts and figures. It is meant to be interactive, to create, like Universal Studios, a contrived reality with an array of costly animatronic men and women, as well as looming dinosaurs. It is part of the drive to make real a non-reality-based world, a world of miracles and magic.

"We take as our philosophy that the whole museum will prove that God's word is true," says Jean Ampt, who leads the tour through the museum.

The danger of creationism is not that it allows followers to retreat into a world of certainty and magic—which it does—but that it allows all facts to be accepted or discarded according to the dictates of a preordained ideology. Creationism removes the follower from the rational, reality-based world. Signs, miracles, and wonders occur not only in the daily life of Christians, but also in history, science, medicine and logic. This belief system becomes the basis for understanding the world, and random facts or data are collected and made to fit into the belief system. If facts can't be made to fit, they are discarded or treated as misguided opinions.

When facts are treated as if they were opinions, when there is no universal standard by which to determine truth in law, in science, in scholarship, or in the reporting of the events of the day, the world becomes a place where lies become true, where people can believe what they want to believe, where there is no possibility of reaching any conclusion not predetermined by those who interpret the official, divinely inspired text.

The museum illustrates the movement's marriage of primitive intolerance with the modern tools of technology, mass communication, sophisticated fund-raising and political organization. Totalitarian systems usually start as propaganda movements that ostensibly teach people to "believe what they want," but that opening gambit is a ruse. This insistence on the primacy of personal opinion regardless of facts destabilizes and destroys the primacy of all fact. This process leads inevitably to the big lie. Facts are useful only if they bolster the message. The use of mass-marketing techniques to persuade rather than brainwash allows millions of followers to accept the toxic totalitarian line, having been tricked into believing it's their own. Ironically, at the outset the movement seemingly encourages people to think "independently" or "courageously." It presents its ideology of creationism, repackaged as "intelligent design," as an alternative to Darwinian theories of evolution. The power of these non-reality-based movements is that they appeal to our deepest-held, most primitive prejudices, our classism, sexism, racism—perversions based on fear of complexity or change. So the propaganda contains much of what we already yearn to believe. Its subversive message is that it's OK to believe what we want, to believe lies.

In the promulgation of the totalitarian belief system, at first we are told we all have a right to an opinion, in short, a right to believe anything. Soon, under the iron control of an empowered totalitarian movement, facts become worthless, kept or discarded according to an ideological litmus test. Lies become true. And once the totalitarians are in power, facts are ruthlessly manipulated or kept hidden to support the lie. Hannah Arendt called the principle behind this process "nihilistic relativism." The goal of creationism is not to offer an alternative. Its goal is the destruction of the core values of the open society—the ability to think for oneself, to draw independent conclusions, to express dissent when judgment and common sense tell you something is wrong, to be self-critical, to challenge authority, to advocate for change and to accept that there are other views, different ways of being, that are morally and socially acceptable.

The museum will cost an estimated $25 million. It is the work of Ken Ham, a schoolteacher, one of the country's leading creationists. Other creationist museums are going up in Arkansas, Texas, California, Tennessee and Florida. The museum is part of a massive push to teach creationism in schools, championed by a vast Christian publishing and filmmaking industry that seeks to rewrite the past and make it conform to the Bible. The front lines of the culture wars are the classrooms, and the battle is one reality-based educators are slowly losing. Twenty states are considering changing the way evolution is taught in order to include creationism or intelligent design.[2] Intelligent design has been the code word of the movement since the Supreme Court ruled in the 1987 *Edwards v. Aguillard* case that creationism cannot be taught in public schools. Intelligent design argues that the slow process of evolution could not have produced something as complex as the living cell. Rather, life was created by an "intelligent agent," one the proponents of intelligent design are careful to specify is unknown, in order to skirt the judicial ban on creationism. Several states, including Pennsylvania, now have state education charters requiring that students be taught the evidence "both for and against" evolution—although there is no scientific evidence against it. And many Americans buy into the myth. When asked for their views on human origins, only 13 percent of respondents in a 2004 Gallup poll said life arose from the strictly natural process of evolution. More than 38 percent believed God guided evolution, and 45 percent said the Genesis account of creation was a true story.[3] Courses on intelligent design have been taught at the universities of Minnesota, Georgia, New Mexico and Iowa State, along with Wake Forest and Carnegie Mellon, not to mention Christian universities that teach all science through the prism of the Bible.

When Charles Lyell's *Principles of Geology* was published in 1830–1833, it challenged the prevailing views of how Earth had been formed. Lyell questioned the assumption that unique catastrophes or supernatural events—such as Noah's flood—shaped Earth's surface. He wrote that a once tumultuous period of change had slowed to today's calmer, more leisurely pace. The date of the Earth's sudden creation, up until then, had been widely accepted as 4004 BC based on the creation story in Genesis. When Charles Darwin published *The Origin of Species* in 1859, his findings further eroded the biblical account of creation. Lyell's and Darwin's works were catastrophic for biblical literalists. Evolution and natural selection shattered the comfortable worldview of many Christians, who saw themselves as created in the image of God. Evolution reduced the human race to the status of a species, one descended from primates. The scientific accounts of creation and the origin of species became in the eyes of fundamentalist believers the materialist foundation for the human race's moral and cultural decline. It dethroned Christians from their self-constructed platform of moral and ethical superiority. It challenged the belief that God intervenes in human affairs to protect and guide believers. The ideological pillars of literalist Christianity, which viewed the universe as revolving around and serving the interests of anointed Christians, were destroyed.

Literalist Christians believe that death did not exist before Adam and Eve were expelled from the Garden of Eden for disobeying God. Death and suffering were introduced by God as a punishment for living in a sinful, fallen world. Jesus' suffering and crucifixion, however, atoned for Adam's sin and made possible a return to a deathless paradise. But if the Darwinian account of evolution is correct, then death and suffering were always and always will be a part of human existence. Evolution implicitly challenges the possibility of miracles, the Second Coming of Christ, the Resurrection, and an apocalyptic end to human existence in which the saved are lifted up into heaven. For believers who have found in the certitude of Christian fundamentalism a shelter from despair, a despair that threatens to consume them again if they return to a reality-based world, evolution is terrifying. The miracles they insist they see performed around them, the presence of the guiding, comforting hand of God in their lives, the notion that there is a divine destiny specially preordained for them, crumbles into dust under the cold glare of evolution. Evolution posits what they fear most: a morally neutral universe. It obliterates the fantastic constructs of their belief system. And the steady efforts by creationists to erode the authority of evolution and discredit Darwin are, because of all this, unrelenting and fierce.

"Unlike the animals, mammals included, man is an immortal being who will live somewhere forever,"[4] reads a passage in *Biology: God's Living Creation,* a creationist textbook popular in Christian high schools. Human beings are discussed in isolation from other mammals, and brief passages interrupt the chapters with headings such as "The Wonders of the Human Hand." "Only an omnipotent and all-wise God could have designed and created the human hand,"[5] students read. Computers can never think, students are told, because "No machine will ever know satisfaction at discovering God's truth."[6] The textbook, with an index of scripture references, states that "according to the laws of probability, the probability that evolution occurred is essentially zero. Yet, evolutionists believe sincerely that it did somehow happen. We marvel at their faith in the impossible."[7]

Creationist publications such as this one blame Darwin for spawning most of the evils of modernity including racism,[8] apartheid,[9] Stalinism,[10] the Holocaust[11] and the Rwandan genocide.[12] It was evolution, the textbook states, that "exploded into a worldwide philosophy of 'kill or be killed' as expressed by Adolf Hitler and the proponents of the religion of Communism."[13] Darwin is usually presented as mentally unbalanced and sadistic. An article put out by the California-based Institute for Creation Research is typical: "Was Charles Darwin Psychotic? A Study of His Mental Health."[14] Believers are told that Darwin, and all evolutionists, were behind the genocides unleashed by all modern tyrants from Hitler and Stalin to Pol Pot.[15] And Christians must be prepared for battle, for war, against satanic forces that lie incubating within America's secular, evolutionist, materialistic, godless society, forces getting ready to begin a new round of mass exterminations, this time of American Christians.[16]

Darwin, students learn, suffered from deep depression, alienation and constant illness and physical pain once he defied God and published his work. He could not escape divine wrath. "He lost all interest in the higher things of life, the things about man that can only be explained by his being a creature made in the image of God," the textbook reads. "He lost his love for poetry, music, and literature, and, of course, he could not pray."[17]

And yet, coming from the modern age, the fundamentalists cannot discount science. They employ jargon, methods and data that appear like science to make an argument for creationism. They have created research and scholarly institutions designed to parallel legitimate scientific organizations. They pump out articles in self-published journals to provide "evidence" that homosexuals can be cured, that global warming is a myth, that abortion can cause breast cancer, that something they call "postabortion syndrome" leads to deep depression and suicide, and that abstinence-only education is an effective form of birth control. Bogus and unsubstantiated claims, all in the service of the ideology, are dressed up to look scientific. This pseudoscience seeps into the public debate, disseminated by a nervous media anxious to give both sides of every argument. Those with contempt for facts and truth, for honest research and inquiry, are given the same platform as those who deal in a world of reality, fact and rationality. The movement's leaders dress up this ideology as scientific to discredit real science. They have created a "fundamentalist science." They cannot return to the pre-Darwinian innocence that let their predecessors believe the Bible alone was enough. They need, in the midst of their flight from reality, to be reassured that science—science not contaminated by secular humanists and nonbelievers—is on their side. In this they are a distinctly modern movement. They need the imprint of science and scholarship to legitimize myth. This is a characteristic they share with all modern totalitarian movements, which work hard to co-opt the disciplines of law, science, medicine and scholarship to give to their primitive and superstitious belief systems, systems that allow the rulers to dictate reality and truth, a modern veneer. The "paraprofessional" organizations formed by the Christian Right—organizations of teachers, journalists, doctors, lawyers and scientists—mimic the activities of traditional professional groups (groups in which the focus really is the profession and not the faith). They seek to challenge the legitimacy and power of these traditional organizations. The duplication of the structures and methods employed by the nontotalitarian world, as Arendt wrote, "proved extremely fruitful in the work of undermining actively existing institutions and in the 'decomposition of the status quo,' which totalitarian organizations invariably prefer to an open show of force." [18]

The Creation Museum presents the creationist argument that Adam and Eve were human beings and that God created everything on the earth in six 24-hour days. Adherents to this worldview do not believe that the earth has existed for millions of years or that the first living cell appeared 3.5 billion years ago or that the dinosaurs roamed the planet for 160 million years before becoming extinct, their reign ending abruptly. They scoff at the notion that the dinosaurs could, as biologists suggest, be the ancestors of birds. Instead, they embrace a strict 6,000-year chronology of the Bible. Men and dinosaurs coexisted and were created during the same six-day cycle, wholly and fully evolved. When the biblical flood covered the earth, dinosaurs, along with other species, were sheltered on Noah's ark. The rest of the dinosaurs were drowned in the flood, and this, as the museum's exhibits explain, accounts for the vast tracts of fossilized dinosaur bones. Animals on the ark, including the dinosaurs, repopulated after disembarking, but environmental changes meant that the dinosaurs could not adapt and died off. The biblical accounts of sea monsters, leviathans and behemoths are, according to the museum's displays, references to dinosaurs. They do not give credence to the concept of the big bang because Genesis states that God created waters and Earth on the third day, and the sun, moon and stars on the fourth day. It is a story hardly more credible than the fantasy of a child, but it fulfills a powerful emotional need.

"The Bible tells us that God created all of the land animals on the sixth day of creation," a brochure from the museum reads. "As dinosaurs were land animals, they must have been made on this day, alongside Adam and Eve, who were also created on Day Six (Genesis 1:24–31). If God designed and created dinosaurs, they would have been fully functional, designed to do what they were created for, and would have been 100 percent dinosaur. This fits exactly with the evidence from the fossil record."

The museum devotes much of its space to trumpeting what it insists are discrepancies in the scientific search for the origins of life. The dearth of fossil ancestors for major life-forms after the "Cambrian explosion" about 550 million years ago, for example, is used by creationists to discredit evolution, although science furnishes a range of persuasive explanations for the paucity of fossils—for example, that primitive life-forms before the Cambrian period lacked hard body parts that could have been fossilized. The fact that we have any fossils of larger life-forms is an amazing piece of luck, since they can exist only in quite specific geologic conditions. But all this is used against science. And a mantra of creationists, one the museum guide repeats a few times, is: "God is not a God of gaps."

The creationists act and look like scientists. They couch their language in the jargon of science. They say they can disprove the theory of evolution with facts and evidence. They talk of research and data. It is not enough these days to argue that God wrote the story of Creation and therefore it is true. The movement needs the veneer of science. This is the goal of the museum. Science will prove the biblical account of creation and the literal interpretation of the Bible. Creationism must be defended in a scientific manner, with scientific conclusions disproving the "theory" of evolution and supporting the words of the Bible. Once the "science" of creationism is accepted, the Bible reigns as the undisputed word of God and the sole arbiter of truth. Leaders who interpret the Bible must be obeyed. Creationism is a key part of a system aimed at building a society that relinquishes the capacity to examine itself.

Museum displays say there is no proof that fossils are millions of years old. Evolution, in the hands of creationists, becomes just another unsubstantiated story about the past since "no scientist was there to see the dinosaurs live through this supposed dinosaur age."

"Some people think that dinosaurs were too big, or there were too many of them, to go on this ark," a museum display reads. It goes on to explain that in fact there were very few different kinds of dinosaurs. And then there is the speculation that perhaps not all the dinosaurs were full-grown when they mounted Noah's gangplank. "Even though there was ample room in the huge ship for large animals," the museum material explains, "perhaps God sent young adults into the ark that still had plenty of room for them to grow."

We stand in a display room called "the dig site." In front of us is a replica of a pit with the re-creation of fossilized bones of the dinosaur. The room is meant to explore, from the biblical perspective the work of paleontologists.

The paleontologist "creates a story based on her assumption about 'millions of years' of earth history with the help of artists and sculptors," reads the sign over the dig site. "She transforms the story into 'believable history' that appears in films, books and papers. The room shows how the false assumptions of evolutionary scientists end up 'as facts' in our public schools and museums."

This pseudoscience is part of a wider assault on all scientific studies that challenge the radical fundamentalist worldview. There are Christian scientists who challenge research regarding global warming, AIDS, and pregnancy prevention. Christian Right organizations such as the Traditional Values Coalition, whose founder, Paul Cameron, once called for AIDS "leper colonies,"[19] are lobbying to end all programs by the National Institutes of Health related to HIV infection. Members of the Christian Right, positioned inside government agencies, have worked to discredit or silence research by public health officials and censored data that conflict with the radical fundamentalist vision, especially regarding birth control.

Self-appointed Christian "experts" produce glossy studies to displace genuine research. Joe McIlhaney, one of the most prominent compilers of this pseudoscience, has published a brochure, *Why Condoms Aren't Safe*, which uses discredited science to prove that condoms do not work. The number of pseudoscientists peddling falsehoods inside the government is part of what triggered the Union of Concerned Scientists in March 2004 to write in its report *Scientific Integrity in Policymaking:* "There is significant evidence that the scope and scale of the manipulation, suppression, and misrepresentation of science by the Bush administration are unprecedented. . . . World-renowned scientific institutions such as the Centers for Disease Control and Prevention and the National Institutes of Health take decades to build a team of world-class scientific expertise and talent. But they can be severely damaged in short order by the scientifically unethical behavior such as that displayed by the current administration."[20]

One of the final displays in the museum shows how "a contemporary family experiences daily life without God." It portrays a household in disarray, with fights and teenager drug use. Licentiousness, alcohol abuse and the breakdown of parental authority are tied to the failure to believe in the creation myth. In this gloomy section of the museum, there is also a darkened, graffiti-covered alley and a sign that asks: "What happens when absolute authority is eliminated and man's opinion is the only measure of good and evil?"

"A walk through an inner-city alley is the backdrop for a virtual and auditory display of the horrors of a culture that had made man's opinion the final authority in life," another sign reads. These displays depict women and men out of control, hooked on drugs, sexually promiscuous, suffering in the stench of a modern Sodom and Gomorrah.

Numerous books purport to offer scientific evidence to back up creationism, including the 550-page *The Genesis Flood*, coauthored by Henry M. Morris and John Whitcomb. The book, published in 1961, has gone through 40 printings and is the movement's opening manifesto, the first assault by creationists against evolution from a "scientific" position. It seeks to lay out "evidence" to support the biblical account of creation, attacking an array of research methods that are usually obscure to the lay reader, such as the modern methods of radiometric dating. The authors write off modern research tools as unreliable and trumpet contradictory studies within the scientific community about issues such as the age of the Earth. The heavy use of scientific jargon gives the work a scholarly appearance.

Whitcomb, a graduate of Princeton, where he arrived in 1942 as "a godless evolutionist," had a conversion experience as a freshman. He interrupted college to serve in the army in World War II, including the Battle of the Bulge, and returned to complete his degree and attend Grace Theological Seminary. He stayed at the seminary for nearly forty years to teach Old Testament. He has spent his life peddling creationism. Soft-spoken, good-humored, he rattles off his theories with the aid of an overhead projector that shows time lines for the account of creation, diagrams of the planets and measurements of Noah's ark. The morning I find him in Independence, Missouri, his audience is made up of several hundred Christian schoolteachers from Midwestern states. They take notes and laugh as he pokes fun at or appears to puncture the research of secular scientists. The audience, at times, is giddy with excitement. Whitcomb assures the teachers they will be amassing the scientific ammunition to demolish the work of geologists, biologists and paleontologists who dismiss the creation account in the Bible.

"Now you say, 'Lord, you don't really expect intelligent, scientifically-minded people to believe that, that the whole universe was created in six days, do you?'" Whitcomb asks. "And God says, 'Dear reader, I have written a chapter in the Bible called Genesis 1. And it's called a time block, which means it is not fluffy, frothy and cannot be manipulated, stretched or accommodated.'"

Whitcomb brings up some of the stickier problems in Genesis, such as the account that God created light on the first day and the sun on the fourth day. He posits that God created a "temporary" light until the sun was formed. The reason for this, Whitcomb explains, is that God wanted to abolish the cult of sun worship.

"And don't think for one minute America has abandoned sun worship, either in public school textbooks, which starts this way on how the world began: 'Billions of years ago, solar radiation bathed the primeval seas and somehow activated lifeless chemicals and coalesced them into highly complex, self-reproducing organisms that have evolved under solar radiation for billions of years, and as long as the sun keeps shining, life will continue, and when the sun dies out, life ends.' What you have just heard was a sun-worship service.

"Friends," Whitcomb concludes, "it took no work at all for Jesus to do this. But astronomers in their debates and arguments on a horizontal, rationalistic level will never discover the correct answer. Don't expect any textbooks, in any university, as long as the world goes on as it is, to ever, ever come to the right conclusion. Only the infallible, inspired, inerrant, unique written revelation of God has the answers."

The lecture is met with rapturous applause. The teachers close their notebooks, and several hurry forward to ask more questions or buy books, many by Whitcomb, on the table outside the door.

Similar seminars are being held by creationists around the country. On an April night at Pennview Christian School in Souderton, Pennsylvania, about a half hour outside of Philadelphia, Dr. Jason Lisle, who works for the Creation Museum, sets up his slide projector for a lecture. He begins his presentation by disabusing his audience of about 150 people, mostly students, teachers and parents, of the notion that dinosaurs were frightful creatures.

"God didn't make monsters," he says, explaining his theory of the dinosaurs' diet. "The first *T. rex* would have eaten plants. Dinosaurs, along with all animals originally, were vegetarians.

"People say, 'Wait a minute—but *T. rex* has those incredibly sharp teeth.' And indeed, *T. rex* had six-inch serrated fangs—perfectly designed for ripping and tearing into watermelons and cantaloupes and cabbages and all kinds of fruits.

"You see, you think of a watermelon as soft. But in order to get to the soft stuff on the inside, you have to cut through the hard outer exterior. But not *T. rex*. He was quite ready to eat it off the vine."

Lisle shows fanciful slides to the audience, of raptors and stegosauruses outfitted with saddles, a caveman fighting an infant *T. rex*, and Adam and Eve strolling in the Garden of Eden alongside triceratops.

"Dinosaurs were docile, gentle, when they were first created," says Lisle. "All life's animals would have been gentle when they were first created."

"People say, 'Wait a minute. Wouldn't *T. rex* try to eat people—try to eat Adam and Eve?'" Lisle asks. But he blames the question on "anti-God, humanistic-based evolution movies" like *Jurassic Park*.

"I'm not saying it's wrong for you to see movies like that. But you need to *think* about things when you watch things like that. How do I process this from the biblical worldview? Is this really accurate?"

He tells the students he did not admit he was a creationist to his professors at Ohio Wesleyan, or at Colorado where he received his PhD in astrophysics. He speaks of the dilemma faced by creationists at secular schools, urging that students not "come out" until after graduate school. "Some professors will just stop you from getting your PhD if you're a creationist."

Lisle's final image on the screen shows a small church with a cross on its roof. Next to it is a large white cross. The large cross has the words "The Church" emblazoned on it. A network of white tree roots, labeled "Creation," secures "The Church" to the earth. Lisle explains that secular science is attacking the biblical view of creation. In his drawing is a salvo of cruise missiles with phrases "Ape = Man," "Millions of Years" and "Evolution" printed on their sides as they head in an arch toward the roots. These attacks, he says, are aimed to bring down the cross, to destroy the church.

He shows a slide picturing a small hut with a radar dish on the roof. The hut is labeled "Answers in Genesis," the church's early warning system. He flips to a new slide.

The church begins firing lasers—emitted from its cross—at the incoming missiles. The cascade of laser beams strikes the missiles, causing them—and their blasphemies—to erupt into flames.

"Come to the Cross and be saved!" proclaims the final slide.[21]

All attempts to seek truth, however elusive and difficult, challenge the blind obedience and suppression of conscience championed by those who teach one "truth" and one way of being. When only one "truth" is allowed, empirical data becomes irrelevant. Intellectual, scientific and moral inquiry becomes unnecessary. In this new world followers are robbed of the capacity to think. The lies, however enormous and absurd, defy criticism and unmasking because the rational world is discredited and finally silenced. The Creation Museum, standing with its imposing pillars, its sea of parking lots for school buses, 52 acres of groomed landscaping, pond, looping nature trails, animatronic dinosaurs and "Christian" paleontologists, presages a society where truth is banished.

CHAPTER SEVEN

The New Class

To tell men that they are equal has a certain sentimental appeal. But this appeal is small compared with that made by a propaganda that tells them they are superior to others, and that others are inferior to them.

—*Karl Popper*, The Open Society and Its Enemies, *Vol. 1*[1]

The elevator at the Hilton Hotel in Anaheim, California, fills floor by floor, as it descends with delegates for the National Religious Broadcasters annual convention. There is a slightly forced camaraderie and an awkward cheerfulness as we head down to the lobby. People glance quickly at the plastic name tags on one another's chests. They smile as new passengers step inside and say good morning. They sprinkle the words of the converted into their banter, talking about how "blessed" they are to be here, beginning brief dialogues with phrases such as "Where is your ministry?" and ending them with "Praise the Lord." This call-and-response is a form of initiation, an easy way to draw the lines between themselves and nonbelievers, to establish the parameters of their exclusive community. All subcultures have their linguistic codes of identification. This new class is no exception.

The convention has brought together some 5,500 Christian broadcasters from radio and television, who reach, according to their figures, an estimated 141 million listeners and viewers across America. And they see themselves as both the persecuted and the powerful. These twin themes run through the event. They are both threatened by conspiratorial forces that seek to destroy them and empowered by the certainty of Christ's return. These emotions bond them together as a crowd, as comrades in the battle against the godless.

Southern California, along with Colorado Springs, is one of the epicenters of the radical movement. Numerous television evangelists, including the disgraced Jimmy and Tammy Faye Bakker, got their start in these huge, soulless exurbs. These large developed tracts of housing are isolated, devoid of neighborhood gathering places, community rituals and routines, even of sidewalks. The isolation, coupled with the long, lonely commutes in a car; the cold, impersonal world of the corporate office; and the banal, incessant chatter of talk radio and television create numbness and disorientation. This destruction of community is one of the crucial factors that has led to the rise of the Christian Right. The megachurches, which have prospered in these environments, have become surrogate communities, places where people can find clubs to pursue common interests, friends, a sense of belonging, and moral direction. In these sprawling churches, which often look like shopping or convention centers, believers are reassured, told that affluence is blessed by God—a sign of their righteousness and the righteousness of their nation—and that in the embrace of the church they have a place, a home.

There is a Starbucks in the Hilton Hotel lobby. Dee Simmons from Dallas is waiting to order a coffee. Around her neck she is wearing a gold cross studded with diamonds, and on her face, smooth and unwrinkled, makeup is artfully applied. The line of men and women, in front and behind us, is conservatively dressed in skirts or coats and ties. They are about to head into the convention hall next door. Simmons and a friend, Samantha Landy, with red hair, are chatty and friendly.

In 1987, Simmons says, she was diagnosed with breast cancer and had a "modified radical mastectomy." Five years later her mother died of cancer. These events led her, she says, to turn her focus away from the designer clothes boutiques she owned in Dallas and New York to nutrition.

"When God gave me my life back, I decided to make a difference in people's lives," she says.

She reaches into her purse and pulls out some pamphlets for Ultimate Living, her company. She tells me about her books, including *The Natural Guide to Healthy Living,* and mentions the numerous Christian talk shows she regularly appears on, including Pat Robertson's *The 700 Club,* as well as *Hope Today, Praise, Something Good Tonight* and the *Armstrong Williams Show.*

"I was saved and found Christ when I was 3," she says. "I'm 64. My daughter is 36."

She appears to wait for the effect of her age, which she will repeat a few more times, to sink in.

"I also have skin care products which are all natural," she says. "I am on *Living the Life* once or twice a month, the show with Terry Meeuwsen, who was Miss America. There is a huge crossover with my nutrition work. Everyone is interested in nutrition, even nonbelievers. I use organically grown papayas. I have eight laboratories where I make Green Miracle. Green Miracle combines greens and roots that are ground up. They have all the vital nutrients. I sell it at cancer hospitals. It is good for diabetes, heart disease, immune support, hormone problems, any issue, really."

Landy tells me she runs "Christian celebrity luncheons" in Palm Springs as part of her work of "salvation outreach for snowbirds." Her ministry, she says, focuses on country clubs and golf courses, places "where people do not often hear the word of God.

"A lot of people go to churches and assume the pastor has a personal relationship with Christ," she says, "but they often do not. I bring in celebrity speakers like Gavin MacLeod, he was the Captain on *Love Boat;* and Rhonda Fleming, she was in over 40 films and starred with Bing Crosby—speakers who have really accomplished things in the world who are Christian. Rhonda Fleming did her own stunts."

Her list of Christian celebrities available to speak includes Donna Douglas from the *Beverly Hillbillies;* Ann B. Davis, who was

Alice on *The Brady Bunch;* and Lauren Chapin, who played Kathy on *Father Knows Best.*

"Tell him about the wedding," Landy prompts.

Simmons's daughter recently got married in Dallas. The wedding was filmed for broadcast on a show called *Sheer Dallas.* She urges me to watch it. The wedding theme, she says, was "Sultan's Palace: Her Majesty the Queen." There were 500 guests who gathered in a building known as the Hall of State and "flowers from all over the world." She says she would rather not mention the cost. Her husband—who, she says, is "very, very wealthy," adding "I don't need to work"—refers, she says, to the wedding expense as "the national debt."

"Her husband is quite a bit older," Landy interjects.

"There was a huge fireworks display," Simmons says, "but I am too embarrassed to tell you how much it cost. When the fireworks stopped, a quartet sang 'God Bless America.' There was a saxophone solo. Everyone had chills."

"It was awesome," Landy says.

The cake took three months to make. There were jewels and semiprecious stones both on the cake and in the bridal bouquet. Both had to be brought the day of the wedding to the Hall of State in an armored truck.

"The bridal gown took five and a half months to make," she says. "It had mink this thick," she adds, holding her thumb and index finger about four inches apart.

The women, minor celebrities in the world of Christian broadcasting, capture the strange fusion between this new, flamboyant gospel of prosperity and America's celebrity-driven culture. Not only are the wealthy blessed by the Lord and encouraged to engage in a frenzy of outlandish consumption, but also those who are famous, those who have achieved any celebrity or notoriety, no matter how minor, or those who have power, are seen as having important things to say about faith. Wealth, fame and power are manifestations of God's work, proof that God has a plan and design for believers. This new class of celebrity, plutocrat Christians fuses with the consumer society, one where the lives and opinions of entertainers, the rich and the powerful are news. The women tell me they are in Anaheim because the yearly convention is the only time they can see all the major Christian broadcasters in one place. But it is clear they also come to be seen.

"These are the people who set up the shows," Simmons says. "This is a good way to see everybody. It is like the gathering of one big family. We have flown in to network."

This is the apotheosis of capitalism, the divine sanction of the free market, of unhindered profit and the most rapacious cruelties of globalization. Corporations, rapidly turning America into an oligarchy, have little interest in Christian ethics, or anybody's ethics. They know what they have to do, as the titans of the industry remind us, for their stockholders. They are content to increase profit at the expense of those who demand fair wages, health benefits, safe working conditions and pensions. This new oligarchic class is creating a global marketplace where all workers, to compete, will have to become like workers in dictatorships such as China: denied rights, their wages dictated to them by the state, and forbidden from organizing or striking. America once attempted to pull workers abroad up to American levels, to foster the building of foreign labor unions, to challenge the abuse of workers in factories that flood the American market with cheap goods. But this new class seeks to reduce the American working class to the levels of this global serfdom. After all, anything that drains corporate coffers is a loss of freedom—the God-given American freedom to exploit other human beings to make money. The marriage of this gospel of prosperity with raw, global capitalism, and the flaunting of the wealth and privilege it brings, are supposedly blessed and championed by Jesus Christ. Compassion is relegated to private, individual acts of charity or left to churches. The callousness of the ideology, the notion that it in any way reflects the message of the gospels, which were preoccupied with the poor and the outcasts, illustrates how the new class has twisted Christian scripture to serve America's god of capitalism and discredited the Enlightenment values we once prized.

The Convention Center, located next door, is a huge, curvy glass structure with gleaming towers. The exhibition hall on the first floor has plush, blue carpeting and 320 display booths. At the far end of the hall lie the twisted remains of an Israeli bus blown up by Palestinian suicide bombers in Jerusalem. The Israeli Ministry of Tourism has the largest display space in the hall. The Christian Law Center, organized to remove "activist judges" in the courts, has people handing out yardsticks of gum. At a booth featuring Valerie Saxion's book *The Gospel of Health*, they are mixing raspberry shakes in blenders. A Virginia Web design company in another booth offers "church Web sites the way God intended." A bearded man dressed as a biblical prophet promotes tours to the Holy Land. Numerous antiabortion booths are staffed by women, who, it often turns out, had multiple abortions before finding Christ. There are fringe groups such as Jews for Jesus and Accuracy in Media, which is passing out a report with the title *American Troops Cheer Attacks on U.S. Media.*

Rows of palm trees are visible through banks of windows, and on the upper floors are technical workshops, such as "Finding God in Hollywood," as well as luncheons. One seminar is entitled "Taking Over Cities for Christ: The Thousand-Day Plan." In the parking lot outside the center is a pickup truck with large hand-painted panels covered with antigay slogans. There is a round red circle with a line through the center superimposed on the faces of two men kissing. "Stop the Insanity" is painted across the top. I walk outside after surveying the hall and pick up one of the pamphlets in a metal box on the side of the truck. "PROTECT YOUR FAMILY & FRIENDS FROM THE DANGERS OF . . . HOMOSEXUALITY: THE TRUTH!" the pamphlet says. It lists "the facts about homosexuality they refuse to teach in Public Schools or report on the Evening News!" including "because of unsanitary sexual practices, homosexuals carry the bulk of all bowel disease in America" and "homosexuals average 500 sexual partners in their short lifetime."

The opening session is held on the third floor, a large room with a round stage surrounded on three sides with rows of folding chairs. The hall is dimly lit. There are a few thousand people. Large television screens are suspended from the ceilings, and the platform in front of us has a podium and a grand piano. The host, Bob Lepine, cohost of the radio show *Family Life Today*, broadcast from Little Rock, Arkansas, is a round-faced man with an easy smile. He begins the session by showing himself in a video wandering the beaches near Anaheim asking surfers and stray Californians, some of whom clearly spent the night sleeping on the beach, what "NRB" means. No one knows, but the guesses evoke laughter from the hall.

"One of the fun things about coming here . . . I was thinking about the old days, you know, when we used to go to Washington to the Sheraton in February, and it's cold, and now we come here and it's warm, and you get to go to the beach and see weird people," he quips. He explains that the evening is sponsored by the Family Research Council and introduces its president, Tony Perkins, who, he notes, "was responsible for the covenant marriage law that got passed in Louisiana," a law that made it harder for couples to divorce.

Perkins is typical of the new class of insider-cum-outsiders. He organized the rallies, broadcast around the nation to church audiences, known as "Justice Sunday," which featured an array of politicians such as Senate majority leader Bill Frist, all pounding home one central theme: the Democrats are at war with "people of faith." The Democrats used the filibuster, viewers were told, to block judicial appointees who were people of faith. Perkins works for James Dobson, who founded the Family Research Council, the lobbying arm of his Focus on the Family empire. Dobson has said the Supreme Court's legalization of abortion with *Roe v. Wade* unleashed "the biggest Holocaust in world history" and has compared the "black-robed men" on the Supreme Court to "the men in white robes, the Ku Klux Klan."[2]

Justice Sunday was part of a strategy devised more than two decades ago by Woody Jenkins, Perkins's political mentor. Jenkins and some 50 conservative men gathered in May 1981 at the northern Virginia home of direct-mail pioneer Richard Viguerie to plot the growth of their movement following Ronald Reagan's presidential victory. They formed the Council for National Policy (CNP), a secretive, right-wing organization that brought together dominionists such as R. J. Rushdoony, Pat Robertson and Jerry Falwell with right-wing industrialists willing to fund them, such as Amway founder Richard DeVos Sr. and beer baron Joseph Coors. As DeVos quipped, the CNP "brings together the doers with the donors."[3]

Jenkins, then a Louisiana state lawmaker, became the CNP's first executive director. He told a *Newsweek* reporter: "One day before the end of this century, the Council will be so influential that no president, regardless of party or philosophy, will be able to ignore us or our concerns or shut us out of the highest levels of government."[4]

In 1999, Texas Governor George W. Bush addressed the group as he launched his bid for the presidency. The media were barred from the event. But those who wrote about the meeting afterward said that Bush, who refused to release a public transcript of his speech, promised to only appoint antiabortion judges if he was elected. The group, which meets three times a year in secret, brings together radical Christian activists, right-wing Republican politicians and wealthy patrons willing to fund the movement. During Bush's presidency, Dick Cheney and Donald Rumsfeld have attended CNP meetings.[5]

Perkins, like other leaders in the movement, has troubling associations with white supremacy groups. They work hard now to distance themselves from these relationships, often quoting Dr.

Martin Luther King Jr. and drawing parallels between their movement and the civil-rights movement. But during the 1996 Senate
campaign of Woody Jenkins, Perkins, who was Jenkins's campaign
manager, signed an $82,500 check to the head of the Ku Klux
Klan, David Duke, to acquire Duke's phone bank list.[6] And as late
as 2001, Perkins spoke at a fund-raiser for the Council of Conservative Citizens, a white nationalist group that has called blacks "a
retrograde species of humanity" on its Web site.[7]

The ties by Christian Right leaders such as Perkins with racist
groups highlight the long ties between right-wing fundamentalists and American racist organizations, including the Klan, which
had a chaplain assigned to each chapter. During the Depression,
when many on the right and in corporate America were openly
flirting with fascism, fundamentalist preachers such as Gerald B.
Winrod and Gerald L. K. Smith fused national and Christian symbols to advocate the country's first crude form of Christo-fascism.
Smith, who openly admired the Nazis, founded a group called the
Christian Nationalist Crusade, whose magazine was *The Cross and
the Flag*. The movement proclaimed that "Christian character is
the basis of all real Americanism."[8]

By the late 1950s these radical Christians had drifted to the
fiercely anticommunist John Birch Society. Many of the ideas
championed by today's dominionists—the bizarre conspiracy theories, the calls for unrestrained capitalism, the war against "liberal" organizations such as the mainstream media and groups
such as the ACLU, along with the calls to dismantle federal agencies that deal with housing or education—are drawn from the ideology of this rabid anticommunist enclave. Timothy LaHaye used
to run John Birch Society training seminars in California. And
Nelson Bunker Hunt, a member of the John Birch Society's national council, worked with LaHaye to help found the CNP.[9]

A baritone voice booms throughout the arena as we watch
video images of the nation's capital: "America's culture was hijacked by a secular movement determined to redefine society,

from religious freedom to the right to life. These radicals were doing their best to destroy two centuries of traditional values, and no one seemed to be able to stop them until now."

"Will Congress undo 200 years of tradition?" the video asks ominously. "Not on our watch."

"This is about calling Christians across this nation to action," Perkins says in the video. "As one who spent nearly a decade in political office and even longer as a minister of the Gospel, I see [the Family Research Council] as a bridge between Christians and between government. Spanning a gulf that has been created by judicial decisions that have taken away the rich soil of this nation, that is this historical soil of Christianity, and by those whose misguided theology have caused Christians to abandon the public square, leaving a cavernous void in public policy. As this bridge, the Family Research Council sends its team to Congress and into the White House on a daily basis, to advocate for family and for our faith."

There was a brief attempt at resistance to the rule of National Religious Broadcasters by these dominionists. Wayne Pederson in 2002 was appointed to replace the group's longtime president, Brandt Gustavson. "We get associated with the far Christian right and marginalized," Pederson told a reporter for the *Star Tribune* in Minneapolis. "To me the important thing is to keep the focus on what's important to us spiritually." [10] His effort to shift the organization's focus away from politics saw the executive committee orchestrate his removal a few weeks later. He was replaced by Frank Wright, who had spent the previous eight years serving as the executive director of Kennedy's Center for Christian Statesmanship, a Capitol Hill ministry that conducts training for politicians on how to "think biblically about their role in government."

Wright, with white hair and a cold, hard demeanor, lacks the easy banter of Lepine or the comforting, bland good looks of Perkins. Wright lauds the transformation in Washington, saying that 130 members of the House of Representatives are "born again." He tells a story, which elicits laughter and applause, of how during a late-night private tour of the capital, he and other pastors stopped and prayed over Hillary Clinton's Senate floor desk.

Wright, like most speakers, begins by talking about his long marriage. It is a reminder that in Christ is stability, that the home and marriage are protected, that Christian men and women achieve bliss denied to others. The movement, he says, is the bulwark against chaos, against a return to lives spinning out of control.

"The Gospel changed not just my life, it changed my marriage to Ruth," he says. "It changed my family. The Gospel changes families, and churches and communities and cities and nations. All of what we call Western civilization today, it has the shape that it has and the character that it has because the Gospel changes things."

And then he warns his listeners about the enemies at the gate, saying that "calls for diversity and multiculturalism are nothing more than thinly veiled attacks on anyone who is willing or desirous or compelled to proclaim Christian truth. Today, calls for tolerance are often a subterfuge, because they'll tolerate just about anything except Christian truth."

The broadcasters' association, he explains, is lobbying in Congress against hate-crime legislation, which, Wright explains to the audience, "is step one to defining what you do as against the law." The broadcasters have worked to thwart the "fairness doctrine," what he calls "the bane of Christian broadcasters.

"A bill was filed in the House of Representatives that would require any programming that was 'controversial,' quote unquote, in nature, to give equal time to opposing viewpoints," he tells the crowd. "Now let me think about this . . . controversial things . . . the divinity of Christ, the virgin birth, the bodily Resurrection. Everything we teach is controversial to someone else. If we had to give equal time to every opposing viewpoint, there would be no time to proclaim the truth that we've been commanded to proclaim. So we will fight the 'fairness doctrine' tooth and nail. It could be the end of Christian broadcasting if we don't."

The preoccupation with legislation, the plethora of speakers who come from Christian lobbying groups based in the capital, attest to a movement that is increasingly as preoccupied with legislation as with saving souls. And those that do not deal with the nuts and bolts of legislation remind those present that there are forces out there that seek to destroy Christians. James MacDonald, an imposing man with a shaved head, runs a church in Arlington Heights, Illinois, and is heard regularly on 600 Christian radio outlets. He fires up the crowd.

"How many of you out there think ministering the Word is unpopular?" he asks, as a sea of hands shoots into the air.

"His eyes are like a flame of fire," MacDonald says, quoting Revelation 19. "Out of his mouth goes a sharp sword, and with it he can strike the nations. He treads the wine press of the fierceness and wrath of the almighty God, and on his robe and on his thigh a name is written: King of Kings and Lord of Lords. Jesus commands all men everywhere to come to the knowledge of Him."

He reminds us that "ages of faith are not marked by dialogue but by proclamation" and "there is power in the unapologetic proclamation of truth. There is power in it. This is a kingdom of power." When he says the word "power," he draws it out for emphasis. He tells the crowd to eschew the "persuasive words of human wisdom." Truth, he says, does "not rest in the wisdom of men but the power of God." And, in a lisping imitation of liberals, he mocks, amid laughter and applause, those who want to "share" and be sensitive to the needs of others.

His antics delight most of the crowd, but not all. Luis Palau, a close protégé of Billy Graham, is one of the few present at the convention who is uncomfortable with the naked and repeated calls for power. Palau is an affable man, an Argentine with a refreshing worldliness about him. He also represents a traditional evangelicalism that has been shunted aside, often ruthlessly, by this new class. His focus is on personal salvation, he says, not the seizing of political power. He refused to become involved in the referendum banning gay marriage in Oregon, where his organization is based, although he, like Graham, is no supporter of gay rights. But he bristles at the coarseness, the naked calls for a Christian state, and the anti-intellectualism. He, like Graham, shuns the movement's caustic, biting humor that belittles homosexuals, those deemed effete intellectuals and those condemned as "secular humanists." The emphasis on abortion and gay marriage to the exclusion of other issues worries him.

"There are some Christians who have gone overboard," Palau says, choosing his words carefully as we talk. "The message has become a little distorted in states where they talk about change yet focus on only one issue. We need a fuller transformation. The great thing Billy Graham did was to bring intellectualism back to fundamentalism.

"I don't think it is wrong to want to see political change, especially in places like Latin America," he says. "Something has to happen in politics. But it has to be based on convictions. We have to overcome the sense of despair. I worked in Latin America in the days when almost every country had a dictator. I dreamed, especially as a kid, of change, of freedom and justice. But I believe that change comes from personal conviction, from leading a more biblical lifestyle, not by Christianizing a nation. If we become called to Christ, we will build an effective nation through personal ethics. When you lead a life of purity, when you respect your wife and are good to your family, when you don't waste money gambling and womanizing, you begin to work for better schools, for more protection and safety for your community. All change, historically, comes from the bottom up. And this means changing the masses from within."

Palau sees his work as focused on the conversion of souls, who, once they become saved, will become a force for "structural, institutional change." But this, he adds, "can take two or three generations."

The emphasis on personal renewal and commitment to Christ—the staple message of evangelists such as Billy Graham and Luis Palau—is an anachronism to the new class. While speakers demand that followers give their lives to Christ, and while the born-again experience is considered the dividing line between believers and nonbelievers, the conversion experience is no longer the dominant theme pounded home from the pulpit or across the airwaves. It has been replaced by the rhetoric of war, the demands of a warrior God who promises blood and vengeance, and by the rhetoric of persecution, by the belief that there are sinister forces that seek the destruction of believers. It has also been replaced by a conspicuous and unapologetic infatuation with wealth, power and fame. As the movement has shifted away from the focus on personal salvation to a focus on power, it has incorporated into its theology the values, or lack of them, of a flagrant consumer society.

The strangest alliance, on the surface, is with Israeli Jews. After all, the movement generally teaches that Jews who do not convert are damned and will be destroyed in the fiery, apocalyptic ending of the world. It is early on Sunday morning in a ballroom on the second floor of the Hilton Hotel. The Israel Ministry of Tourism is hosting a breakfast. Several hundred people are seated at round tables with baskets of bread, fruit plates and silver pitchers of coffee. Waiters are serving plates of scrambled eggs and creamed spinach. Nearly everyone is white. On the platform is a huge picture of the Dome of the Rock, the spot where the Temple will be rebuilt to herald the Second Coming. Some 700,000 Christian tourists visit Israel each year, and with the steep decline in overall tourism, they have become a valued source of revenue in Israel.

Dominionists preach that Israel must rule the biblical land in order for Christ to return. The belief that Jews who do not convert will be killed is unmentioned at the breakfast. The featured speakers include Avraham Hirschsohn, the new Israeli minister of tourism; and Michael Medved, a cultural conservative and a nationally syndicated radio talk-show host. Medved is one of the most prominent Jewish defenders of Mel Gibson's *The Passion of the Christ* and of the radical Christian Right. He wears a yarmulke and is warmly greeted by the crowd.

"A more Christian America is good for the Jews," he says. "This is obvious. Take a look at this support for Israel. A more Christian America is good for America, something Jewish people need to be more cognizant about and acknowledge. A more Jewish community is good for the Christians, not just because of the existence of allies, but because a more Jewish community is less seduced by secularism."

A former left-wing radical, who in later life embraced Orthodox Judaism, he lambastes other Jews for their hostility to Christianity.

"When you see Jews who are part of the attack on Christmas," he says, "you know they have rejected their own faith."

He ticks off causes in which both Jewish and Christian people have been active, including the call for prayer in schools and the fight against abortion (although abortion is legal in Israel). He defends his Jewish integrity by saying he does not believe in the Rapture. But this is more than a religious alliance. It is a political alliance. It unites messianic Christians with right-wing messianic Jews, who believe God has anointed them to expand their dominion throughout the Middle East at the expense of the Arab majority.

This is soon made clear by the next speaker, Glenn Plummer, a black minister from Detroit who is active in the Republican Party. It is his role—I suspect because his status as an inner-city black minister makes expression of such sentiments "all right"— to unleash the audience's vituperative hate against Muslims. He says he knows about Muslims because "I come from Detroit, where the biggest mosque in America is. It didn't take 9/11 to show me there is a global battle going on for the souls of men. . . . When Islam comes into a place it is intent on taking over everything, not only government, but the business, the neighborhoods, everything."

The Christian writer Kay Arthur, who can barely contain her tears when speaking of the Jews and Israel, assures those in the room that, although she loves America, if she had to choose between America and Israel, "I would stand with Israel, stand with Israel as a daughter of the King of Kings, stand according to the word of God." She goes on to quote at length from the Book of Revelation, repeating many of the familiar passages that inspire the movement, and speaks of Jesus seated in a throne floating about Jerusalem as believers are raptured up toward him in the sky. The fate of unreconstructed Jews, including—one would assume—those hosting the breakfast, is omitted.

A popular radio host, Janet Parshall, who also leads tours to the Holy Land, speaks to the group of her dialogue with the Lord about taking tourists to a place where there are suicide bombings and attacks.

"'God, the Holy Land has terrorists,' I said. But God said, 'Janet, you're from Washington DC,'" a quote that elicited laughter.

Hirschsohn, Israel's minister of tourism, says to the gathering: "You stood with us for the last four years when nobody else would. Thank you."

"The Bible tells us the Lord spoke to Abraham in the land where today American troops are defending freedom," he says. He announces that the Israeli tourism ministry will build a "pilgrim center" for Christian tourists in the Galilee.

The charred remains of Israeli Public Bus 19 are in the neighboring convention hall. The bus, owned by a Christian Zionist group called the Jerusalem Connection, was blown up by Palestinian suicide bombers in January 2004. The president of the organization, retired U.S. Brigadier General James Hutchens, according to information from the group, "looks at the conflict in Israel within a biblical context." Bus 19 has, since the group acquired it, been displayed around the world, including in The Hague and in numerous "Remember Israel" rallies in the United States. On a table next to the bus, a seated Jerusalem Connection official hands out pamphlets reading, "Bring Bus #19 To Your Community!"

One of the reasons to bring the bus, the pamphlet says, is that "for Christians, you will increase in stature, appreciation and acceptance by Jews."

An Egyptian woman, a Christian who is manning a booth near the bus that advertises Christian broadcasts to the Arab world, is periodically reduced to tears by enraged conventioneers who, after visiting the bus, tell her Arabs are "terrorists."

Onlookers climb onto a platform alongside the bus to peer within. Its sides are scorched black, center doors twisted, steel frame bent and shattered. Bus 19 has been adorned with banners bearing biblical quotations, including: "I will plant Israel in their own land, never again to be uprooted from the land I have given them" (Amos 9:15); "And I will bless those who bless you. And whoever curses you I will curse" (Genesis 12:3), and "Those who say come, let us destroy them as a nation, that the name of Israel be remembered no more. . . . They form an alliance against God" (Psalm 83:4–5).

There are cards of condolences from American schoolchildren, flowers on the flooring of the bus, and at the base of the raised platform large photos and biographies of those killed in the attack. A poster reads: "When Palestinians love their children, more than they hate Israel, then there will be peace in Palestine." The poster shows six photos of children holding weapons or strapped with explosives.

"Over 50 public transportation buses just like this one have been bombed in Israel," reads another sign. "In three and a half years, suicide bombers have killed more than 975 people in Israel. They are represented here."

But some of the Israelis in the hall are uncomfortable with the Bus 19 display. They are telling conventioneers, whom they are trying to get to visit Israel, that the bus represents an old phase in the conflict, and that Israel is now moving toward peace. One Israeli is Marina, who has long, blond hair, a brown shirt, and knee-high leather boots. She immigrated to Israel from Holland and lives on a cooperative mango farm near the Sea of Galilee. She says she is "embarrassed" to be at the convention. "These people are anti-Semitic," she says, speaking softly as conventioneers move past the large Israeli display space. She is unhappy with the bigotry toward Muslims expressed by the speakers. When asked why the ministry is here, she answers curtly: "money."

"No one else visits Israel," she says.

In this version of the Christian Gospel, the exploitation and abuse of other human beings is a good. Homosexuality is an evil. And this global, heartless system of economic rationalism has morphed in the rhetoric of the Christian Right into a test of faith. The ideology it espouses is a radical evil, an ideology of death. It calls for wanton destruction, destruction of human beings, of the environment, of communities and neighborhoods, of labor unions, of a free press, of Iraqis, Palestinians or others in the Middle East who would deny us oil fields and hegemony, of federal regulatory agencies, social welfare programs, public education—in short, the destruction of all people and programs that stand in the way of a Christian America and its God-given right to dominate the rest of the planet. The movement offers, in return, the absurd but seductive promise that those who are right with God will rise to become spiritual and material oligarchs. They will become the new class. Those who are not right with God, be they poor or Muslim or unsaved, deserve what they get. In the rational world none of this makes sense. But believers have been removed from a reality-based world. They believe that through Jesus all is possible. It has become a Christian duty to embrace the exploitation of others, to build a Christian America where freedom means the freedom of the powerful to dominate the weak. Since believers see themselves as becoming empowered through faith, the gross injustices and repression that could well boomerang back on most of them are of little concern. They assuage their consciences with the small acts of charity they or their churches dole out to the homeless or the mission fields. The emotion-filled religious spectacles and spiritual bromides compensate for the emptiness of their lives. They are energized by hate campaigns against gays or Muslims or liberals or immigrants. They walk willingly into a totalitarian prison they are helping to construct. They yearn for it. They work for it with passion, self-sacrifice and a blinding self-righteousness. "Evil when we are in its power is not felt as evil but as a necessity, or even a duty," Simone Weil wrote in *Gravity and Grace*. And it is the duty of the Christian foot soldiers to bring about the Christian utopia. When it is finished, when all have been stripped of legal and social protection, it will be too late to resist. This is the genius of totalitarian movements. They convince the masses to agitate for their own incarceration.

CHAPTER EIGHT

The Crusade

One of the most striking traits of the inner life of a crowd is the feeling of being persecuted, a peculiar angry sensitiveness and irritability directed against those it has once and forever nominated as enemies. These can behave in any manner, harsh or conciliatory, cold or sympathetic, severe or mild—whatever they do will be interpreted as springing from an unshakable malevolence, a premeditated intention to destroy the crowd, openly or by stealth.

—*Elias Canetti*, Crowds and Power[1]

Pastor Russell Johnson stands against the backdrop of a huge American flag with the Christian cross superimposed on the Stars and Stripes. He calls his Christian warriors to battle. He invokes the legacy of the civil-rights movement, speaking of Dr. Martin Luther King Jr. and Rosa Parks. He talks of embattled Christians in America. A war of values and morals, of decency and goodness pitted against forces of darkness and evil, has enveloped the country, and he issues a strident call to arms. He calls Ohio "the tip of the spear to turn back the nation.

"We're on the beaches of Normandy, and we can see the pillbox entrenchments of academic and media liberalism," he says. "We'll take back our country for Christ."

Johnson, who leads the Ohio Restoration Project, is on a 10-city tour in Ohio. The Christian group's credo is "Pray, Serve, Engage." The rallies across the state are thinly disguised campaign events for "Christian" candidates, such as Ohio Secretary of State J. Kenneth Blackwell, the Republican nominee for governor. But the speakers also pound home the message that Christians must protect the family, ban abortion, bring back school prayer and register voters who will create a Christian Ohio. There are voter registration cards available, and the few hundred people at the rally are urged to join the "Patriot Pastors"—some 2,000 Ohio pastors, each of whom has promised to recruit 100 new "Intercessors" or "Faithful Servants of Prayer" and 200 "Minutemen Volunteers" to work in the upcoming election. The goal of the movement is to register 300,000 new voters. Johnson has called for a monthly voter-registration Sunday where clergy will show a PowerPoint presentation on how to register, collect cards and send them directly to the office of the secretary of state. These new voters will, in a phrase repeated often at the rally, be like "salt and light for America." They will stem the forces out to destroy them and the nation. They will return America to the Christian path—which, Johnson claims, was the intent and goal of the nation's founders.

The fusion of Christian and national symbols marks a completion for those at the rally of America's new state religion, a Christo-fascism. A choir sings rousing patriotic and Christian hymns while pictures of American troops fighting in Iraq flash on huge screens. There are moments of prayer and a somber honoring of the men and women in uniform, with all veterans in the room asked to stand. Looming above it all is a huge American flag with the Christian cross superimposed on it. On another wall is a flag with a superimposed George Washington, sword by his side, kneeling in prayer. Christian rallies like these are also being held in other states such as Texas and Pennsylvania.

Johnson warns about the "secular jihadists" who have "hijacked" America, removing public prayer from schools, the 10 Commandments and the Bible from public places. He accuses the public schools, which he says promote an ideology of secular humanism, of neglecting to teach that Hitler was "an avid evolutionist." There can be no negotiation, no compromise, no deals cut with the enemy. And the enemy lives in your neighborhood, teaches in your schools and works in your office. The battle lines are being demarcated in the suburbs of Dayton and across America.

Johnson likens America's predicament to that of Nazi Germany. He tells the gathering of about 400 supporters that church congregations in Germany would sing so that they could not hear the passing of trainloads of crying Jews headed for nearby concentration camps. He accuses Christians in America of leading "Neville Chamberlain lives," referring to the British prime minister who naively signed a neutrality pact with Adolf Hitler. As Johnson speaks, pictures of Hitler and Chamberlain flash on the screens. If Christians do not begin to act, they will be next. They will be hauled off in freight cars like the Jews in Nazi Germany and murdered.

The rhetoric creates an atmosphere of being under siege. It also imparts the warm glow of comradeship, the feeling that although outside these walls there is a dangerous, hostile world, here we are all brothers and sisters. It is clear to whom Christians bear a moral obligation: to fellow Christians. The world is divided into friends and enemies, neighbors and strangers. A moral obligation, Freud wrote, only increases with our affection for an individual. In this room, the commandment to "Love your neighbor as yourself" is twisted, in ways Freud could understand, to "Love your fellow Christians as yourself." Loving one's neighbor presupposes a bond, a shared sense of belonging, but it was a presupposition Freud pointed out was absurd. "If this grandiose commandment had run 'love thy neighbor as thy neighbor loves thee,' I should not take exception to it," he wrote.[2] Loving a stranger, Freud said, was counter to human nature: "If he is a stranger to me . . . it will be hard for me to love him."[3] And those outside the Christian community are effectively made strangers. They are no longer worthy of being loved. The distinction creates a world where there are only two types of people. There are godly men and women who advance Christian values, and there are nonbelievers—many of them liberal Christians—who peddle the filth and evil of secular humanism. This dividing line is nothing

other than the distinction between human and nonhuman, between the worthy and those unworthy of life, between saved and
unsaved, between friend and foe.

In rallies like those in Johnson's Ohio tour, friends, neighbors,
colleagues and family members who do not conform to the ideology are gradually dehumanized. They are tainted with the de-
spised characteristics inherent in the godless. This attack is
waged in highly abstract terms, to negate the reality of concrete,
specific and unique human characteristics, to deny the possibility
of goodness in those who do not conform. Some human beings,
the message goes, are no longer human beings. They are types.
This new, exclusive community fosters rigidity, conformity and intolerance. In this new binary world segments of the human race
are disqualified from moral and ethical consideration. And because fundamentalist followers live in a binary universe, they are
incapable of seeing others as anything more than inverted reflections of themselves. If they seek to destroy nonbelievers to create
a Christian America, then nonbelievers must be seeking to destroy them. This belief system negates the possibility of the ethical life. It fails to grasp that goodness must be sought outside the
self and that the best defense against evil is to seek it within.
When people come to believe that they are immune from evil,
that there is no resemblance between themselves and those they
define as the enemy, they will inevitably grow to embody the evil
they claim to fight. It is only by grasping our own capacity for evil,
our own darkness, that we hold our own capacity for evil at bay.
When evil is purely external, then moral purification always entails the eradication of others.

This rhetoric of depersonalization creates a frightening moral
fragmentation, an ability to act with compassion and justice toward those within the closed, Christian circle yet allow others outside the circle to be abused, silenced and stripped of their rights.
And the passivity of many in America who do not acknowledge the
danger of this rhetoric, and the moral fragmentation it inspires,

lends itself to the pleasant fiction that these radicals are fundamentally decent, that they do not mean what they say, that they will never actually persecute homosexuals or nonbelievers or execute abortion providers. Such passivity only accelerates the probability of evil. Extremists never begin as extremists. They become extremists gradually. They move gingerly forward in an open society. They advance only so far as they fail to meet resistance. And no society is immune from this moral catastrophe.

The Christian Right, for now, is forced to function within the political system it seeks to destroy. Judges continue to judge. Teachers continue to teach. The media continues to report. Politicians continue to campaign. But in the world of fundamentalist rhetoric, only "Bible-believing" judges are worthy of respect. Only Christian teachers are true educators. And only the pseudo-reporters seen and heard on Christian broadcasts, who portray the course of historical and world events as conforming to purported biblical prophecies, report the real news. Finally, it is only the men of God, those who champion the Christian state, who have the right to rule. The movement is creating a parallel system, complete with parallel Christian organizations, to replace the old one. It is a slow and often imperceptible process, but Johnson's Ohio rally is the outward expression of vast subterranean shifts that are methodically reorienting the lives of literalist Christians and the country.

Students in Christian schools are being inculcated with the intolerant, heavy-handed political doctrine on display at the rally. The Accelerated Christian Education curriculum, one of the country's three major publishers of Christian textbooks, defines "liberal" in its schoolbooks as "referring to philosophy not supported by Scripture" and "conservative" as "dedicated to the preserving of Scriptural principles."[4] And "Conservative Christian schools," identified by their affiliation with one of four national school organizations that define themselves as evangelical and Christian, are the fastest-growing segment within the private school system. Such schools now represent 15.4 percent of all pri-

vate school enrollment. The National Center for Education Statistics shows a 41 percent growth in the total enrollment at conservative Christian schools between 1992 and 2002.[5] The National
Center for Education Statistics estimates that the number of
home schoolers rose from 850,000 to 1.1 million between 1999
and 2003. Of those surveyed, 72 percent of parents cited the desire to give religious and moral instruction as a top reason for
home-schooling.[6]

In texts published by A Beka, one of the big fundamentalist
publishing houses, African religious beliefs are described as
"false."[7] Hinduism is "pagan"[8] and "evil."[9] The lack of Christian
conversion among Africans is blamed on "Satan's strong hold on
these people," according to a Bob Jones University Press history
textbook for seventh graders.[10] A Beka's high school world history
textbook blames the poverty and political chaos in most of Africa
on a lack of faith. It skips over the repressive colonial European
regimes that exploited the continent and decimated the population in countries such as the Congo, explaining:

> For over a thousand years, there was no clear Christian witness
> in the vast heartland of Africa; the fear, idolatry, superstition,
> and witchcraft associated with animism (the belief that natural
> objects and forces are inhabited by mostly malignant spirits) pre-
> vented most Africans from learning how to use nature for man's
> benefit.[11]

Another A Beka textbook argues that "witchcraft and spirit worship" caused most postcolonial self-governments in Africa to descend into dictatorships.[12] Hinduism is described as "devastating
to India's history."[13] Hindus are "incapable of writing history [be-
cause] all that happens is dissipated in their minds into confused
dreams. What we call historical truth and veracity—intelligent
comprehension of events, and fidelity in representing them—
nothing of this sort can be looked for among the Hindus."[14]

The Muslim prophet Muhammad is portrayed as deceiving followers about his "supposed encounters with angels," and Buddha is criticized because he desired to "leave his wife and newborn son"[15] in a search for enlightenment. The deaths of Muhammad and Buddha, set against the risen Christ, are taken as proof that Islam and Buddhism are false religions. And while the movement works alongside right-wing Catholic groups, within its own circle it spits venom at the Catholic faith. The A Beka textbook calls Catholicism "distorted" and explains that in Catholic countries such as Ireland children "grow up believing the traditions of the Roman Catholic Church without knowing of God's free salvation."[16] The Catholic empires of France and Spain failed to colonize the United States, students are told, because God wanted to make America a Christian nation.

The college protesters of the 1960s were largely the instruments of communists "seeking to exploit youthful rebellion in order to advance their own goals."[17] Riots occurred in black neighborhoods because "power-hungry individuals stirred up the people."[18] Those dependent on the welfare programs of the 1960s "became more susceptible to politicians that preyed on economic insecurity. . . . In this way politicians literally bought the votes of millions of Americans."[19] And Joseph McCarthy becomes a patriot, with a textbook stating, "McCarthy's conclusions, *although technically unprovable, were drawn from the accumulation of undisputed facts.*"[20]

It is this binary worldview that informs those around me at the rally. The room falls silent to watch a video that will precede the talk by Blackwell. It begins with images of the life of Christ. The text that accompanies the images is lifted from a passage in LaHaye's final apocalyptic novel *Glorious Appearing*. The novel reprints a sermon by the late Dr. Shadrach Meshach Lockridge, who served as the pastor of the Calvary Baptist Church in San Diego from 1952 to 1993. It is pounded out in a raplike beat, the voice deep and sonorous. The narrator slowly builds momen-

tum, and the crowd shouts, rises and erupts in thunderous applause. Blackwell regularly uses the video as a campaign prop.

> The Bible says my king is a seven-way king. He's the king of the
> Jews; that's a racial king. He's the king of Israel; that's a national
> king. He's the king of righteousness. He's the king of the ages.
> He's the king of heaven. He's the king of glory. He's the king of
> kings. Besides being a seven-way king, He's the Lord of lords.
> That's my king. Well, I wonder, do you know Him?[21]

The video builds on this refrain, all the while listing attributes of
the king. The beat and pace of the words infect the crowd, which
shouts, "Amen!"

> He's indescribable. He's incomprehensible. He's invincible. He's ir-
> resistible. Well, you can't get Him out of your mind. You can't get
> Him off of your hand. You can't outlive Him and you can't live
> without Him. The Pharisees couldn't stand Him, but they found
> they couldn't stop Him. Pilate couldn't find any fault in Him.
> Herod couldn't kill Him. Death couldn't handle Him, and the
> grave couldn't hold Him. That's my king![22]

It is on this euphoric note that gubernatorial candidate Blackwell
rises to speak. He turns to the cheering crowd, now on their feet,
and shouts: "He is my King! Do you know Him?"

Blackwell is the only candidate for governor to appear at the
rallies. He has posted on his Web site a list of 20 requirements for
people of "high character." He helped make Ohio a "State of Character," part of a movement within the Christian Right that includes the states of Alabama, Arkansas, Delaware, Georgia and
Oklahoma. There are also more than 160 American cities and
towns of "high character," 36 counties and 47 foreign cities, most
of them in the Philippines. Blackwell has put funding and resources aside to train citizens and leaders on how to be people of

character. To all potential candidates he sends out forms to fill out to declare they are persons of character and posts the names of those who abide by the request on his Web site.

Woven into Blackwell's 20-point list, which deftly eschews all religious terminology, is a blueprint for an authoritarian state, one where questioning power is unpatriotic and only those with "high character," as rigidly defined by Christians like Blackwell, have the right to lead and be heard. Individualism, the right to privacy, the belief that other political viewpoints and moral systems have value—all are attacked as disruptive to social cohesion.

Within the movement there is an open call for a uniform moral code, one that needs to be enforced in the public and private realms. In the section titled "Unity," followers are told:

> *High-character people strive to build relationships that foster oneness among others who are bound with them to a common promise, vision, mission or purpose. Ethical organizations seek uniformity in their people's shared character ethics and unity among their otherwise richly diverse people. Without a persevering commitment to shared character ethics, there is no hope for sustainable unity. (Observable Virtues: reconciler.)*[23]

In section 7, titled "Accountability," followers are told how to enforce this unity:

> *High-character people scrutinize themselves and welcome the scrutiny of others. They acknowledge that human nature compels us toward independence. Our preference for independence results in isolation from one another. Isolation breeds temptation to unethical conduct. High-character people resist this chain reaction by adopting transparent life- and work-styles that invite inspection. They place themselves in relationships that motivate self-examination and encourage constructive critique from others, particularly those they serve. (Observable Virtues: an open, up-front, disclosing spirit.)*[24]

Point 14, titled "Honoring Authority," is a reminder that without moral guides, people of "high character" can go astray and deviate from the ethical standards imposed from above:

> All people are imperfect, requiring boundaries for behavior. High-character people willingly yield to the authority of those who are charged with upholding those boundaries. They help shape and then abide by the legitimate laws, rules and boundaries established by legitimate authorities and strive to live within those boundaries for the betterment of all people. When those given authority violate conscience-convicting character ethics, high-character people take wise action to justly hold them accountable. (Observable Virtues: yieldedness, submission/"aligned with the mission.")[25]

Toward the end of the list, in point 19, under a heading titled "Our Ability to Change," there is a section titled "Submission to Truth":

> Truth transforms people only when we submit to it. People who seek truth cannot not transform. Eventually everyone confronts the power of truth. When people of conscience are confronted by what is true, they feel convicted to replace or "put off" their lower character by pursuing and "putting on" high-character ethics. Taking action on this choice can occur overnight or over a long and often painful period.[26]

All the points ask people of "high character" to give over all authority for moral and political decisions to leaders who tell them what is true and what is right. All must, if they have "high character," invite scrutiny by these leaders, by the organs of the state and by their neighbors. These tenets are the pillars of the police state, the state where all are told to watch for social and political deviants, where there is only one orthodox truth, where all dissent is heresy, where those who are not of "high character," those who do not submit and do what they are told, are not allowed to contaminate the public domain. Those of "high character," those who abide by these moral tenets, become servile, afraid, bound to the tasks laid out by their leaders, willing to be punished for failing to achieve the moral standards and goals imposed by the state and ready to denounce those around them.

Rod Parsley, the head of the World Harvest Church, is one of the Christian Right's shining lights, not least because of his crossover appeal among African Americans, who make up about 45 percent of his 12,000–member congregation. Parsley works crowds like a revival preacher. His spitfire phrases tumble out of his mouth. His face is swiftly covered with sweat, which he periodically swipes clean with a white handkerchief. Often, as he did at a rally at Columbus with former Attorney General John Ashcroft, Parsley orders the secular media to leave. He was instrumental in mobilizing voters to support the gay marriage ban during the 2004 presidential elections in Ohio, an effective tool in getting the religious right to the polls to vote for President Bush.

Parsley represents the new breed of Christian Right leaders. His worship services resemble freewheeling chats between him and the congregation. Traditional hymnals and choreographed, predictable liturgies, as well as suits and dresses, have been replaced by a casual come-as-you-are attitude, electric guitars and dancing in the aisles. But the service revolves around Parsley. He exudes the aura of a rock star and the moral authority of a prophet. Parsley, although white, changes easily into the traditional rhythms and cadences of the black church. He questions the biological basis for homosexuality. He argues that the gay lifestyle is morally and physically damaging to homosexuals. He says that liberals defend homosexuality to erode the moral fiber of the nation. Islam, he says, is "an anti-Christ religion" that intends to use violence to conquer the world. Allah, Parsley contends, is a demon spirit.[27] And Christian America has been mandated by God to do battle and defeat all demons to usher in the reign of Christ.

Charismatic and funny, he peppers the language of war and violence into his sermons, which usually rouse his audiences to their feet. I heard him speak in Washington, where, in a naked call to battle, he soon had those in the hall standing and shouting. (Part of his peroration appears above, in Chapter 1.)

Throughout history, countries and kingdoms have been birthed on the battlefield of a revolutionary movement. Such crusades have been championed by soldiers and citizens who have refused to be denied or delayed or detoured in their pursuit to take up a cause they believed deserving of even death itself. Now, the effect of such an upheaval has been the escalation of every religious, political, and social event from Communism to feminism, from Marxism to Nazism, from mayhem to martyrdom, from anarchy to democracy.

A moral revolution is dependent upon the moral virtue of the people. It becomes necessary when the vice and ignorance, or virtue and intelligence, of a people demand it. At that point, negotiation and compromise become void and revolution is inevitable. . . .

The church that claims to hold the cause of right, yet condemns confrontation, is little more than a social club. They want rain with no thunder, and rain with no lightning. They long to avoid confrontation by dwelling in what I call the devil's demilitarized zone, inside the safety of their sanctuary. . . . in order that they might preserve their little façade of peace at any price. But there are those in this room with pigmentation in their skin a little darker than mine that understand this terminology: power—real power—concedes nothing without demand. Somebody's got to speak up and be seen and be heard. Somebody's got to say, "I'm not going to the back of the bus, not one single solitary time more. My father owns the bus line; I will sit where I please." [Applause]. . . .

I don't know if you've noticed it or not, but we are at a point of crisis. Our culture is in chaos. The moral foundations once constructed by the tenets of our faith are quickly crumbling around us with no sign of a cure. We are at a point of crisis. We are at a strategic inflection point. And we are this morning faced with a choice. Let me share it with you this way: when complacency exceeds your desire and mine for change, the consequence is concession and chaos. But when comfort and contentment no longer pacify the people, the cry "Freedom at any cost" can be heard, and it alone becomes the catalyst which produces confrontation, which gives birth to change.

Such upheaval was apparent in the early church. Men and women became martyrs and misfits. They didn't fit in. They were mocked and ridiculed by the social, political, and religious leaders of their day. But . . . they could not bow, and they would not burn.

I don't know if you've noticed it or not, but I see the embers starting to flicker again. I see a glorious church just about to rise out of the blurs of indistinction. I see a remnant of people here this morning that are glad to give their lives to a cause greater than themselves.

There's no greater drama than the sight of a few remnant believers gathered for breakfast, scorned by a succession of adversaries, multiplying miraculously from a world that still doesn't understand where it came from. We've multiplied miraculously. The more they afflict us, the more we prosper and grow. I'm here to tell you, if you think 2004 was something, we have not begun to reach critical mass. We are the largest special-interest group in America.

We're giving order to chaos. We're fighting the sword with the Word. We're fighting savagery with hope. We're rescuing the downtrodden, restoring the disheartened, reviving the life of Christ in the hearts of humanity. Look at them. Look at us. We're people and we're battered, but we are not bowing. Why? Because we are propelled—here's what they don't get—we're propelled by a power that is greater than ourselves.

Christians, evangelical Christians, are the original obsessive-compulsive people. We put down one arm and the other goes up. We cover our mouths, and the gaze of our eyes shouts a hallelujah of victory. We're compelled by a power greater than ourselves, compelled to serve an infallible leader, an irresistible power which is based upon absolute truth.

Listen, when you get hold of truth—I'm not talking about tolerance, that's what secular humanism has done to the church of Jesus Christ across America. It has turned us into secular humanists, where we try to use the Bible as a tool to make God give us what we want. It's time to start singing old songs again, like "I Surrender All": "All to Jesus I surrender./All to him I freely give./I will ever love and trust him./In his presence daily live. I surrender all. Though none go with me, still I will follow." A thousand men may fall at my left and ten thousand at my right, but it shall not come nigh thee. With God before me, who can be against?

Men and women of such moral stock will not cave in at the sight of first opposition. You don't need anybody. Just give us somebody. Give us somebody like David in the Valley of Elah, with five smooth stones, crying out, "Is there another cause?" Give us somebody like Moses. They don't have to have perfect speech. Give us a Moses to stand in front of Pharaoh, saying, "L-l-l-l-l-let my— better let 'em go."

Give us somebody. Give us somebody like Martin—what poor whites called Dr. King. Give us somebody like Martin to stand over Washington Mall again, and say, "God hasten that day when all God's children, black men and white men, Jews and gentiles, Protestants and Catholics, may join hands and sing in the words of that old Negro spiritual, 'Free at last, free at last, thank God Almighty, we're free at last.' "

We don't need everybody. Just give us a Patrick Henry, who at the birth of the American Revolution cried out, "Is life so dear and peace so sweet that it is to be purchased at the price of these chains and slavery? Forbid it, Almighty God! I know not what cause others may take, but as for me, give me liberty or give me death!"

Now, this revolution is not for the temperate. This revolution—that's what it is—is not for the timid and the weak, but for the brave and strong, who step over the line out of their comfort zone and truly decide to become disciples of Christ. I'm talking about red-blooded men and women who don't have to be right, recognized, rewarded, or regarded. Something unimaginable happens when names and logos and egos are set aside. [Applause.] I'm talking about people who don't have to be right, recognized, rewarded, or regarded . . . don't need a position at the front table. They're just happy to be in the battle.

So my admonishment to you this morning is this. Sound the alarm. A spiritual invasion is taking place. The secular media never likes it when I say this, so let me say it twice. Man your battle stations! Ready your weapons! They say this rhetoric is so inciting. I came to incite a riot. I came to effect a divine disturbance in the heart and soul of the church.

Man your battle stations. Ready your weapons. Lock and load—for the thirty-forty liberal pastors who filed against our ministry with the Internal Revenue Service. One of their complaints was that they wouldn't give their names to the media because they "feared retribution." I asked them, "What do they mean?" One of the newspapermen said, "Well, they're afraid you're going to call out the troops." I said, "I already have. We've been in prayer every night for them since they filed." I don't think that's the answer he was looking for.

Spiritual invasion is taking place; if you believe it, say, "Yes." Let the struggle begin. Let it begin in your heart today with a shout unto Him who has called us to war—not only that, He has empowered you and I to win. I will be silent no more. Our times demand it, our history compels it, our future requires it, but most importantly, God is still watching.

Parsley swings deftly from anger and bellicosity to sentimentality. He is arrogant and self-righteous and then maudlin and ingratiating. He shapes and fashions the moods and emotions of those who stand before him. And he, like many of these preachers, is rich. He collects his millions of dollars by promoting the gospel of prosperity, the promise that if his followers, mostly of modest means, tithe 10 percent of their salaries, God will reward them a hundredfold. This money is in addition to the collections he often solicits two or three times during a service. He has, in the past, urged followers to burn their household bills and give the money to him to be free from debt.[28]

"I just love to talk about money," Parsley once said. "I just love to talk about your money. Let me be very clear—I want your money. I deserve it. The church deserves it."[29]

He peddles "covenant swords" and "prayer cloths" that he claims will bring the buyer freedom from financial troubles as well as from physical or emotional ailments. He has written that "one of the first reasons for poverty is a lack of knowledge of God and His Word," and that "the Bible says that to withhold the tithe is to rob God." Parsley lives lavishly in a 7,500-square-foot house valued at more than $1 million. He refuses to disclose information about the church's income or expenditures and has fought off several allegations from former employees charging gross misuses of church funds.[30]

Parsley is one of the masters at peddling this message of greed, hatred and intolerance as gospel truth. The Christian rhetoric, on the surface, is often the same. It is comfortable and predictable. The gestures are familiar. The reverence to God and nation, the deference to the authority of the Bible, do not appear to have changed. But the heart of the Christian religion, all that is good and compassionate within it, has been tossed aside, ruthlessly gouged out and thrown into a heap with all the other inner organs. Only the shell, the form, remains, its empty carcass wrapped around these wolves like a cloak. Christianity is of no use to Parsley, Blackwell and the others. In its name they kill it.

CHAPTER NINE

God: The Commercial

There can be no liberty for a community which lacks the means
by which to detect lies.

—*Walter Lippmann*[1]

Arthur Blessitt sits with his large dark wooden cross, a wheel
attached to the base, on a couch in the studios of the Trinity
Broadcasting Network (TBN) in Tinicum, California. He and the
host, Paul Crouch Jr., watch as Paul's younger brother Matt fin-
ishes an interview in the studio in Hollywood. The two men wait
for the cue signaling they are on the air.

Blessitt, who has just completed a book called *Give Me a J,* is a
frequent guest on the network's most popular nightly two-hour
variety show, *Praise the Lord.* He played a role in the conversion of
George W. Bush after meeting him in 1984 in Midland, Texas. The
owners and founders of Trinity Broadcasting, Paul Crouch Sr. and
Jan Crouch, have carried out fund-raising appeals so Blessitt, who
has a citation in the *Guinness Book of World Records* for "World's
Longest Walk," can carry his cross along roadsides in foreign countries. The show this evening, filled with the usual uplifting Christian music and interviews with Christian celebrities, such as the
former NBA basketball star A. C. Green, is about to turn to the supernatural portion of the program, the moment when the power of
Jesus to perform miracles is, the hosts say, made visible and real.

"There is more excitement and joy in living with Jesus for one
hour than all the carnal pleasures in a lifetime," Blessitt says into
the camera when they begin.

"Amen," Paul Crouch Jr. adds.

The conversation centers on Blessitt's campaign, which began on Christmas day 1969, to traverse the globe carrying the wooden cross on his shoulder. Blessitt, with a mop of gray hair, explains that he has walked "over 37,000 miles, almost one and a half times around the world, through 305 nations, island groups and territories" and taken "over 64 million steps.

"When you calculate the weight of each step with the weight of the cross," he says, he has carried "over 8 billion pounds, and I don't have one callus, one bunion, and I'm 65 years old and I never felt better in my life."

The taped applause track prompts the small studio crowd to clap.

"The obvious question is: Why?" asks Crouch, leaning toward his guest.

"Because Jesus spoke to me, I love Him," Blessitt answers. "And in 1969 one night I was praying and Jesus said, 'Take the cross off the building on Sunset Boulevard'—where I had a Jesus night club on Sunset Strip—'put the cross on your shoulder, and carry it on the roadsides of the world and identify My message where the people are.' And by the grace of God, I've walked through 50 countries at war. I've been in jail 24 times. I've been through Iraq, Iran, Afghanistan, Saudi Arabia, North Korea, Sudan, Somalia, everyplace, lifting up the cross, preaching Jesus. There are no walls. There are no barriers. The world is open. Jesus said, 'Go,' and you go to live or die, but you go to do His will."

"You took the great commission literally," Crouch says, referring to the belief that Christians must leave their homes to convert nonbelievers.

"Yes, yes," Blessitt says.

"To go into all the world. And you are just about to do that," Crouch adds. "You have a few little island nations—"

"—well, they are not nations," Blessitt says. "I have been to every nation, but there are a few remote islands, like the Chatham Islands and Zanzibar and some of these places. To have been in every inhabited place—"

"—Wow—"

"—and Jesus has given the strength to do that and it is just amazing," Blessitt says. "I look at the pictures on my wall. I look at everything and it is a living miracle of what God has done."

Blessitt and his wife, Denise Irja, have just adopted a baby and recently moved to work out of the Heritage Christian Center in Denver, Colorado. He is on *Praise the Lord* to give tips on how to witness and "reach a hurting world," but first Crouch promises dramatic video footage from a TBN documentary called *Arthur Blessitt: A Pilgrim.*

The men sit back and watch the clip.

NARRATOR: *(Over pictures of a younger Blessitt)* In 1979, Arthur journeyed into one of the most politically unstable areas of the world, Central America. The trip was sponsored by the Trinity Broadcasting Network.

PAUL CROUCH SR.: *(Over dark, ominous music)* We saw the phones ring and the money pledged to buy what we lovingly dubbed the Holy Roller, the little four-wheel drive vehicle that had been given by the partners to assist Arthur in his travel and his journey down through Central America.

(Paul and Jan Crouch, who is wearing a flowing dress that looks like a square-dancing outfit, climb out of the cab of a jeep that is pulling a small caravan and hand the keys to Blessitt.)

PAUL CROUCH SR.: This absolutely unreal drama unfolded, and we were to learn later the most frightening and dangerous experiences of Arthur Blessitt's entire life.

(Jan Crouch, her champagne-colored wig cascading down her shoulders, sits on a bed under muted lighting.)

JAN CROUCH: *(Speaking in a breathless whisper)* I really wasn't thinking about Arthur Blessitt. . . . when all of a sudden I looked up and the entire ceiling in the bedroom where we were sleeping had lit up. And I saw like it was a movie screen what was going on, what was happening in Nicaragua.

ARTHUR BLESSITT: I heard a banging on the side of the trailer. I opened the trailer caravan door, and gunmen burst into our trailer.

JAN CROUCH: When I opened my eyes to look at it, I saw Arthur and he was just looking at me, and I had never really seen that look before. There was no fear. It was just like, "Pray, Jan, pray."

ARTHUR BLESSITT: They took me near the side of the van, the four-wheel drive vehicle, and they stood me there and they lined up, seven gunmen and two on a truck with machine guns. They said they were going to kill me. When they raised the guns up and took aim, I realized at that moment, "They are going to literally shoot me now."

JAN CROUCH: And I stopped and I said, "Honey, Arthur Blessitt is in trouble and we have got to pray."

PAUL CROUCH SR.: All of a sudden, Jan descended on me and half frightened me to death. . . . She seized my arm and said, "Honey, Arthur's in trouble, and we've got to pray for him."

NARRATOR: Blessitt explains that he decided he would not die without a Bible in his hand.

ARTHUR BLESSITT: In a momentary decision, as I heard the guy say, "Uno, dos," I turned instantly with my prayer: "Jesus, help me hit the keyhole." And I turned and stuck the key into the door, right in the hole first time, right in the door, and they were saying, "Don't move" in Spanish. I thought, "It doesn't matter if I get shot in the front or the back." I opened the door, picked up a box that had Bibles in it. I set the box down and started tearing off the top of the box, and it had these cords on it. It was very difficult to get the box open. I could see the gunmen's feet around me. They were pulling on my shoulder trying to get me to stand up. Finally, I got a whole load and put the Bibles in my arm and thought I would give them all a Bible. I was really anticipating getting one for myself, but I thought I would give them all a Bible before they shot me.

PAUL CROUCH SR.: We fell to our knees, right there in the bedroom in that little cottage in Phoenix, and began to cry out to God and pray and receive, knowing nothing about what Arthur was experiencing at that moment.

JAN CROUCH: We jumped down by the bed very quickly. . . . We held hands across the bed and prayed for our friend Arthur. And all of a sudden I said, "Father, I ask you to send 12 big angels to fight for him right now."

ARTHUR BLESSITT: And when I stood up, there wasn't one gunman standing there. And I looked and there were six on the ground about 15 feet away and one with his feet sticking out the door of the trailer who had been knocked inside. I didn't know what had happened. I heard nothing. I saw nothing.

NARRATOR: Blessitt says he went over to the ones on the ground and offered them a Bible and some water, but they were terrified and ran for the truck and sped away. When he walked in the trailer, his friend Don said he thought he had been killed.

DON: I have just been saved a couple of years, and I grew up in bars. I know meat against meat. I heard blows and then the gunmen fell by the door, and one fell into the door. Didn't you hit them?

ARTHUR BLESSITT: I said no, I didn't do anything. The people in the village came running up and said they saw God here. They said they saw a bright flash of light and God was here. And all I could do was stand in the midst of that whole situation and say, "Somebody must have been praying for me."

"Oh, man," Paul Crouch Jr. says as the camera switches back to the studio amid heavy applause.

"It is very moving to look at that," Blessitt tells his host.

"What are you feeling?" Crouch asks softly.

"I feel the love that Paul and Jan had," he says. "I don't understand all about prayer, but God had them pray."

"Amen," Crouch says.

"And there was a literal miracle that took place," Blessitt says. "I feel the presence of God."

"Amen," Crouch says.

"The only thing I can say is, I have lived now for 36 years of walking around the world in the presence of God," Blessitt says.

"Amen," Crouch says.

"I carried the cross," Blessitt says. "I know His presence."

"Amen," Crouch says.

"And really, that is how I live," Blessitt says. "I know Jesus is with me. I know that I know that I know that I know."

"How do you know?" Crouch asks in a whisper.

"I know because His word says so," Blessitt says as the applause track is again turned up, prompting the audience to clap. "Jesus said, 'I will be with you always.' I believe what He said."

"Tell them," Crouch encourages.

"And I believe another scripture: 'Where two or three are gathered in my name there am I in the midst of them.'"

"Amen," Crouch says, as an electric piano plays soft music in the background.

"And Paul, I have been so many times in places where there is not one believer around me," Blessitt says. "I have been with soldiers. I have been with terrorist groups. And I will just say to them, 'Would you say the name "Jesus"?' And when they say the name 'Jesus,' the presence of Christ comes into that atmosphere. And really, that is how I share Christ; that is how I witness."

The scene, with its high drama and emotion, its story of a miracle and the divine intervention mediated by Paul and Jan Crouch, is typical fare for Trinity Broadcasting. As Blessitt launches into a short pitch on the importance of knowing and accepting Jesus into your heart, Crouch reminds viewers that they can call prayer counselors at the toll-free number shown on the bottom of the screen. It is a short step from a prayer counselor to making a "love gift" and becoming a partner in Trinity Broadcasting. Above all else, this is a business, a huge one, and those who know how to run it well, the Paul and Jan Crouches, the Pat Robertsons and Benny Hinns, have grown wealthy and built massive media and personal empires on the gospel of prosperity.

The Crouches, who began their television evangelism with the disgraced Jim and Tammy Faye Bakker, wear gaudy costumes and sit during their popular nightly program in front of stained-glass windows that overlook faux Louis XIV sets awash in gold rococo and red velvet, glittering chandeliers and a gold-painted piano. The emblem of the station, which Paul Crouch wears on the pocket of his blue double-breasted blazer, is a crest with a British lion and unicorn on each side and a white dove of peace in the middle. The couple, who collect nearly $1 million a year in salary from the network, also have use of 30 ministry-owned homes, including two sprawling multimillion-dollar oceanfront mansions in the resort town of Newport Beach, California, a mountain retreat near Lake Arrowhead and a ranch in Texas. They travel in a $7.2 million, 19-seat Canadair Turbojet, drive luxury cars, and charge everything from dinners to antiques on company credit cards, according to former employees. They run their empire with 400 employees, out of walnut-paneled offices with plush velvet furniture. The offices occupy half of the top floor of the network's headquarters in Costa Mesa.[2]

Jan, who is caked in makeup and appears to have undergone extensive plastic surgery—including, allegedly, breast implants—wears garish outfits and huge, flowing wigs. Her tear-filled stories of miracles—such as how her pet chicken was brought back to life when she was a child—or her accounts of prayer requests from listeners, are used to extract money from viewers.[3] She and her husband speak as if they have a direct connection with God, an implication reinforced by constant stories of their personal involvement in divine miracles, such as the event involving Blessitt.

Their message, however, also has a dark side. Those who do not support their ministry, the Crouches often say, will see God turn against them. Viewers who have struggled with deep despair, and who believe that the world of miracles and magic is the only thing holding them back from the abyss, often find the threat potent and frightening. Better, many feel, to send in money and not take a chance.

"If you have been healed or saved or blessed through TBN and have not contributed to [the] station, you are robbing God and will lose your reward in heaven," Paul Crouch said in a *Praise the Lord* broadcast on November 7, 1997.[4] Crouch said: "God, we proclaim death to anything or anyone that will lift a hand against this network and this ministry that belongs to You, God. It is Your work, it is Your idea, it is Your property, it is Your airwaves, it is Your world, and we proclaim death to anything that would stand in the way of God's great voice of proclamation to the whole world. In the name of Jesus, and all the people said, 'Amen!'"[5]

Trinity Broadcasting Network is the world's largest televangelist organization, with programming beamed from some two dozen satellites and thousands of cable and terrestrial channels in some 75 countries. It owns interests in stations in El Salvador, Spain and Kenya and has contracts with numerous other cable and satellite companies and station owners. Its programming is carried on more than 6,000 stations in the United States and abroad as well as the Internet.[6] The network is the platform for some of the Christian Right's most reactionary and bizarre preachers, including many from other countries. The success of the network lies in its array of programming and the variety of different "faith" messages it is willing to incorporate. It provides religious entertainment, children's programming, gospel music concerts from

Nashville, live coverage of Christian events, lifestyle shows, health and beauty tips, financial counseling and prosperity tips, news and current events, Christian documentaries and feature films, teaching programs, worship services at megachurches and spirited revivals. The messages range from the theologically conservative— embodied in the Southern Baptist preachers Charles Stanley and Adrian Rogers—to Catholic Ministries' Father Michael Manning, to those who preach the gospel of prosperity, such as Kenneth Copeland, Creflo Dollar and John Avanzini. The network broadcasts Dr. D. James Kennedy, who is at the forefront of the movement to create a theocratic America, and it gives a voice to some of the outer fringes of the movement, such as the Christian exorcist Bob Larson and the popular healer Benny Hinn, who says that Adam was a superhero who could fly to the moon and claims that one day the dead will be raised by watching TBN from inside their coffins.[7] In a *Praise the Lord* broadcast on October 19, 1999, Hinn told viewers that he will one day be able to raise the dead through his television broadcasts, that soon those who have lost loved ones will refuse to bury them but

> place him in front of that TV set for 24 hours. I see rows of cas-
> kets lining up in front of this TV set, and I see them bringing them
> closer to the TV set, and as people are coming closer I see loved
> ones picking up the hands of the dead and letting them touch the
> screen, and people are getting raised as their hands are touching
> that screen.[8]

Hinn, who says he is a prophet who speaks with God daily, also tells followers that he has been transported to heaven and regularly receives visions and revelations. He has predicted that one day Jesus would appear at one of his crusades. He claims to be able to heal the sick and told Larry King he had healed himself by watching a previously recorded broadcast of one of his sermons.[9] He also, like the Crouches, lashes out at his critics, once saying: "Sometimes I wish God would give me a Holy Ghost machine gun. I'd blow your head off!"[10] This sentiment was echoed by the elder Crouch, who has attacked critics as "heresy hunters" and lambastes them as enemies of God who will soon feel God's wrath.

In an April 2, 1991, "Praise-a-Thon," Crouch let loose on his critics:

> To hell with you! Get out of my life! Get out of the way! I say, get out of God's way! Quit blocking God's bridges or God's going to shoot you—if I don't. I don't even want to even talk to you or hear you! I don't want to see your ugly face.[11]

The Crouches have repeatedly been embroiled in scandals in their three decades on television, including battles with the Federal Communications Commission over the legality of some of their station licenses.[12] Lonnie Ford, Paul Crouch's chauffeur, said he had a homosexual relationship in 1996 with Crouch, something Crouch has vehemently denied. But Ford was, the network admitted, paid $425,000 and given housing in settlement when he threatened to go public with the charges shortly after the affair allegedly took place. The story was first reported six years later by the *Los Angeles Times*.[13] Disgruntled former employees complain about the lavish lifestyles of the Crouches, paid for by contributors who are often of modest means.

None of this seems to dampen the enthusiasm—or lessen the coffers—of the network. The promise of miracles, coupled with the fear of falling out of the favor of God (and the Crouches), compels loyal "partners" to mail in monthly "love offerings." The network, expanding in areas such as the Middle East, dubs its programs in 11 different languages. It is watched by viewers in more than 5 million households in the United States each week and millions more overseas. And televangelists such as Pat Robertson, despite having networks that once dwarfed TBN, now buy time on the TBN network to reach a wider audience. The network generates more than $170 million a year in revenue, according to tax filings reported by the *Los Angeles Times*. Viewers' contributions make up two-thirds of the income, and the rest comes from fees imposed on those who want to buy airtime.[14]

Crouch encourages viewers to send in checks for $1,000, even if they cannot afford it. Write the check anyway, he tells them, as a "step of faith," and the Lord will repay them many times over. "Do you think God would have any trouble getting $1,000 extra to you somehow?" he asked during one Praise-a-Thon.[15]

The constant appeals for money, the fantastic stories about angels and healings and miracles, and the opulence of the Crouches' lifestyles are defended by many viewers who cling to the network. The Crouches' wealth is merely proof, many say, of God's blessing and a sign that such blessings will one day flow to them as well, as long as they mail in their prayer offerings and love gifts and have faith.

The triviality of American popular culture, its emptiness and gossip, accelerates this destruction of critical thought. It expands the void, the mindlessness that makes the magic, mythology and irrationality of the Christian Right palatable. Television, the movement's primary medium, allows viewers to preoccupy themselves with context-free information. The homogenized empty chatter on the airwaves, the banal amusement and clichés, the bizarre doublespeak endlessly repeated on cable news channels and the huge spectacles in sports stadiums have replaced America's political, social and moral life, indeed replaced community itself. Television lends itself perfectly to this world of signs and wonders, to the narcissism of national and religious self-exaltation. Television discourages real communication. Its rapid frames and movement, its constant use of emotional images, its sudden shifts from one theme to an unrelated theme, banish logic and reason with dizzying perplexity. It, too, makes us feel good. It, too, promises to protect and serve us. It, too, promises to lift us up and thrill us. The televangelists have built their movement on

these commercial precepts. The totalitarian creed of the Religious
Right has found in television the perfect medium. Its leaders
know how television can be used to seduce and encourage us to
walk away from the dwindling, less exciting collectives that protect and nurture us. They have mastered television's imperceptible, slowly induced hypnosis. And they understand the
enticement of *credo quia absurdum*—I believe because it is absurd.

Arlene Jacques, in dark-framed rectangular glasses and with
her hair pulled back, is wearing a bright red sequined shirt, flashy
red sequin earrings and fire-engine red nail polish. She is brows-
ing with her 35-year-old daughter Brandy in the Gold, Frankin-
cense and Myrrh gift shop on the ground floor of the Costa Mesa
TBN headquarters, situated next to the San Diego Freeway. The
headquarters is a gaudy, white wedding cake of a building with a
dramatic front lobby that holds two spiral staircases winding up-
ward, their railings ornate, gold-painted ironwork. Set in colored
marble at the foot of the staircases, directly in front of the double
glass doors, is the imperial-looking emblem of the network.
Above the shoppers, the staircases converge on a huge white
statue of the archangel Michael slaying the dragon, a 13-inch
replica of which is on sale in the gift shop. The walls have gold-
tinted mirrors and huge windows that allow visitors to look at the
fountains, reflecting pools, sculptures, neoclassical colonnades,
manicured lawns and white lights that outline the building and
the shrubs. It's Christmastime: elaborate light displays outline
reindeer and hug the palm trees. On the top of the building, lights
spell out "Happy Birthday Jesus."

Jacques, from Visalia, California, looks at the displays of books
by various members of the Crouch family, the clothing with the
TBN emblem, and trinkets such as the Mary and Baby Jesus Deco-
rator Plate or the Coming King Medallion. This is her first visit to
TBN, although she has been a "partner" of the network for many
years and has long made regular monthly contributions. She busily
snaps pictures, including shots of herself in front of a gold grand

piano on the second floor, with her daughter Brandy, who is a nurse. They visited the virtual reality theater earlier in the day and walked through the re-creation of the Via Dolorosa, the route through Jerusalem by which Jesus carried the cross to his crucifixion. In the 50-seat theater she has seen one of the *End Time* movies, which portray the apocalyptic end of the world, the death of nonbelievers and saving of the righteous, and she has felt the seats tremble during projected quakes and storms. She is about to head to the Heavenly Bistro for something to drink. The network has a similar complex near Dallas and a Christian entertainment center outside of Nashville. But there are few visitors today and the headquarters is nearly empty.

Jacques turned to the network 30 years ago at a time when she was "in a lot of pain." She was living in a tiny, run-down apartment with her two small daughters, Brandy and Raquel, and had been recently divorced.

"I had never been a working parent," she says. "I was scared to death to go out into the working world. I was not real churched at the time. They were speaking to me, Paul and Jan and the people at TBN, about my spiritual side. I knew Jesus, but I did not have a personal relationship with Jesus. God could know you personally, they told me, and I could know Him personally."

She met with a neighbor to pray and talk about changing her life. She watched the broadcasts, the promises of salvation, the stories about how finding God changes lives, melts away problems and leads to financial and emotional security. The broadcasts gave her comfort.

"I got down on my knees by myself by the couch," she remembers. "I got a great big Bible, a 90-pound Bible that my husband got overseas, it was a big white one with gold print, and I put my hands on it and said, 'God, please touch me, my life and children.' Then I cried for three hours. I saw a slide show in front of my eyes. It seemed like every single wrong thing I had ever done flashed before my eyes and I was truly sorry."

She visited various churches, but nothing gave her the glow of the TBN broadcasts. She began to pray daily, sometimes for long stretches. And she began to watch, slowly drawn into the culture and the message preached by Paul and Jan Crouch.

"I was taking a load of clothes down to the washing machine in the basement of the apartment building," she says. "We were poor, living on welfare and food stamps, and when I came back upstairs I felt that I wanted to kneel by the bed and pray. I lifted up my hands and started to talk in a loud language I had never heard before. I thought, 'It's happening. My mind is thinking one thing and something different is coming out of my mouth. I am speaking in prayer language.'"

She found a job driving a school bus, but her emotional life remained in turmoil and the family often had a hard time paying bills. She struggled with depression. There were nights she could not sleep. She felt as if she was hanging on by her fingertips and there were few people listening or willing to help.

"I don't know if you have ever been in a place in your life where it takes effort to walk from one room to the next," she says. "It takes so much effort. I was in those places several times. But just by hearing the worship on TBN, by listening to different people speak the word of God, it gave me strength. The network is on 24 hours a day, seven days a week. The pastor of your church and all your wonderful friends do not want you to call them up at four a.m. in tears when you feel such total despair. But you can call TBN. You can call TBN and there are people who actually speak to you. You can speak to a real, live person. They ask who you are and what you want to pray about. You can do this 24 hours a day.

"There is power in prayer," she says. "Not only do you feel different; you feel more peaceful. In time you see answers to those prayers. Nothing happened instantly, but you know you can actually live another day, and you get to a place where you can keep on living."

When she called the toll-free "prayer line," the number of which is always visible at the bottom of the TV screen, she was asked by a "prayer warrior" on the other end for her name and address. The information was put into a direct-mail database, one of the network's most successful fund-raising tools. Her calls to prayer partners, she says, gave her strength. But they also led her, a young, single mother on welfare, to take some of her meager income and mail it to the network.

"I was living on welfare, collecting food stamps," she says, "and I would tape fifteen cents to one of their little cards and mail it back."

Her life had always been turbulent. She started working very young, in her father's restaurant. There was little time for school. She says she came from a "dysfunctional family" in which there was "no value of people, no value for life, for relationships and how to talk and relate to people.

"I didn't know kids didn't work," she says. "My parents were divorced early on, and I lived with my dad and my stepmother since I was about 10. I did not know some kids got to eat dinner with their family, do their homework and go to bed."

She barely made it through high school and eloped a couple years later with a man in the Navy. They went to Los Angeles and got married. He was sent to Vietnam. When he came back from the war, the marriage was tempestuous. They split and reconciled numerous times until they finally gave up.

"I remember as a little girl living in that apartment," says Brandy. "My mom was a total Jesus freak. She used to bring homeless people in from the park and feed them and pray over them. She loved everybody with the love of God."

Arlene baptized homeless people who visited in a small inflatable children's pool. The pool was where she also baptized her daughters. She taught her daughters that, as Paul and Jan Crouch said, faith alone would be enough to let them survive. Jesus, if you had enough faith, would take care of you.

"For us, for my sister and I, to this day we know that God is so real," Brandy adds. "We know God brought us through and protected us. One time me and my sister and mom got on our knees and prayed for our rent money. We left. We went to do the laundry at the laundromat. When we got back, there was a check in the middle of the floor, not like it was pushed under the door, but right in the middle of the floor. It was for our rent, and it was signed by Jesus Christ, and Wells Fargo cashed it."

But the gospel of prosperity has a more insidious effect than the personal enrichment of leaders such as Paul and Jan Crouch at the expense of gullible, desperate and often impoverished followers. When it is faith alone that will determine your well-being, when faith alone cures illness, overcomes emotional distress and ensures financial and physical security, there is no need for outside, secular institutions, for social-service and regulatory agencies, to exist. There is no need for fiscal or social responsibility. Although many of the followers of the movement rely, or have relied in the past, on government agencies to survive, the belief system they embrace is hostile to all secular intervention. To put trust in secular institutions is to lack faith, to give up on God's magic and miracles. The message being preached is one that dovetails with the message of neoconservatives who want to gut and destroy federal programs, free themselves from government regulations and taxes and break the back of all organizations, such as labor unions, that seek to impede maximum profit.

The popular Christian textbook *America's Providential History* cites Genesis, which calls for mankind to "have dominion over the fish of the sea, and over the birds of the air, and over the cattle, and over all the earth, and over every creeping thing that creeps upon the earth" (Genesis 1:26–27) as evidence that the Bible calls for "Bible-believing Christians" to take dominion of America and the world: "When God brings Noah through the flood to a new earth, He reestablishes the Dominion Mandate but now delegates to man the responsibility for governing other men."[16] The authors write that God has called the United States to become a Christian nation and "make disciples of all nations."[17]

The book fuses the Christian message with the celebration of unrestricted capitalism. It denounces income tax as "idolatry" and property tax as "theft," and in a chapter titled "Christian Economics," calls for the abolishment of inheritance taxes.[18] This indoctrination is designed to form a cadre of young believers who will follow biblical rather than secular law. They are told that when the two laws clash, they as believers must defy secular authorities. And they are taught to judge others not by what they do but by their fidelity to Christian doctrine.

"Even if Christians manage to outnumber others on an issue and we sway our Congressman by sheer numbers, we end up in the dangerous promotion of democracy," the book reads. "We really do not want representatives who are swayed by majorities, but rather by correct principles."[19]

The book also teaches students that a Christian's primary responsibility is to create material wealth. God will oversee the increase and protection of natural resources. *America's Providential History* belittles secular environmentalists, who see natural resources as fragile and limited, and says of those who hold these concerns that they "lack faith in God's providence and consequently, men will find fewer natural resources. . . . The Christian knows that the potential in God is unlimited and that there is no shortage of resources in God's earth." The book blithely dismisses the threat of global warming and overpopulation, saying, "Christians know that God has made the earth sufficiently large with plenty of resources to accommodate all the people."[20]

Nietzsche wrote that man needs lies. And the Jan and Paul Crouches of the world are perfect emissaries of the belief system needed to dismantle the power of the federal government and unleash the fetters on corporations. Moral life is reduced in their ideology to personal, individual piety. All well-being lies in the hands of God—or, more specifically, the hands of those who pose as ambassadors for God. The power of the supreme collective, of the corporation, is increasingly unchecked when a society accepts that fate is determined by a personal relationship with Jesus Christ. In this world individual rights—once safeguarded through the competing collectives of diverse social, religious or ethnic groups, trade unions, government regulatory agencies, advocacy groups, independent media and judiciaries, and schools and universities that do not distort the world through an ideological lens—are neutered.

This new world of signs and wonders, of national and religious self-exaltation and elaborate spectacle, makes people feel good. It offers the promise of God's protection and service. This new world promises to lift them up and thrill them, all the while calling on them to do away with the dwindling collectives that in fact heretofore have protected them. When individuals are finally emasculated and alone, bereft of the help of competing collectives, they cannot defend their rights or question the abuses of their overlords. When there is no other place to turn for help other than the world of miracles and magic, mediated by those who grow rich off those who suffer, when fealty to an ideology becomes a litmus test for individual worth, tyranny follows.

CHAPTER TEN

Apocalyptic Violence

... This was a "moment of madness"—a revolutionary, romantic moment when an entire society seems to be up for grabs. In these moments, fundamental change appears irresistible; for a brief moment, "all seems possible, all within reach." Across time, people who get caught up in moments of madness imagine that their own "radiant vision" is at hand: a workers' paradise, a grassroots democracy, fraternité-egalité-liberté, or the Second Coming of Jesus. The utopian imagination is—suddenly, powerfully, briefly—inflamed by the immediate prospect of radical change, by visions of an apocalypse now.

—*Stephen D. O'Leary describing the "Great Awakening"*
of the 1700s[1]

The Gilead Baptist Church outside of Detroit is on a four-lane highway called South Telegraph Road. The drive down South Telegraph Road to the church, a warehouse-like structure surrounded by black asphalt parking lots, is a depressing gauntlet of boxy, cut-rate motels with names like Melody Lane and Best Value Inn. The highway is flanked by a flat-roofed Walgreens, Blockbuster, discount liquor stores, Taco Bell, McDonald's, Bob's Big Boy, Sunoco and Citgo gas stations, a Ford dealership, Nails USA, the Dollar Palace, Pro Quick Lube and U-Haul. The tawdry display of cheap consumer goods, emblazoned with neon, lines both sides of the road, a dirty brown strip in the middle. It is a sad reminder that something has gone terribly wrong with America, with its inhuman disregard for beauty and balance, its obsession with speed and utilitarianism, its crass commercialism and its oversized SUVs and trucks and greasy junk food. This disdain for nature, balance and harmony is part of the deadly, numbing assault against community. Ten or fiften minutes negotiating the traffic down South Telegraph Road make the bizarre attraction of the End Times—the obliteration of this world of alienation, noise and distortion—comprehensible. The manufacturing jobs in the Detroit auto plants nearby are largely gone, outsourced to other nations with cheaper labor. The paint is flaking off the cramped two-story houses that lie in grid patterns off the highway. The plagues of alcoholism, divorce, drug abuse, poverty and domestic violence make the internal life here as depressing as the external one. And the congregation gathering today in this church waits for the final, welcome relief of the purgative of violence, the vast cleansing that will lift them up into the heavens, and leave the world they despise, the one they ruined or that was ruined for them, to be wracked by plagues and flood and fire until it, and all those they blame for the debacle of their lives, are consumed and destroyed by God. It is a theology of despair. And for many, the apocalypse can't happen soon enough.

The guru of the End Times movement is a small, elderly, gnomelike man with his hair dyed coal black, a battery-powered earpiece and a pedantic, cold demeanor. His name is Timothy LaHaye, a Southern Baptist minister and coauthor, along with Jerry Jenkins, of the *Left Behind* series of Christian apocalyptic thrillers that provide the graphic details of raw mayhem and cruelty that God will unleash on all nonbelievers when Christ returns and raptures Christians into heaven. Astonishingly, the novels are among the best-selling books in America with more than 62 million in print. They have been made into movies, as well as a graphic video game in which teenagers can blow away nonbelievers and the army of the Antichrist on the streets of New York City. These books have come to express, for many in the Christian Right, the yearning they feel for the Rapture, the end of history, the end of time. Once Christ returns and believers are lifted into heaven, the Earth will, they are told, enter a period of tribulation.

The tribulation will lead to a final, gruesome battle between Christ and the forces of the Antichrist, with "bodies bursting open from head to toe at every word that proceeded out of the mouth of the Lord as he spoke to the captives within Jerusalem."[2] In the novels those Christians, who hastily converted once the righteous were lifted into the clouds, have to drive carefully to avoid hitting splayed and filleted corpses of men and women and horses. The soldiers in the army of the Antichrist, facing the warrior Christ, are defeated in the final moments as "their flesh dissolved, their eyes melted, and their tongues disintegrated." And after pages of graphic violence, readers are told that the soldiers of the Antichrist "stood briefly as skeletons in now-baggy uniforms, then dropped in heaps of bones as the blinded horses continued to fume and rant and rave."[3]

LaHaye and Jenkins had to distort the Bible to make all this fit—the Rapture, along with the graphic details of the end of the world and the fantastic time line, is never articulated in the Bible—but all this is solved by picking out obscure and highly figurative passages and turning them into fuzzy allegory to fit the apocalyptic vision. This stygian nightmare is, rather, a visceral and disturbing expression of how believers feel about themselves and the world. The horror of apocalyptic violence— the final aesthetic of the movement—feeds fantasies of revenge and empowerment. It is an ominous reminder that failing to follow God's commands will ensure their own eternal damnation. LaHaye has a checkered past that includes years working for the John Birch Society and many more peddling quack theories such as "temperament analysis," which purports to be a system to identify predominant characteristics, strengths and weaknesses to help people make vocational, personal and marital decisions. He was previously known for books such as *Spirit Controlled Temperament*, *Transformed Temperaments*, *The Male Temperament* and *Your Temperament: Discover Its Potential*, all variants of astrology.[4] In short, before becoming the champion of a Christian America and the apocalypse he made his living as a fortune-teller. LaHaye has helped found and lead numerous right-wing groups, including the Council for National Policy, and he is not only the nation's best-selling author, but also one of the dominionists' most powerful propagandists.

LaHaye has come to the conference with his wife, Beverly, who founded Concerned Women of America, an antifeminist group with 540,000 women "who were committed to protecting the rights of the family through moral activism."[5] They were the early pioneers in the Christian Right's attack on the school textbook industry, helping to orchestrate a series of lawsuits against publishers who printed material they found offensive or anti-Christian. They sit together at a table to sign their books, and the line snakes down the corridor, with many people clutching multiple books for signatures. LaHaye, along with two other well-known apocalyptic preachers—including Gary Frazier, the glib, silver-tongued founder of the Texas-based Discovery Ministries, Inc., which leads "Walking Where Jesus Walked" tours in Israel—travels the country holding daylong End Time conferences, such as today's event at the Gilead Baptist Church. Tickets to the event in Detroit cost $20. Frazier and LaHaye also take pilgrims to visit Israel, where they stand on the hill of Megiddo—better known as Armageddon—that in the Book of Revelation is the site of the final battle between the forces of Christ and the Antichrist. In the lobby of the church, just outside the sanctuary, a television set on a stand continuously runs one of the tapes of a "Walking Where Jesus Walked" tour next to a table filled with Frazier's books, CDs and DVDs.

LaHaye insists that everything in the Bible is literally true. All events in the modern world are described and represented, he says, in the Bible. All has been predicted. The Bible is primarily a book of prophecies that predict the events that will take place shortly before the worldwide cataclysm. This belief relies on a curious hybrid of allegory and literal interpretation. When Revelation

9:1–11 says that monsters will appear whose faces are "like human faces," with "hair like women's hair," "teeth like lions' teeth," "scales like iron breastplates" and "tails like scorpions and stings," LaHaye assures us they will appear. These monsters, which will have what look like crowns of gold on their heads, will torture unbelievers for five months, although not kill them. He quotes from some of the more disturbing passages in the Book of Revelation to remind his listeners of how terrible it will be for nonbelievers: "And in those days men will seek death and will not find it; they will long to die and death will fly from them" (Revelations 9:6).

"Everything we believe is based on the principles of this book," LaHaye tells the group from the church pulpit, holding up his Bible.

"How do we know this is a supernatural book?" LaHaye asks. "Fulfilled prophecies prove that this was not written by men," he says. "One thousand prophecies, as the Bible tells us, five hundred of which have already been fulfilled."

The apocalyptic fantasy calls on believers to turn their backs on the crumbling world around them. This theology of despair is empowered by widespread poverty, violent crime, incurable diseases, global warming, war in the Middle East and the threat of nuclear war. All these events presage the longed-for obliteration of the Earth and the glorious moment of Christ's return. In this scenario, the battle at Armageddon will be unleashed from the Antichrist's worldwide headquarters in Babylon once the Jews again have control of Israel. The war in Iraq, along with the conflict between Israel and the Palestinians, only brings the world one step closer to the end.

LaHaye, his head poking up from behind the wooden pulpit, tells the story of the origins of his series of apocalyptic books to those in the pews in front of him. He was on an airplane, he says, watching a pilot flirt with an attractive flight attendant. The pilot had a wedding ring. The flight attendant did not. He wondered what would happen if the Rapture happened at that moment.

What would happen if hundreds of millions of saved Christians were raptured into heaven and the unsaved left behind, including those who were insufficient Christians, along with Muslims, Catholics and Jews? He convinced Jerry Jenkins, a former sportswriter, to help him set his vision down in a series of novels. He and Jenkins went on to imagine the Rapture and what would happen when it set loose the Tribulation and a worldwide war. In their vision, this war would be waged by a band of new believers, called the Tribulation Force, against Satan and the Antichrist. In the end, seas and rivers would turn to blood, searing heat would burn men alive, ugly boils would erupt on the skin of the disfavored, and 200 million ghostly, demonic warriors would sweep across the planet, exterminating one-third of the world's population. Those who join forces with the Antichrist in the *Left Behind* series, true to LaHaye's conspiracy theories, include the United Nations, the European Union, Russia, Iraq, all Muslims, the media, liberals, freethinkers and "international bankers." The Antichrist, who heads the United Nations, eventually moves his headquarters to Babylon. These demonic forces battle the remaining Christian believers—those who converted after the Rapture took place, remnants of extremist American militia groups, who in the novels are warriors for Christ, and the 144,000 Jews who convert. This, through pages of dense, stilted and leaden prose, is what has captivated tens of millions of American readers. And LaHaye tells those in front of him that he believes that their generation may be the "terminal" generation. He warns his listeners to get right with God as fast as they can because there is not much time left.

Gary Frazier, with his thick head of silver hair, is the most engaging of the speakers. He has a soft Texas twang, at times a soaring eloquence and easy cadence. He begins by flashing a drawing of a monster, taken, he says, from a dream of Nebuchadnezzar that was interpreted for the king by Daniel in Second Daniel. King Nebuchadnezzar sees in his dream a statue with a head of gold, iron teeth, bronze claws, arms and chest of silver, stomach and thighs of bronze, legs of iron, and feet of iron and clay.

"'Here's what it means,'" Frazier quotes Daniel as saying. "'You, Nebuchadnezzar, are the head. That's the Babylonian Empire. You rule over the whole world, but there'll come a second empire behind you,' and historically, we know now as we look back, that was the Medo-Persian Empire." Frazier explains that the stomach and thighs of bronze are the Hellenistic Empire. The two legs of iron, he says, represent the Roman Empire.

"You see what God did was in this simple dream of Daniel, God set the boundaries, the parameters, that there would never be more than four world empires in the entire history of time," Frazier explains. "It would be the Babylonians defeated by the Medes and the Persians, who were then later defeated by the Greeks, who were defeated by Rome, but the interesting part is found in the two feet and the ten toes of part iron and part plate."

He tells the congregation that the 10 toes stand for ethnically mixed cultures that will unite and rise up to dominate the world before the Rapture. He describes this empire as the European Union, or what he says is a revived form of the Roman Empire. This final empire will be destroyed by God to usher in the 1,000-year reign of Christ.

Frazier says the final chapter in human history started in 1948 with the foundation of the state of Israel, something predicted by the Bible. Less noticed but equally important, he tells the crowd, was the 1948 Benelux Conference that brought together Holland, Luxembourg and Belgium. This too, he says, fulfilled biblical prophecy. Just as God had to restore Jews to the land of Israel before the End Times, so too did God have "to raise Europe back up in order to bring to pass this revived form of the ancient Roman Empire."

He explains that while each of the other empires fell, Rome "has never gone away," his voice dipping ominously. Instead of falling to an outside invader, Rome "collapsed," "imploded," due to its own "degradation and perversion." "You see, there's never been a society in the history of the world that has openly accepted and embraced homosexuality and lesbianism that has survived," he explains, because while homosexuals and lesbians may not reproduce, "they are busy recruiting."

"We're seeing the shaping, the rebirthing, the revising of the ancient Roman Empire that will ultimately be the world power," Frazier says of the European Union, the figure of the metallic man with the iron legs on the screen behind him.

He explains that Europe, because it has so few Bible-believing Christians, will not see large sections of its population lifted to heaven in the Rapture. The United States, however, will be devastated when tens of millions of its Christians disappear, including half of the military. America will suddenly become "a Third World" power, and Europe, ruled by the Antichrist, will dominate the planet.

"These prophecies were never given to scare us but to prepare us for the second coming of Jesus Christ," he says.

The second sign of the End Times, he says, will be the rise of radical Islam. This too, he says, is predicted in the Bible.

"Now," he says, "I realize that we're living in a community that has a large Arab constituency. I want you to know something as I begin this portion of this particular message. Not all Muslims are terrorists. I want you to know that. But I also want you to know that to date every terrorist has been a Muslim. Hello? I want you also to know that the scripture's clear on a couple of things, and I'm going to say some things today in the next few moments that may be construed as being intolerant. I want you to understand that. I've been called that on more than one occasion. And if you get mad at me about it, you'll get over it, all right?

"In the days following 9/11," Frazier says, "I heard our leadership say that we're not at war with the religion of Islam, that there were Islamic radicals who had taken over the religion and they're the ones we have a problem with. Folks, I'm here to tell you right now, I want to apologize to you on behalf of our president and our political leadership because they lied to us. We *are* at war with the religion of Islam, and it is not a handful of radical Islamists who are taking over the religion and hijacking it."

He speaks about the child martyrs in the war between Iran and Iraq, in which the Iranian clerics sent young boys into the minefields to clear the way for troops and returned their remains, Frazier says, in urns to their families.

"Can you explain to me how in the West that we would understand a person who would strap dynamite upon themselves and blow themselves up along with innocent men and women and children with the promise that they would have seventy brown-haired—I mean blond-haired, blue-eyed—virgins for their unlimited sexual pleasure in this place called paradise? And the parents of that person then throw a party celebrating the destruction of their child. You want to tell me you understand that kind of mentality?

"Islam," Frazier says dramatically, "is a satanic religion."

He tells the crowd that his honesty and candor have brought him threats. He insists he has Muslim friends and that some Muslims who live in America love this country. But he warns about "a second kind of Muslim" who is in America for "the wrong reasons."

These Muslims want to export their religion and achieve their goal of "world domination," he explains.

"You show me a country that is dominated by Muslims, and I'll show you a country where people are dying, where there are no freedoms or rights, and people being persecuted on a daily basis," he says. "God help us if they ever were to get in control, in charge here in the United States of America."

He warns of Muslim "sleeper cells" waiting to carry out new terrorist attacks. He illustrates his point with a hypothetical story about a Muslim doctor forced to accept a nefarious mission or receive the heads of his three children in a box.

Frazier stops, pauses and slowly scans the crowd, which sits silently, expectantly for his next sentence.

"I thank God for our men and women who are fighting over there because if they weren't fighting there, we'd be fighting right here in the streets of America. I'm convinced of that," he says, and the sanctuary erupts in loud applause.

Once the Antichrist takes power, the second temple in Jerusalem will be rebuilt. Followers of the Antichrist will be branded on their hands and foreheads with "the mark of the Beast," which Frazier says could well be "biochips" implanted under the skin. It will be impossible to buy and sell in the new world without this mark. Those who convert to Christ will receive "the mark of the Father" on their foreheads, but they will become outcasts and persecuted in the Antichrist's worldwide empire. Most will be martyred and killed.

"Do you see this?" he asks. "We're the first generation that's ever had the possibility of this happening in our lives.

"Does that apply to you?" he asks. "Do you have to be concerned about taking the mark? Absolutely not. You can't have but one mark. You're safe if you already have it—the blood of Jesus Christ that cleanses away my sin and yours."

He goes on to say that the loved ones of many in this room, who are not saved, will be branded with the mark of the Beast because they will be left behind.

America, according to Frazier, LaHaye and many other leaders in the movement, is being ruled by evil, clandestine organizations that hide behind the veneer of liberal, democratic groups. These clandestine forces seek to destroy Christians. They spread their demonic, secular-humanist ideology through front groups such as the American Civil Liberties Union, the National Association for the Advancement of Colored People, the National Organization for Women, Planned Parenthood, the Trilateral Commission and "the major TV networks, high-profile newspapers and newsmagazines," the U.S. State Department, major foundations (Rockefeller, Carnegie, Ford), the United Nations, "the left wing of the Democratic Party," Harvard, Yale "and 2,000 other colleges and universities."

America must repent, Frazier tells his audience. It must ask God to cleanse the moral stains that infect the nation and its godless inhabitants. The nation must swiftly dismantle the barriers between church and state and bring God back into the schools, the government, the media, the entertainment industry, the workplace, the courts and the home. Time is running out. If America, as a nation, does not get right with God very soon, it will face terrible retribution. The sins that have befallen America, the moral license, the high rates of premarital sex, homosexuality, abortion, pornography, the adultery and the greed and lust that have beset the country must be stamped out. America must become submissive and heed God's prophets or be destroyed. If the Christians in this room fail, if they do not wipe out vice, sin and corruption, if they do not establish a Christian America soon, God will begin to carry out acts of vengeance.

Frazier ends the conference with a call for those in the room to commit or recommit their souls to Christ.

"This afternoon as we bring our time together to a close, it's not about being a Baptist; we went through that earlier. It is not about being a Methodist, or charismatic, or Assembly of God or an Episcopalian," he says softly. "It is about knowing in your soul."

He asks those before him if they are sure that if Christ appeared today they would go to heaven.

"I'm not trying to trick you," he implores the bowed heads. "I'm trying to reason with you. For you see, one day the life that you and I know will be over. So I just wonder, is there a stirring in your heart? Am I speaking to you? Is He calling your name? He is. He is knocking on the door of your life? The door handle is on the other side. Where does it open? You have to open it. How do you do that? Well, the way I did it years ago was to call on the name of the Lord, and I prayed. I'm going to ask you this afternoon if there is a stirring in your heart." He prays:

"Dear Lord Jesus, I know that I'm a sinner, and right now as an act of my own free will, I agree with You that I have sinned, and I want to ask You to forgive me of the sin that separates me from You. Come into my life; save my soul—and right now, with heads bowed and eyes closed, I just wonder if any of you have prayed that prayer. Here is what I'm going to ask you to do: Will you lift your head and look at me and make eye contact with me? I just want to see your face. No one is looking around. If you prayed that prayer, here is what I'm going to ask you to do—will you lift your head and look at me and make eye contact with me? I just want to see your face. No one is looking around. If you prayed that prayer and you really mean it then just lift your head, look at me so I can see your . . . God bless you, God bless you . . . I can't really see the balcony because of the angle here, but if you are in the balcony will you slip your hand up for just a moment . . . God bless you, God bless you, yep, yeah, God bless you . . . you . . . you . . . and God bless you back there."

Several people in the pews begin weeping softly.

Frazier tells them God has taken their sins away.

"And now when God looks at you, he doesn't see your sins, your mistakes, He sees the blood of Jesus that washed your sin away," he intones.

He invites all those who raised their hands or looked him in the eye to stand and come down to the front of the church. A couple dozen people slowly make their way past those in the pews to walk down the aisles to the front. Frazier gathers them around him in a tight circle. As the group forms, several church members wearing tags that say "counselor" silently enter the sanctuary through the double doors at the back. They wait, hands folded in front of them, to pray with the new converts, to tell them they need to come to church and to offer to help guide them toward new life.

Frazier thanks God for looking past the congregation's sins.

He tells the small group in front of him not to go back to their friends or family, not to retrieve their belongings from the pews.

"We are going to ask you to walk right back to that door," he says, pointing to where the counselors with the name tags are waiting to receive the group. "Would you all just step right through that door? And while they are going, folks, can we just do what the angels in heaven are doing?"

He starts to clap. The crowd follows his lead. The men and women file down the aisle as the crowd applauds, each being met by an individual counselor who takes their arm and guides them to a secluded corner in the lobby. The process begins.

Dr. James Luther Adams, my ethics professor at Harvard Divinity School, told us that when we were his age—he was then close to 80—we would all be fighting the "Christian fascists."

The warning, given to me nearly 25 years ago, came at the time Pat Robertson and other radio and televangelists began speaking about a new political religion that would direct its efforts at taking control of all institutions, including mainstream denominations and the government. Its stated goal was to use the United States to create a global Christian empire. It was hard, at the time, to take such fantastic rhetoric seriously, especially given the buffoonish quality of leaders in the Christian Right who expounded it. But Adams warned us against the blindness caused by intellectual snobbery. The Nazis, he said, were not going to return with swastikas and brown shirts. Their ideological inheritors in America had found a mask for fascism in patriotism and the pages of the Bible.

Adams was not a man to use the word "fascist" lightly. He was in Germany in 1935 and 1936 and worked with the underground anti-Nazi church, known as the Confessing Church, with dissidents such as Dietrich Bonhoeffer. Adams was eventually detained and interrogated by the Gestapo, who suggested he might

want to consider returning to the United States. It was a sugges-
tion he followed. He left on a night train with framed portraits of
Adolf Hitler placed over the contents inside his suitcase to hide
the rolls of home movie film he took of the so-called German
Christian Church, which was pro-Nazi, and the few individuals
who defied them, including the theologians Karl Barth and Albert
Schweitzer. The ruse worked. The border police lifted the tops of
the suitcases, saw the portraits of the Führer and closed them up
again. I watched hours of the grainy black-and-white films as he
narrated in his apartment in Cambridge.

He saw in the Christian Right, long before we did, disturbing
similarities with the German Christian Church and the Nazi
Party, similarities, he said that would, in the event of prolonged
social instability, catastrophe or national crisis, see American fascists, under the guise of Christianity, rise to dismantle the open
society. He despaired of liberals, who he said, as in Nazi Germany,
mouthed empty platitudes about dialogue and inclusiveness that
made them ineffectual and impotent. Liberals, he said, did not
understand the power and allure of evil or the cold reality of how
the world worked. His long discussions with church leaders and
theologians in Nazi Germany—some of whom collaborated with
the regime, some of whom resisted and most of whom remained
silent—were the defining experiences of his life. He was preoccupied with how liberal democracies, which could never hope to
compete with the fantastic, utopian promises of personal and collective salvation offered by totalitarian movements, could resist.
Adams was a close friend of the theologian Paul Tillich, a vocal
opponent of the Nazis who in 1933 became the first non-Jewish
professor barred from German universities and soon went into
exile. Tillich, he reminded us, taught that the role of the church
was in society, that the depth of its commitment and faith were
measured by its engagement with politics and culture. It was this
engagement that alone gave faith its vibrancy and worth. Tillich
did not retreat from the looming crisis around him. He spoke out

against the intolerance and hatred preached by the Nazis before they came to power. And Tillich angrily chastised those in the church who, preoccupied with narrow Christian piety, were passive. He thundered against this complacency and begged Christians to begin to "take time seriously."

Adams had seen how the mask of religion hides irreligion. He reminded us that "our world is full to bursting with faiths, each contending for allegiance." He told us that Hitler claimed to teach the meaning of faith. Mussolini used to shout, "Believe, follow, and act," and told his followers that fascism, before being a party, had been a religion. Human history is not the struggle between religion and irreligion, Adams said. "It is veritably a battle of faiths, a battle of the gods who claim human allegiance."

Democracy is not, as these Christo-fascists claim, the enemy of faith. Democracy keeps religious faith in the private sphere, ensuring that all believers have an equal measure of protection and practice mutual tolerance. Democracy sets no religious ideal. It simply ensures coexistence. It permits the individual to avoid being subsumed by the crowd—the chief goal of totalitarianism, which seeks to tell all citizens what to believe, how to behave and how to speak. The call to obliterate the public and the private wall that keeps faith the prerogative of the individual means the obliteration of democracy. Once this wall between church and state, or party and state, is torn down, there is an open and subtle warfare against love, which in an open society is another exclusive prerogative of the individual. In the totalitarian world, there are those worthy of love and those unworthy of it. In the totalitarian world, the private sphere becomes the concern of the state. This final restriction of the freedom to love—the freedom of a Christian to love a Muslim or the freedom to love those branded by the state as the enemy—heralds the death of the open society. The promises of Christian harmony, unity, happiness—in short a utopia—held forth by the dominionists have a seductive quality that will never be countered by the tepid offerings of democrats, who at best can offer citizens the opportunity to seek their own happiness and construct their own meaning.

We must, Adams also told us, watch closely what these new fascists accused their opponents of planning. For radical movements expose their own intentions and goals by tarring their enemies with their own nefarious motives. These movements assume that those they attack are, like themselves, also hiding their true agenda, also plotting to silence and eradicate opponents. This common form of "projection" was, on a smaller scale, on display during the Florida recount in 2000. The Republicans accused Al Gore of attempting to steal the election through court fiat, the very theft being secretly orchestrated by the Republicans. Richard Hofstadter was one of the first to grasp the role of projection in "The Paranoid Style in American Politics":

> It is hard to resist the conclusion that this enemy is on many counts the projection of the self; both the ideal and the unacceptable aspects of the self are attributed to him. The enemy may be the cosmopolitan intellectual, but the paranoid will outdo him in the apparatus of scholarship, even of pedantry. Secret organizations set up to combat secret organizations give the same flattery. The Ku Klux Klan imitated Catholicism to the point of donning priestly vestments, developing an elaborate ritual and an equally elaborate hierarchy. The John Birch Society emulates Communist cells and quasi-secret operation through "front" groups and preaches a ruthless prosecution of the ideological war along lines very similar to those it finds in the Communist enemy. Spokesmen of the various fundamentalist anti-Communist "crusades" openly express their admiration for the dedication and discipline the Communist cause calls forth.[6]

Adams, like Bonhoeffer, did not believe that those who would fight effectively in coming times of turmoil, a fight that for him was an integral part of the biblical message, would arise from the institutional church or the liberal, secular elite. His critique of the prominent research universities, along with the media, was withering. These institutions—self-absorbed, compromised by their close relationship with government and corporations, given enough of the pie to be complacent—were unwilling to deal with the fundamental moral questions and inequities of the age. They had no stomach for a battle that might cost them their prestige and comfort. He saw how easily the German universities had been Nazified. He told me, I suspect only half in jest, that if the Nazis took over America, "60 percent of the Harvard faculty would begin their lectures with the Nazi salute." He had seen academics at the University of Heidelberg, including the philosopher Martin Heidegger, raise their arms stiffly to students before class. Adams also reminded us that American intellectuals and industrialists openly flirted with fascism in the 1930s. Mussolini's "corporatism," which created an unchecked industrial and business aristocracy, appealed to many American industrialists at the time, who saw it as an effective counterweight to Roosevelt's New Deal. In July 1934, *Fortune* magazine lavished praise on the Italian dictator for his defanging of labor unions and his empowerment of industrialists at the expense of workers. And Sinclair Lewis's 1935 novel *It Can't Happen Here* told the story of a conservative politician, "Buzz" Windrip, backed by a nationally syndicated radio host, Bishop Peter Paul Prang, who is elected president and becomes a dictator to save the nation from welfare cheats, sex, crime and a liberal press.

The New York Times in 1944 asked Vice President Henry Wallace to answer the questions: What is a fascist? How many fascists have we? How dangerous are they? The Vice President's answers were published on April 9, 1944, as the war against the Axis powers and Japan was drawing to a close. He wrote:

> *The really dangerous American fascist . . . is the man who wants to do in the United States in an American way what Hitler did in*

Germany in a Prussian way. The American fascist would prefer not to use violence. His method is to poison the channels of public information. With a fascist the problem is never how best to present the truth to the public but how best to use the news to deceive the public into giving the fascist and his group more money or more power.

They claim to be superpatriots, but they would destroy every liberty guaranteed by the Constitution. They demand free enterprise but are the spokesmen for monopoly and vested interest. Their final objective toward which all their deceit is directed is to capture political power so that, using the power of the state and the power of the market simultaneously, they may keep the common man in eternal subjugation.[7]

Adams knew that resentments and bigotry lurk below the surface of all democratic societies and can be roused, under the right conditions, to promote a creed that calls for the destruction of democracy. What is evil about these systems of intolerance and persecution is not the foot soldiers who carry out the crimes, but the organization that mobilizes and unleashes these dark passions. He worried that such a movement was, late in his life, again on the march. It was more sophisticated than in the past, more cleverly packaged, and this time without serious opposition. The hatreds were again being stoked. The labor unions and progressives who had been able to battle back in the 1930s were spent forces. The despair of tens of millions of Americans, unable to find manufacturing jobs or work that offered fair wages and benefits, would lead them, he knew, into the arms of these fanatical preachers. The rage of those abandoned by the economy, the fears and concerns of a beleaguered and insecure middle class, and the numbing isolation that comes with the loss of community, would be the kindling for a dangerous mass movement. If these dispossessed were not reincorporated into mainstream society, if they eventually lost all hope of finding good, stable jobs and opportunities for themselves and their children—in short, the promise of a brighter future—the specter of American fascism would beset the nation. This despair, this loss of hope, this denial of a future, led the desperate into the arms of those who promised miracles and dreams of apocalyptic glory. Adams had seen it once. He knew what it looked like. He feared it was coming again.

Toward the close of the Second World War, Adams was asked to give a lecture about the Nazi faith to a large group of U.S. Army officers preparing for service in the occupation army in Germany. He described the views expressed by the officers at the meeting as "an orgy of self-righteousness." Bigotry, in all its forms, had to be vigorously fought. He was not going to let this opportunity escape him. Adams wrote later:

> *This self-righteousness, I decided, ought somehow to be checked. Otherwise I might succeed only in strengthening the morale of a bumptious hundred-percent "Americanism," and that was not the faith we were supposed to be fighting for. Toward the end of the lecture I recapitulated the ideas of the Nazi "faith," stressing the Nazi belief in the superiority of the Teutons and in the inferiority of other "races." I also reminded the officers of similar attitudes to be observed in America, not only among the lunatic and subversive groups but also among respectable Americans in the army of democracy. Then I asked these Army officers to pose one or two questions to be answered by each man in his own conscience. First: "Is there any essential difference between your attitude toward the Negro and the Jew, and the Nazi attitude toward other 'races'— not the difference in brutality but a difference in basic philosophy?" "If there is an essential difference," I said, "then the American soldier might logically become a defender of the Four Freedoms [freedom of speech, freedom of religion, freedom from want, and freedom from fear], but if there is no essential difference between your race philosophy and that of the Nazis, a second question should be posed: "What are you fighting for?"*

I blush when I think of some of the responses I received. I was immediately besieged with questions like these: "Do you think we should marry the nigger?" "Aren't Negroes a naturally indolent and dirty race?" "Haven't you been in business, and don't you know that every Jew is a kike?" Questions like these came back to me for over an hour. I simply repeated my question again and again: "How do you distinguish between yourself and a Nazi?" Seldom have I witnessed such agony of spirit in a public place.

Many of these Americans who could not distinguish between themselves and Nazis came from "religious" homes, or they claimed to be representatives (or even leaders) of the American faith. Apparently their faith was quite different from the faith behind the Four Freedoms. On the other hand, many of them no doubt would have disclaimed possessing anything they would call faith, yet all of them, whatever their answers to these questions, spoke the faith that was in them, and for many of them it was a trust in white, gentile supremacy—faith in the blood.[8]

Adams, finally, told us to watch closely what the Christian Right did to homosexuals. The Nazis had used "values" to launch state repression of opponents. Hitler, days after he took power in 1933, imposed a ban on all homosexual organizations. He ordered raids on places where homosexuals gathered, culminating in the ransacking of the Institute for Sexual Science in Berlin and the permanent exile of its director, Magnus Hirschfeld. Thousands of volumes from the institute's library were tossed into a bonfire. The stripping of homosexuals of their civil rights was largely cheered by the German churches. But this campaign legitimized tactics, outside the law, that would soon be employed against others. Adams said that homosexuals would also be the first "social deviants" singled out and disempowered by the Christian Right. We would be the next.

Those arrayed against American democracy are waiting for a moment to strike, a national crisis that will allow them to shred the Constitution in the name of national security and strength. And those in the movement often speak about such a moment with gleeful anticipation. Howard Phillips, a right-wing strategist who helped Jerry Falwell create the Moral Majority, has warned Christians to be ready. "My friends, it is time to leave the 'political *Titanic*' on which the conservative movement has for too long booked passage," he told the Council for National Policy. "Instead, it is our task to build an ark so that we can and will be ready to renew and restore our nation and our culture when God brings the tides to flood."[9]

Debate with the radical Christian Right is useless. We cannot reach this movement. It does not want a dialogue. It is a movement based on emotion and cares nothing for rational thought and discussion. It is not mollified because John Kerry prays or Jimmy Carter teaches Sunday school. Naive attempts to reach out to the movement, to assure them that we, too, are Christian or we, too, care about moral values, are doomed. This movement is bent on our destruction. The attempts by many liberals to make peace would be humorous if the stakes were not so deadly. These dominionists hate the liberal, enlightened world formed by the Constitution, a world they blame for the debacle of their lives. They have one goal—its destruction.

Alvin Toffler wrote that if you don't have a strategy you end up being part of someone else's strategy. There are isolated groups and individuals who, at some cost, are fighting back. The nonviolent protests of the Reverend Mel White's Soulforce outside of Christian universities and service academies that discriminate against gays and lesbians are, according to the ideas of theologians such as Adams and Tillich, acts of faith. The clergy and rabbis who have banded together in Ohio to challenge the tax-exempt status of the megachurches that promote "Christian" candidates are performing an act of faith. The rulings of independent judges—such as the Republican-appointed Judge John E. Jones III in Dover, Pennsylvania—who have prohibited the teaching of creationism in public schools because it is not science, are acts of faith. Cardinal Roger Mahony, the head of the Archdiocese of Los Angeles, the nation's largest, has called on Catholics to be prepared to defy the laws now being considered in Congress and backed by the Christian Right that make it a felony to shield or protect or offer support to illegal immigrants. Such civil disobedience would be an act of faith. The hate-crimes legislation now stalled in Congress because of bitter opposition from the Christian Right must be made law. Its passage would be an act of faith. Programs to protect or establish community, to direct federal and state assistance to those truly left behind, those trapped in America's urban ghettos and blighted former manufacturing towns, are acts of faith. And the valiant struggle by former Vice President Al Gore and others to wake us up to the impending catastrophe that will beset us if we do not curb global warming is an act of faith. The accelerated rate of global warming could, within a decade, bring about epic destruction involving extreme weather, floods, droughts, epidemics and killer heat waves. To face this challenge, to do something about it, is to embrace a theology of hope, of life. To do nothing, to paint these ecological catastrophes as messages from an angry God rather than the folly of humankind, to believe blithely that global warming is a fiction and God alone determines human fate, is to accept this theology of despair, this radical evil.

Finally, we must dismantle the corporate state. American democracy has become a consumer fraud. If we do not halt the corporations that, in the name of globalization, are cannibalizing the country for profit, we will never blunt the appeal of the radical Christian Right to those the corporate state casts aside. We must redirect our national wealth and resources to fund a massive antipoverty campaign. We must end corporate welfare, corporate crime, the hundreds of billions of dollars in corporate bailouts and seriously address issues such as labor law reform. We must curb the cycle of perpetual war that enriches the military—industrial complex—and by extension the two political parties that dominate Washington. If we do not, we must accept an inevitable Christo-fascism.

Corporations have poured hundreds of millions into pseudo think tanks, such as the Heritage Foundation, to invent bogus disciplines including cost-benefit and risk-management analysis, all geared to change the debate from health, labor and safety issues to the rising cost of big government. They run sophisticated ad campaigns to beguile voters. These corporations have wrenched apart, through corruption, lavish campaign donations, and shady lobbying, the ties between public interest groups and the Democratic Party. Washington is now besieged with 25,000 corporate lobbyists and 9,000 corporate action committees.

These corporations, and their enraged and manipulated followers in the Christian Right, tens of millions of them, if left unchecked will propel us into despotism. The corporate state has now rigged our system, hollowed out our political process and steadily stripped citizens of constitutional rights, as well as federal and state protection and assistance. This may be the twilight of American democracy. And it is better to stand up and fight, even in vain, than not to fight at all.

There are battles, big and small, that we can join. Many of them are being waged nearby, at our local school board. So much of maintaining a democracy is simply about showing up, and Adams felt that none of us had a right to profess our faith without this daily involvement in the life and well-being of our community, our nation and the planet Earth. "Repeatedly," Adams told us, "I heard anti-Nazis say, 'If only 1,000 of us in the late twenties had combined in heroic resistance, we could have stopped Hitler.'"

The Adventures of Huckleberry Finn by Mark Twain ends with Huck facing the moral dilemma we now face: whether to pay homage to a false moral code, one which has become law, or to damn ourselves in the eyes of many by opposing it. Here is Huck, faced with the choice of turning in his friend and escaped slave Jim, or living in defiance:

> So I was full of trouble, full as I could be; and didn't know what to do. At last I had an idea; and I says, I'll go and write the letter—and then see if I can pray. Why, it was astonishing, the way I felt as light as a feather right straight off, and my troubles all gone. So I got a piece of paper and a pencil, all glad and excited, and set down and wrote:
>
> Miss Watson, your runaway nigger Jim is down here two mile below Pikesville and Mr. Phelps has got him and he will give him up for the reward if you send. Huck Finn.
>
> I felt good and all washed clean of sin for the first time I had ever felt so in my life, and I knowed I could pray now. But I didn't do it straight off, but laid the paper down and set there thinking—thinking how good it was all this happened so, and how near I come to being lost and going to hell. And went on thinking. And got to thinking over our trip down the river; and I see Jim before me, all the time in the day, and in the night-time, sometimes moonlight, sometimes storms, and we a-floating along, talking, and singing, and laughing. But somehow I couldn't seem to strike no places to harden me against him, but only the other kind. I'd see him standing my watch on top of his'n, stead of calling me, so I could go on sleeping; and see him how glad he was when I come back out of the fog; and when I come to him again in the swamp, up there where the feud was; and such-like times; and would always call me honey, and pet me, and do everything he could think of for me, and how good he always was; and at last I struck the time I saved him by telling the men we had smallpox aboard, and he was so grateful, and said I was the best friend old Jim ever had in the world, and the only one he's got now; and then I happened to look around and see that paper.
>
> It was a close place. I took it up, and held it in my hand. I was

a-trembling, because I'd got to decide, forever, betwixt two things,
and I knowed it. I studied a minute, sort of holding my breath,
and then says to myself:
   "All right, then, I'll go to hell"—and tore it up.[10]

The radical Christian Right calls for exclusion, cruelty and intolerance in the name of God. Its members do not commit evil for evil's sake. They commit evil to make a better world. To attain this better world, they believe, some must suffer and be silenced, and at the end of time all those who oppose them must be destroyed. The worst suffering in human history has been carried out by those who preach such grand, utopian visions, those who seek to implant by force their narrow, particular version of goodness. This is true for all doctrines of personal salvation, from Christianity to ethnic nationalism to communism to fascism. Dreams of a universal good create hells of persecution, suffering and slaughter. No human being could ever be virtuous enough to attain such dreams, and the Earth has swallowed millions of hapless victims in the vain pursuit of a new heaven and a new Earth. Ironically, it is idealism that leads radical fundamentalists to strip human beings of their dignity and their sanctity and turn them into abstractions. Yet it is only by holding on to the sanctity of each individual, each human life, only by placing our faith in tiny, unheroic acts of compassion and kindness, that we survive as a community and as individual human beings. These small acts of kindness are deeply feared and subversive to these idealists, as the Russian novelist Vasily Grossman wrote in *Life and Fate.*

I have seen that it is not man who is impotent in the struggle
against evil, but the power of evil that is impotent in the struggle
against man. The powerlessness of kindness, of senseless kindness,
is the secret of its immortality. It can never be conquered. The
more stupid, the more senseless, the more helpless it may seem, the
vaster it is. Evil is impotent before it. The prophets, religious

teachers, reformers, social and political leaders are impotent before it. This dumb, blind love is man's meaning.

Human history is not the battle of good struggling to overcome evil. It is a battle fought by a great evil struggling to crush a small kernel of human kindness. But if what is human in human beings has not been destroyed even now, then evil will never conquer.[11]

Plato and Aristotle defended slavery and often attacked Athenian democracy, but this does not mean they should not be read for their deep and penetrating insights into political systems and ethics. Sigmund Freud understood little about love, viewed religion as infantile regression and viewed nearly every human motive through the lens of human sexuality, but at the same time Freud gave us one of the most powerful windows into and vocabularies for the workings of the subconscious. The Bible was written by numerous people over hundreds of years with wide and often varying concerns, some of which were and are morally indefensible. Within its pages, however, lie powerful passages that help illuminate our lives and our place before the mystery of human existence. I, too, struggle, like the writers of the Bible, to understand. I, too, often get it wrong. But it is the honesty and rigor of the search, the doubts and reverses, the mistakes and regrets, the ability to stand up again and keep trying that ultimately express faith. This humility before the unknowable, the acceptance that there is much we will never understand, makes possible self-criticism, self-awareness, self-possession and self-reflection. They make possible compassion and acts of kindness. They allow us to see ourselves in the stranger, to reach out in solidarity to those who travel with us on this dusty, brief and often lonely road of life. This honesty and humility make possible a diverse and tolerant human community. They sustain life and, in the midst of it all, impart hope.

I do not deny the right of Christian radicals to be, to believe and worship as they choose. But I will not engage in a dialogue with those who deny *my* right to be, who delegitimize my faith and denounce my struggle before God as worthless. All dialogue must include respect and tolerance for the beliefs, worth and dignity of others, including those outside the nation and the faith. When this respect is denied, this clash of ideologies ceases to be merely a difference of opinion and becomes a fight for survival. This movement seeks, in the name of Christianity and American democracy, to destroy that which it claims to defend. I do not believe that America will inevitably become a fascist state or that the Christian Right is the Nazi Party. But I do believe that the radical Christian Right is a sworn and potent enemy of the open society. Its ideology bears within it the tenets of a Christian fascism. In the event of a crisis, in the event of another catastrophic terrorist attack, an economic meltdown or huge environmental disaster, the movement stands poised to manipulate fear and chaos ruthlessly and reshape America in ways that have not been seen since the nation's founding. All Americans—not only those of faith—who care about our open society must learn to speak about this movement with a new vocabulary, to give up passivity, to challenge aggressively this movement's deluded appropriation of Christianity and to do everything possible to defend tolerance. The attacks by this movement on the rights and beliefs of Muslims, Jews, immigrants, gays, lesbians, women, scholars, scientists, those they dismiss as "nominal Christians," and those they brand with the curse of "secular humanist" are an attack on all of us, on our values, our freedoms and ultimately our democracy. Tolerance is a virtue, but tolerance coupled with passivity is a vice.

Notes

Chapter One: Faith

1. Karl Popper, *The Open Society and Its Enemies* (Princeton, NJ: Princeton University Press, 1971), 1:263.
2. Quotations from the Bible are taken from the Revised Standard Version unless otherwise noted.
3. Reinhold Niebuhr, as reported to me by Reverend Coleman Brown.
4. William Sloane Coffin, *Credo* (Louisville, KY: Westminster John Knox, 2004), 159.
5. Richard K. Fenn, *Dreams of Glory: The Sources of Apocalyptic Terror* (Burlington, VT: Ashgate, 2006), 60.
6. William Sloane Coffin, *The Heart Is a Little to the Left* (Hanover, NH: University Press of New England, 1999), 44.
7. Alfred Lord Tennyson, *In Memoriam A.H.H.*, stanza 96, in *The Poetic and Dramatic Work of Alfred Lord Tennyson* (New York: Houghton Mifflin, 1899), 246.
8. Reinhold Niebuhr, *The Irony of American History* (New York: Charles Scribner's Sons, 1952), 37.
9. Robert O. Paxton, *The Anatomy of Fascism* (New York: Alfred A. Knopf, 2004), 218.
10. Ibid., 219.
11. Davidson Loehr, *America, Fascism and God: Sermons from a Heretical Preacher* (White River Junction, VT: Chelsea Green, 2005), 88.
12. Rousas John Rushdoony, *The Institutes of Biblical Law* (Dallas, TX: Craig, 1973), 585–590.
13. In September 2002, Tommy Thompson, then U.S. Secretary of Health and Human Services, announced the award of 21 grants from the White House's new faith-based initiative. More than 500 institutions had applied. Operation Blessing was one of the winners, receiving more than $500,000. See remarks by Barry Lynn, executive

director of Americans United for the Separation of Church and State, in a Pew forum titled "The Faith-Based Initiative Two Years Later: Examining Its Potential, Progress and Problems," March 5, 2003, Washington, DC, http://pewforum.org/events/index .php?EventID=41. More than 7 percent of the $2,154,246,246 going to faith-based grants was awarded to abstinence-only education programs. See "Federal Funds for Organizations That Help Those in Need," Office of Faith-Based and Community Initiatives, http:// www.whitehouse.gov/government/fbci/grants-catalog02-06.pdf.

14. Katherine Yurica, "What Did Mr. Bush's 2nd Inaugural Address Really Mean? Biblical Code Unraveled," *The Yurica Report*, February 24, 2005, http://www.yuricareport.com/BushSecondTerm/WhatMr Bush2ndInauguralMeans.html.
15. Rushdoony, *Institutes of Biblical Law*, 581; 583–584.
16. Mark A. Beliles and Stephen K. McDowell, *America's Providential History* (Charlottesville, VA: Providence Foundation, 1991), 26.
17. "The Vision of GRN," Global Recordings Network, http://global recordings.net/topic/vision.
18. "True Liberty," Global Recordings Network, http://globalrecord ings.net/script/ENG/171.
19. Joseph Goebbels, *Signale der neuen Zeit* (Munich: Eher, 1934), 34; Gerd Albrecht, *Nationalsozialistische Filmpolitik: Eine soziologische Untersuchung über die Spielfilme des Dritten Reiches* (Stuttgart: Ferdinand Enke, 1969), 464.
20. Claudia Koonz, *The Nazi Conscience* (Cambridge, MA: Belknap Press, 2003), 73.
21. Paxton, *Anatomy of Fascism*, 202.
22. Garry Wills, *Under God: Religion and American Politics* (New York: Simon & Schuster, 1990), 15. The Gallup data are found in George Gallup and Jim Castelli, *The People's Religion: American Faith in the 90s* (New York: Macmillan, 1989), 56, 58, 61, 63 and 75. Data on the Rapture are found in Marlene Tufts, "Snatched Away Before the Bomb: Rapture Believers in the 1980s" (PhD dissertation, University of Hawaii, 1986), vi.
23. Michelle Goldberg, *Kingdom Coming: The Rise of Christian Nationalism* (New York: W. W. Norton, 2006), 9.
24. Crane Brinton, *The Anatomy of Revolution* (New York: Random House, 1965), 154–155.
25. Ibid., 157–158.

26. Ibid. 164.
27. I heard Kennedy say this at my seminar with him at the Coral Ridge Presbyterian Church.
28. Curtis White, "The Spirit of Disobedience," *Harper's,* April 2006.
29. The Christian Coalition of America lists 15 issues as key to its "Legislative Agenda." Its 2004 "Congressional Scorecard" rated (on a 100-point scale) members of the House of Representatives on 13 of these issues; *163* members of the House received an overall rating of 90 or higher on all 13. Members of the Senate were rated on six issues; *42* members of the Senate received an overall rating of 100 on all six. See "Congressional Scorecard," Christian Coalition of America, http://www.cc.org/2004scorecard.pdf. Also Glenn Scherer, "The Godly Must Be Crazy," *Grist,* October 27, 2004.
30. "American Values: The Triumph of the Religious Right," *Economist,* November 11, 2004, http://www.economist.com/printedition/displayStory.cfm?Story_ID=375543; Transcript of interview with Jim DeMint, *NBC News' Meet the Press,* October 17, 2004, http://www.msnbc.com/id/6267835; Hanna Rosin, "Doctor's Order: Oklahoma Republican Tom Coburn Is Back on Capitol Hill, Budgetary Scalpel at the Ready," *Washington Post,* December 12, 2004, D1, http://www.washingtonpost.com/wp-dyn/articles/A58361-2004Dec11.html.
31. MSNBC.com, "Exit Polls—President," http://www.msnbc.msn.com/id/5297138.
32. President Bush created the Office of Faith-Based and Community Initiatives by executive order on January 29, 2001, just nine days after his inauguration. Congress has not passed legislation allowing for faith-based initiatives, so President Bush has repeatedly used executive orders to push the policy through. See "Executive Orders," Office of Faith-Based and Community Initiatives, http://www.whitehouse.gov/government/fbci/executive-orders.html. In February 2006, President Bush signed the Deficit Reduction Act of 2005, reauthorizing welfare reform for another five years and extending the "charitable choice" policy, which allows faith-based groups to continue receiving funding "without altering their religious identities or changing their hiring practices." See "Fact Sheet: Compassion in Action: Producing Real Results for Americans Most in Need," Office of Faith-Based and Community Initiatives, http://www.whitehouse.gov/news/releases/2006/03/print/20060309-3.html.

33. In fiscal year 2003, $1.17 billion out of a $14.5 billion budget in competitive social-service grants were awarded to FBOs. See "Grants to Faith-Based Organizations FY 2003," Office of Faith-Based and Community Initiatives, http://www.whitehouse.gov/government/fbci/final_report_2003.pdf.

34. President George W. Bush, "President Highlights Faith-Based Results at National Conference," http://www.whitehouse.gov/news/releases/2006/03/20060309-5.html.

35. Out of $19,456,713,768 in grants, $2,004,491,549 went to FBOs. See "Grants to Faith-Based Organizations FY 2004," Office of Faith-Based and Community Initiatives, http://www.whitehouse.gov/government/fbci/final_report_2004.pdf.

36. Out of $19,715,661,808 in grants, $2,154,246,246 went to FBOs. See "Grants to Faith-Based Organizations FY 2005," Office of Faith-Based and Community Initiatives, http://www.whitehouse.gov/government/fbci/final_report_2005.pdf.

37. David M. Fine, "Ohio Counties to Adopt Diebold Voting Machines," *The Mill*, January 18, 2004, http://www.gristforthemill.org/010418diebold.html.

38. Ibid.

39. Mark Crispin Miller, "None Dare Call It Stolen," *Harper's*, September 7, 2005, http://www.harpers.org/ExcerptNoneDare.html; Bob Fitrakis and Harvey Wasserman, "Hearings on Ohio Voting Put 2004 Election in Doubt," *Columbus Free Press*, November 18, 2004, http://www.commondreams.org/cgi-bin/print.cgi?file=views04/1118-30.htm.

40. Ray Beckerman, "Basic Report from Columbus," November 4, 2004, http://www.freepress.org/departments/php/display/19/2004/834.

41. Mark Crispin Miller, "None Dare Call It Stolen."

42. The National Center for Education Statistics in the U.S. Department of Education estimated that 1.1 million students were home-schooled in 2003, a 29 percent increase from 1999. The National Home Education Research Institute says that 1.7 million to 2.1 million children were home-schooled during the 2002–2003 academic year. From Michelle Goldberg, *Kingdom Coming*, 2.

43. Barbara Parker and Christy Macy, "Secular Humanism, the Hatch Amendment, and Public Education," People for the American Way, Washington, DC, 1985, 8.

44. Quoted in Bill Moyers, "9/11 and the Spirit of God," address at

Union Theological Seminary, September 7, 2005, http://www.uts
.columbia.edu/index.php?id=605.

45. Sunsara Taylor, "Battle Cry for Theocracy," Truthdig.com, May 11,
2006, http://www.truthdig.com/report/item/20060511_battle_cry
_theocracy.

46. Augustine, quoted in William Sloane Coffin, *The Heart Is a Little to
the Left*, 6.

Chapter Two: The Culture of Despair

1. Fritz Stern, *The Politics of Cultural Despair: A Study in the Rise of the
Germanic Ideology* (Berkeley: University of California Press, 1974),
xii.

2. Beth Shulman, "Working and Poor in the USA," *Nation*, February 9,
2004.

3. Robert Morley, "The Death of American Manufacturing," *Trumpet*,
February 2006, http://www.thetrumpet.com/index.php?page=arti
cle&id=1955.

4. Martin Crutsinger, "United States Cites China and Other Nations in
Report on Unfair Trade Practices," Associated Press, March 31, 2006.

5. Dale Maharidge, "Rust and Rage in the Heartland," *Nation*, September 20, 2004, http://www.thenation.com/doc/20040920/maharidge.

6. Pam Belluck, "To Avoid Divorce, Move to Massachusetts," *New York
Times*, November 14, 2004, as quoted in Michelle Goldberg, *Kingdom
Coming*, 67.

7. By 2010, according to the Center on Budget and Policy Priorities, if
the proposed federal cuts remain in place, elementary and secondary education funding will be cut by $11.5 billion, or 12 percent;
670,000 fewer women and children will receive assistance through
the Women, Infants and Children Supplemental Nutrition Program;
120,000 fewer children will be served through Head Start; and
370,000 fewer low-income families, elderly people and people with
disabilities will receive rental assistance with rental vouchers. See
Sharon Parrott, Jim Horney, Isaac Shapiro, Ruth Carlitz, Bradley
Hardy, and David Kamin, "Where Would the Cuts Be Made under
the President's Budget?: An Analysis of Reductions in Education,
Human Services, Environment, and Community Development Programs," Center on Budget and Policy Priorities, February 28, 2005,
http://www.cbpp.org/2-22-05bud.html.

8. Dale Maharidge, "Rust and Rage."

9. Arlie Hochschild, "The Chauffeur's Dilemma," *American Prospect* 16: 7 (July 2005), 53.

10. Ibid.

Chapter Three: Conversion

1. Dietrich Bonhoeffer, *Life Together: The Classic Exploration of Faith in Community* (New York: HarperCollins, 1954), 330.

2. D. James Kennedy, *Evangelism Explosion*, 4th ed. (Wheaton, IL: Tyndale House, 1996), 59.

3. Ibid.

4. Ibid., 60.

5. Ibid., 137.

6. Ibid., 2.

7. Ibid., 139.

8. Ibid., 103.

9. Ibid., 22.

10. Margaret Thaler Singer, *Cults in Our Midst: The Continuing Fight Against Their Hidden Menace* (San Francisco: Jossey-Bass, 2003), 114.

11. Robert Jay Lifton, cited in Denise Winn, *The Manipulated Mind* (Cambridge, MA: Malor Books, 2000), 21.

12. William James, *The Varieties of Religious Experience* (Mineola, NY: Dover, 2002), 187

13. "Staff Biography: 'Dr. James Kennedy,'" Center for Reclaiming America for Christ, http://www.reclaimamerica/org/pages/About Us.aspx?pg=djk.

14. "Dr. Kennedy's Profile," *The Kennedy Commentary*, http://www .kennedycommentary.org/default.asp?pg=djk; *Truths That Transform*, Coral Ridge Ministries, http://www.truthsthattransform. org/ITT.asp?page=about; "About the Coral Ridge Hour," *The Coral Ridge Hour*, http://www.coralridgehour.org/coralridgehour.asp?/ page=crh.

15. Terry Gross, "Closing the Gap Between Church and State," *Fresh Air from WHYY*, May 18, 2005.

16. Ibid.

17. Bob Moser, "The Crusaders," *Rolling Stone*, April 7, 2005, http:// www.rollingstone.com/politics/story/7235393/the_crusaders/?md =1140382586732&has-player=false.

18. Ibid.
19. Ashley Fantz, "Cross Purposes: The Rev. D. James Kennedy Teaches That Homosexuality Is a Sin. Richard Murphy Loves Him Anyway," *Broward–Palm Beach New Times,* May 2, 2002.
20. *Worthy Creations,* http://www.worthycreations.org.
21. Rob Boston, "D. James Kennedy: Who Is He and What Does He Want?" *Americans United for Separation of Church and State,* http://www.au.org/site/News2?page=NewsArticle&id=5936&abbr=cs_.
22. Kennedy, *Evangelism Explosion,* 72.
23. Ibid.
24. Ibid., 73.
25. Ibid., 84.
26. Ibid., 42.
27. Ibid.
28. Paul Tillich, "You Are Accepted," in *The Shaking of the Foundations* (New York: Charles Scribner's Sons, 1948), 155.
29. Kennedy, *Evangelism Explosion,* 48.
30. D. James Kennedy and Jerry Newcombe, *The Gates of Hell Shall Not Prevail* (Nashville, TN: Thomas Nelson, 1996), 135.
31. "Aggregated Grants to Coral Ridge Ministries, Coral Ridge Presbyterian Church and Evangelism Explosion" (grants cover January 1998 to February 2004), *Media Transparency,* http://www.mediatransparency.org/coralridgeaggregate.php.

Chapter Four: *The Cult of Masculinity*

1. Klaus Theweleit, *Male Fantasies* (Minneapolis, MN: University of Minnesota Press, 1987), 1:218.
2. Francis FitzGerald, "A Disciplined, Charging Army," *New Yorker,* May 18, 1981, 53, quoted in Robert Smart, "*The Passion of the Christ:* Reflections on Mel's Monstrous Messiah Movie and the Culture Wars," *Jump Cut* 47 (Winter 2005), http://www.ejumpcut.org/archive/jc47.2005/melsPassion/text.html.
3. Karen McCarthy Brown, "Fundamentalism and the Control of Women," in *Fundamentalism and Gender,* ed. John Stratton Hawley (New York: Oxford University Press, 1994), 176.
4. Ibid., 182–183.
5. "Dobson's Choice: Religious Right Leader Becomes Political Power Broker," *People for the American Way Foundation,* February 24, 2005,

http://www.pfaw/general/default.aspx?oid=17932&print=yes& units=all.

6. James Dobson, *Dare to Discipline* (New York: Bantam, 1977), 23.

7. "Dobson's Choice."

8. "Right Wing Organizations: Focus on the Family," *People for the American Way Foundation,* http://www.pfaw/general/default.aspx ?oid=257#.

9. "Dobson's Choice."

10. James Dobson, "The Gender Gap," *Focus on the Family,* http:// www.family.org/married/comm/a0009661.cfm.

11. Mark Edmundson, "Freud and the Fundamentalist Urge," *New York Times,* April 30, 2006.

12. Ibid.

13. Susan Friend Harding, *The Book of Jerry Falwell: Fundamentalist Language and Politics* (Princeton, NJ: Princeton University Press, 2000), 176.

14. Joost A. M. Meerloo, *Mental Seduction and Menticide: The Psychology of Thought Control and Brain-Washing* (London: Jonathan Cape, 1957), 163–164, 184.

15. B. A. Robinson, "Promise Keepers, Pro and Con: Part 1," *Ontario Consultants on Religious Tolerance,* November 2, 2003, http://www .religioustolerance.org/chr_pk.html.

16. Jena Recer, "Whose Promise Are They Keeping?" *National NOW Times,* August 1995, http://www.now.org/nnt/08–95.html.

17. James Dobson, "Building Moral Character in Kids," radio broadcast, *Focus on the Family International,* February 8, 2006, http://www.one place.com/Ministries/Focus_on_the_Family_International/?swndate =2/8/2006.

Chapter Five: Persecution

1. Tony Kushner, *Angels in America* (New York: Theatre Communications Group, 1995), 46.

2. James Dobson, *Marriage under Fire: Why We Must Win This Battle* (Sisters, OR: Multnomah, 2004), 41.

3. "Focus on the Family," *Citizen Magazine* January 2003, quoted in Jeff Lutes, *A False Focus on My Family* (Lynchburg, VA: Soulforce, 2004), 8.

4. Dobson, *Marriage Under Fire,* 49.

5. James Dobson, *Bringing Up Boys* (Wheaton, IL: Tyndale House, 2001), 127.

6. Robert Knight, "The Homosexual Agenda in Schools," Family Research Council, quoted in Matthew Shepard, "Nazi Anti-Jewish Speech vs. Religious Right Anti-Gay Speech," *Hatecrime.org*, http://www.hatecrime.org/subpages/hitler/hitler.html.

7. P. Gibson, "Gay Males and Lesbian Youth Suicide," in M. R. Feinleib, ed., *Report of the Secretary's Task Force on Youth Suicide, Volume 3: Prevention and Interventions in Youth Suicide* (Rockville, MD: U.S. Department of Health and Human Services; Public Health Service; Alcohol, Drug Abuse, and Mental Health Administration, 1989; DHHS publication ADM 89–1623), 110.

8. Pat Robertson, quoted in Richard K. Fenn, *Dreams of Glory*, 8.

9. Kavan Peterson, "Washington Gay Marriage Ruling Looms," *Stateline.org*, March 7, 2006, http://cms.stateline.org/working/ViewPage.action?siteNodeId=136&contentId=20695; "Same-Sex Marriage Measures on the 2004 Ballot," *National Conference of State Legislatures*, November 2004, http://www.ncsl.org/programs/cyf/samesex.htm.

10. Mel White, *Stranger at the Gate* (New York: Penguin, 1995), 25.

11. Ibid., 22–23.

12. Ibid., 29.

13. Ibid., 14.

14. Ibid., 49–50.

15. Ibid., 96.

16. Ibid., 107.

17. Ibid., 142.

Chapter Six: The War on Truth

1. Hannah Arendt, *The Origins of Totalitarianism* (New York: Harcourt, 1979), 353.

2. Scott LaFee, "Local Scientists, Doctors and Professors Talk About 'Intelligent Design,'" *San Diego Union Tribune*, June 8, 2005, F-1.

3. Frank Newport, "Third of Americans Say Evidence Has Supported Darwin's Evolution Theory," *Gallup Poll*, November 19, 2004, http://poll.gallup.com/content/default.aspx?ci=14107&pg=1.

4. Keith Graham, *Biology: God's Living Creation* (Pensacola, FL: A Beka, 1986), 404.

5. Alfred M. Rehwinkel, *The Wonders of Creation* (Minneapolis, MN: Bethany House, 1974), in Graham, *Biology*, 133.

6. Graham, *Biology*, 163.

7. Graham, *Biology*, 351.

8. Carl Wieland, "Darwin's Bodysnatchers: New Horrors," *Creation* 14:2 (March 1992), 16–18.

9. Carl Wieland, "Apartheid and 'The Cradle of Humankind,'" *Creation* 26:2 (March 2004), 10–14.

10. "What Happened When Stalin Read Darwin?" *Creation* 10:4 (September 1998), 23.

11. Jerry Bergman, "Darwinism and the Nazi Race Holocaust," *Technical Journal* 13:2, 101–111.

12. "Evolution and the Hutu-Tutsi Slayings," *Creation* 21:2 (March 1999), 47.

13. Graham, *Biology*, 347.

14. Jerry Bergman, "Was Charles Darwin Psychotic? A Study of His Mental Health," *Impact* (January 2004).

15. Raymond Hall, "Darwin's Impact—The Bloodstained Legacy of Evolution," *Creation* 27:2 (March 2005), 46–47.

16. Graham, *Biology*, 347.

17. Ibid., 349.

18. Hannah Arendt, *Origins of Totalitarianism*, 371.

19. "Intelligence Report," *Southern Poverty Law Center* (Spring 2005), 4. http://www.splcenter.org/intelreport/article.jsp?pid=869.

20. Union of Concerned Scientists, "Scientific Integrity in Policy Making: An Investigation into the Bush Administration's Misuse of Science," March 2004, 2; 32, http://www.ucsusa.org/assets/documents/scientific_integrity/RSI_final_fullreport_1.pdf.

21. This lecture was taped and transcribed by Timothy Nunan of Princeton University.

Chapter Seven: The New Class

1. Karl Popper, *The Open Society and Its Enemies* (Princeton: Princeton University Press, 1971), 1:96.

2. Max Blumenthal, "Justice Sunday Preachers," *The Nation*, May 9, 2005 (Web edition only), http://www.thenation.com/doc/20050509/blumenthal.

3. Ibid.

4. Ibid.

5. David Kirkpatrick, "Club of the Most Powerful Gathers in Strictest Privacy," *The New York Times*, August 28, 2004.

6. Ibid.
7. Max Blumenthal, "Who Are Justice Sunday's Ministers of Ministry?" *Talk To Action,* January 6, 2006, http://www.talk2action.org/story/2006/1/6/103859/7034.
8. Quoted in Daniel Lev, *The Terrorist Next Door* (New York: Thomas Dumae/St. Martin, 2002), 27.
9. Jean Hardisty, *Mobilizing Resentment* (Boston: Beacon Press, 1999), 107–108; Rob Boston, "If Best-Selling End-Times Author Tim La-Haye Has His Way, Church-State Separation Will Be . . . Left Behind," *Church & State Magazine,* February 2002.
10. Mariah Blake, "Stations Of The Cross: How evangelical Christians are creating an alternative universe of faith-based news," *Columbia Journalism Review,* May/June 2005.

Chapter Eight: The Crusade

1. Elias Canetti, *Crowds and Power* (New York: Farrar, Straus and Giroux, 1973), 22.
2. Sigmund Freud, *Civilization and Its Discontents,* edited and translated by James Strachey (New York: W. W. Norton, 1961), 67.
3. Ibid., 66.
4. Steve Blow, "Turning Textbooks into the Good Book," *Dallas Morning News,* March 5, 2006.
5. Mary Ann Zehr, "School of Faith," *Education Week,* December 7, 2005.
6. See http://www.ed.nces.gov.
7. Laurel Elizabeth Hicks, *Old World History and Geography* (Pensacola, FL: A Beka, 1991), 247, as cited in Frances Patterson, "Teaching Religious Intolerance," *Rethinking Schools Online,* http://www.rethinkingschools.org/special_reports/voucher_report/v_into162.shtml.
8. Hicks, *Old World History and Geography,* 210, as cited in Patterson, "Teaching Religious Intolerance."
9. Hicks, *Old World History and Geography,* 213 and 214, as cited in Patterson, "Teaching Religious Intolerance."
10. Patterson, "Teaching Religious Intolerance," 2.
11. Jerry Combee, *History of the World in Christian Perspective* (Pensacola, FL: A Beka, 1997), 86.
12. Patterson, "Teaching Religious Intolerance," 2.
13. Hicks, *Old World History and Geography,* 47, as cited in Patterson, "Teaching Religious Intolerance."

14. Combee, *History of the World,* 279.
15. Hicks, *Old World History and Geography,* 212, as cited in Patterson, "Teaching Religious Intolerance."
16. *Heritage Studies for Christian Schools 6* (Greenville, SC: Bob Jones University Press, 1998), 41.
17. Kurt S. Grussendorf, Michael R. Lowman, and Brian S. Asbaugh, *America, Land I Love—Teacher Edition* (Pensacola, FL: A Beka, 1994), 636.
18. Ibid., 631.
19. Ibid., 630.
20. Ibid., 593. Italics added.
21. Tim LaHaye and Jerry B. Jenkins, *Glorious Appearing: The End of Days* (Wheaton, IL: Tyndale House, 2004), 10.
22. Ibid., 12.
23. "UnCommonSense," *J. Kenneth Blackwell, Ohio Secretary of State,* http://www_sos.state_oh.us/sos/initiatives/OCCC.aspx?Section=108.
24. Ibid.
25. Ibid.
26. Ibid.
27. Andrew Welsh-Huggins, "Ohio Televangelist Takes to Politics," *FortWayne.com,* December 3, 2005, http://www.fortwayne.com/mld/journalgazette/living/13319862.htm.
28. Sarah Posner, "With God on His Side," *American Prospect,* November 2005.
29. Jim Bebbington, "An Empire of Souls," *Columbus Monthly,* May 1993, 35, quoted in G. Richard Fisher, "Rod Parsley: The Raging Prophet," *Personal Freedom Outreach,* 1999.
30. Posner, "With God on His Side."

Chapter Nine: God: The Commercial

1. Walter Lippmann, *Liberty and the News* (New York: Harcourt, Brace and Howe, 1920), 64.
2. William Lobdell, "The Prosperity Gospel; Pastor's Empire Built on Acts of Faith and Cash," *Los Angeles Times,* September 19, 2004, B1.
3. Ibid.
4. Andre Gumbel, "Scandal, Sex and Sanctimony," *New Zealand Herald,* September 18, 2004, B16.

5. Paul Crouch Sr., *Praise the Lord,* November 7, 1997, quoted in "Paul Crouch and TBN," *On Doctrine,* http://www.ondoctrine.com/10tbn.htm.
6. Lobdell, "Prosperity Gospel."
7. Gumbel, "Scandal, Sex and Sanctimony."
8. Benny Hinn, *Praise the Lord,* October 19, 1999, quoted in "Paul Crouch and TBN."
9. Benny Hinn, *Larry King Live,* quoted in "Benny Hinn—Truth or Consequences, Part 3," *Let Us Reason Ministries Apologetics Index,* http://www.apologeticsindex.org/h04.html.
10. Gumbel, "Scandal, Sex and Sanctimony."
11. Paul Crouch Sr., *Praise-a-Thon,* April 2, 1991, quoted in "Paul Crouch and TBN."
12. Gumbel, "Scandal, Sex and Sanctimony."
13. William Lobdell, "Ex-Worker Accusing TBN Pastor Says He Had Sex to Keep His Job," *Los Angeles Times,* September 22, 2004, B1.
14. Lobdell, "Prosperity Gospel."
15. Ibid.
16. Mark A. Beliles and Stephen K. McDowell, *America's Providential History,* 19
17. Ibid., 3.
18. Ibid., 214.
19. Ibid., 265.
20. Ibid., 197.

Chapter Ten: Apocalyptic Violence

1. Stephen D. O'Leary, quoted in James A. Morone, *Hellfire Nation: The Politics of Sin in American Society* (New Haven, CT: Yale University Press, 2004), 108.
2. Tim LaHaye and Jerry B. Jenkins, *Glorious Appearing: The End of Days,* 286.
3. Ibid., 273.
4. Katherine Yurica, "Tim LaHaye, the Richest Divinator in the World," *The Yurica Report,* http://www.yuricareport.com/Revisited Bks/TimLaHayeDivinator.html.
5. Ibid.
6. See Richard Hofstadter, "The Paranoid Style in American Politics," *Harper's,* November 1964, 77–86.

7. Cited in Davidson Loehr, *America, Fascism and God*, 81–82.
8. James Luther Adams, *The Essential James Luther Adams: Selected Essays and Addresses*, ed. George Kimmich Beach (Boston: Skinner House, 1998), 25–26.
9. Quoted by Michelle Goldberg, *Kingdom Coming*, 187.
10. Samuel Clemens, *The Adventures of Huckleberry Finn* (New York: Charles L. Webster, 1885), 270–272.
11. Vasily Grossman, *Life and Fate*, trans. Robert Chandler (New York: Harper and Row, 1985), 410.

Bibliography

Agee, James, and Walker Evans. *Let Us Now Praise Famous Men*. Boston: Mariner Books, 1988.

Albrecht, Gerd. *Nationalsozialistische Filmpolitik: Eine soziologische Untersuchung über die Spielfilme des Dritten Reiches*. Stuttgart: Ferdinand Enke, 1969.

Alter, Robert, and Frank Kermode, eds. *The Literary Guide to the Bible*. Cambridge, MA: Belknap Press, 1987.

Arendt, Hannah. *The Origins of Totalitarianism*. New York: Harcourt, 1979.

Armstrong, Karen. *The Battle for God*. New York: Alfred A. Knopf, 2000.

Ault, James M., Jr. *Spirit and Flesh: Life in a Fundamentalist Baptist Church*. New York: Alfred A. Knopf, 2004.

Barton, David. *A Spiritual Heritage: Tour of the United States Capitol*. Aledo, TX: WallBuilder Press, 2000.

Bartov, Omer. *Mirrors of Destruction: War, Genocide, and Modern Identity*. New York: Oxford University Press, 2000.

Beach, George Kimmich, ed. *The Essential James Luther Adams: Selected Essays and Addresses*. Boston: Skinner House Books, 1998.

Beliles, Mark A., and Stephen K. McDowell. *America's Providential History*. Charlottesville, VA: Providence Foundation, 1989.

Bellant, Russ. *The Coors Connection: How Coors Family Philanthropy Undermines Democratic Pluralism*. Boston: South End Press, 1991.

———. *Old Nazis, the New Right, and the Republican Party: Domestic Fascist Networks and Their Effect on U.S. Cold War Politics*. Boston: South End Press, 1991.

Belt, Don, ed. *The World Of Islam*. Washington, DC: National Geographic, 2001.

Biros, Florence W. *Crossing Paths Treasury*. Vol. 1. New Wilmington, PA: Son-Rise Publications, 1998.

Bonhoeffer, Dietrich. *Life Together: The Classic Exploration of Faith in Community*. Translated by John W. Doberstein. New York: HarperCollins Publishers, 1954.

Brinton, Crane. *The Anatomy of Revolution.* New York: Random House, 1965.

Brown, Karen McCarthy. "Fundamentalism and the Control of Women." In *Fundamentalism and Gender.* Edited by John Stratton Hawley. New York: Oxford University Press, 1994.

Burke, Theresa, and David C. Reardon. *Forbidden Grief: The Unspoken Pain of Abortion.* Springfield, IL: Acorn Books, 2002.

Cantor, David. *The Religious Right: The Assault on Tolerance and Pluralism in America.* Edited by Alan M. Schwartz. New York: Anti-Defamation League, 1994.

Carter, Jimmy. *Our Endangered Values: America's Moral Crisis.* New York: Simon & Schuster, 2005.

Chrnalogar, Mary Alice. *Twisted Scriptures: Breaking Free From Churches That Abuse.* Grand Rapids, MI: Zondervan Publishing House, 2000.

Clarkson, Frederick. *Eternal Hostility: The Struggle Between Theocracy and Democracy.* Monroe, ME: Common Courage Press, 1997.

Coffin, William Sloane. *The Heart Is a Little to the Left: Essays on Public Morality.* Hanover, NH: University Press of New England, 1999.

Cohen, Edmund D. *The Mind of the Bible Believer.* Amherst, NY: Prometheus Books, 1988.

Crossan, John Dominic. *Jesus: A Revolutionary Biography.* New York: Harper-Collins Publishers, 1994.

Crossman, Richard H., ed. *The God That Failed.* Chicago, IL: Regnery Gateway, Inc., 1949.

De Vries, Hentde, and Samuel Weber, eds. *Religion and Media.* Stanford, CA: Stanford University Press, 2001.

Diamond, Sara. *Not by Politics Alone: The Enduring Influence of the Christian Right.* New York: The Guilford Press, 1998.

———. *Roads to Dominion: Right-Wing Movements and Political Power in the United States.* New York: The Guilford Press, 1995.

———. *Spiritual Warfare: The Politics of the Christian Right.* Boston: South End Press, 1989.

Dobson, James. *Bringing Up Boys.* Wheaton, IL: Tyndale House Publishers, 2001.

———. *Dare to Discipline.* New York: Bantam Books, 1970.

———. *Marriage Under Fire: Why We Must Win This Battle.* Sisters, OR: Multnomah, 2004.

Douglass, Frederick. "What, to the Slave, Is the Fourth of July? (1852)." In *Lift Every Voice: African American Oratory, 1787–1900.* Edited by

Philip S. Foner and Robert James Branham. Tuscaloosa: University of Alabama Press, 1998.

————. *Narrative of the Life of Frederick Douglass, an American Slave, Written by Himself (1845)*. New York: Signet Books, 1968.

Ehrman, Bart D. *The New Testament: A Historical Introduction to the Early Christian Writings*. Third Edition. New York: Oxford University Press, 2004.

Fenn, Richard K. *Dreams of Glory: The Sources of Apocalyptic Terror*. Burlington, VT: Ashgate Publishing Company, 2006.

Frank, Thomas. *What's the Matter with Kansas: How Conservatives Won the Heart of America*. New York: Henry Holt and Company, 2004.

Frazier, Gary. *Signs of the Coming of Christ*. Arlington, TX: Discovery Ministries, 1998.

Freud, Sigmund. *Civilization and Its Discontents*. Edited and translated by James Strachey. New York: W. W. Norton and Company, 1961.

Friedman, Richard Elliott. *Who Wrote the Bible*. New York: HarperCollins Publishers, 1989.

Gallup, George, Jr., and Jim Castelli. *The People's Religion: American Faith in the 90s*. New York: Macmillan, 1989.

Ghosh, Amitav. *Incendiary Circumstances: A Chronicle of the Turmoil of Our Times*. New York: Houghton Mifflin Company, 2005.

Goebbels, Joseph. *Signale der neuen Zeit*. Munich: Eher, 1934.

Goldberg, Michelle. *Kingdom Coming: The Rise of Christian Nationalism*. New York: W. W. Norton and Company, 2006.

Goodrich, Chris. *Faith Is a Verb: On the Home Front with Habitat for Humanity in the Campaign to Rebuild America (and the World)*. Brookfield, CT: Gimlet Eye Books, 2005.

Green, John C., Mark J. Rozell, and Clyde Wilcox, eds. *The Christian Right in American Politics: Marching to the Millennium*. Washington, DC: Georgetown University Press, 2003.

Grossman, Vasily. *Life and Fate*. Translated by Robert Chandler. New York: Harper and Row, 1985.

Harding, Susan Friend. *The Book of Jerry Falwell: Fundamentalist Language and Politics*. Princeton, NJ: Princeton University Press, 2000.

Harris, Sam. *The End of Faith: Religion, Terror, and the Future of Reason*. New York: W. W. Norton and Company, 2004.

Hassan, Steven. *Combatting Cult Mind Control*. Rochester, VT: Park Street Press, 1998.

Heinemann, Larry. *Black Virgin Mountain: A Return to Vietnam*. New York: Doubleday, 2005.

Hitchcock, Mark. *101 Answers to the Most Asked Questions About the End Times*. Sisters, OR: Multnomah Publishers, 2001.

Hoover, Stewart M., and Lynn Schofield Clark, eds. *Practicing Religion in the Age of the Media: Explorations in Media, Religion, and Culture*. New York: Columbia University Press, 2002.

Horton, Ronald A., ed. *Christian Education: Its Mandate and Mission*. Greenville, SC: Bob Jones University Press, 1992.

Hughes, Richard T. *Myths America Lives By*. Urbana, IL: University of Illinois Press, 2004.

James, William. *The Varieties of Religious Experience*. Mineola, NY: Dover Publications, Inc., 2002.

Jenkins, Jerry B., Tim LaHaye, with Chris Faby. *The Rise of False Messiahs: Left Behind: The Kids*. Wheaton, IL: Tyndale Press, 2004.

Juergensmeyer, Mark. *Terror in the Mind of God: The Global Rise of Religious Violence*. Third Edition. Los Angeles: University of California Press, 2003.

Kaplan, Esther. *With God on Their Side: How Christian Fundamentalists Trampled Science, Policy, and Democracy in George W. Bush's White House*. New York: New Press, 2004.

Kennedy, D. James. *Evangelism Explosion*. Fourth Edition. Wheaton, IL: Tyndale House Publishers, 1996.

Kennedy, D. James, and Jim Nelson Black. *Character and Destiny: A Nation in Search of Its Soul*. Grand Rapids, MI: Zondervan Publishing, 1994.

Kennedy, D. James, with Jerry Newcombe. *The Gates of Hell Shall Not Prevail*. Nashville, TN: Thomas Nelson Publishers, 1996.

———. *Lord of All: Developing a Christian World-and-Life View*. Wheaton, IL: Crossway Books, 2005.

———. *What If America Were a Christian Nation Again?* Nashville, TN: Thomas Nelson Publishers, 2003.

Kepel, Gilles. *The War for Muslim Minds: Islam and the West*. Cambridge, MA: Belknap Press, 2004.

Kintz, Linda, and Julia Lesage, eds. *Media, Culture, and the Religious Right*. Minneapolis: University of Minnesota Press, 1998.

Klemperer, Victor. *I Will Bear Witness 1933–1941: A Diary of the Nazi Years*. Translated by Martin Chalmers. New York: Modern Library, 1999.

———. *I Will Bear Witness 1942–1945: A Diary of the Nazi Years*. Translated by Martin Chalmers. New York: The Modern Library, 1999.

Koonz, Claudia. *The Nazi Conscience*. Cambridge, MA: Belknap Press, 2003.

Kugel, James L. *The Bible As It Was*. Cambridge, MA: Belknap Press, 1997.

LaHaye, Tim, with Steve Halliday. *The Merciful God of Prophecy: His Loving Plan for You in the End Times*. New York: Warner Faith, 2002.

LaHaye, Tim, and Ed Hindson. *The Popular Bible Prophecy Workbook*. Eugene, OR: Harvest House Publishers, 1982.

LaHaye, Tim, and Thomas Ice. *Charting the End Times*. Eugene, OR: Harvest House Publishers, 2001.

LaHaye, Tim, and Jerry B. Jenkins. *Apollyon: The Destroyer Is Unleashed*. Wheaton, IL: Tyndale House Publishers, 1999.

———. *Armageddon: The Cosmic Battle of the Ages*. Wheaton, IL: Tyndale House Publishers, 2003.

———. *Assassins: Assignment: Jerusalem, Target: Antichrist*. Wheaton, IL: Tyndale House Publishers, 1999.

———. *Desecration: Antichrist Takes the Throne*. Wheaton, IL: Tyndale House Publishers, 2001.

———. *Glorious Appearing: The End of Days*. Wheaton, IL: Tyndale House Publishers, 2004.

———. *The Indwelling: The Beast Takes Possession*. Wheaton, IL: Tyndale House Publishers, 2000.

———. *Left Behind: A Novel of the Earth's Last Days*. Wheaton, IL: Tyndale House Publishers, 1995.

———. *The Mark: The Beast Rules the World*. Wheaton, IL: Tyndale House Publishers, 2000.

———. *Nicolae: The Rise of Antichrist*. Wheaton, IL: Tyndale House Publishers, 1997.

———. *Remnant: On the Brink of Armageddon*. Wheaton, IL: Tyndale House Publishers, 2002.

———. *Soul Harvest: The World Takes Sides*. Wheaton, IL: Tyndale House Publishers, 1998.

———. *Tribulation Force: The Continuing Drama of Those Left Behind*. Wheaton, IL: Tyndale House Publishers, 1996.

Lakoff, Mark. *Moral Politics: How Liberals and Conservatives Think*. Second Edition. Chicago: University of Chicago Press, 2002.

Larson, Edward J. *Summer for the Gods: The Scopes Trial and America's Continuing Debate over Science and Religion*. Cambridge, MA: Harvard University Press, 1997.

Leonard, Bill J. *Baptists in America*. New York: Columbia University Press, 2005.

Lewis, Sinclair. *It Can't Happen Here*. New York: Penguin Books, 1963.

Lifton, Robert Jay. *Thought Reform and the Psychology of Totalism: A Study of Brainwashing in China*. New York: W. W. Norton and Company, 1961.

Loehr, Davidson. *America, Fascism and God: Sermons from a Heretical Preacher*. White River Junction, VT: Chelsea Green Publishing Company, 2005.

Maharidge, Dale, with photographs by Michael Williamson. *And Their Children After Them: The Legacy of Let Us Now Praise Famous Men: James Agee, Walker Evans, and the Rise and Fall of Cotton in the South*. New York: Seven Stories Press, 2004.

————. *Denison, Iowa: Searching for the Soul of America Through the Secrets of A Midwest Town*. New York: Free Press, 2005.

————. *Homeland*. New York: Seven Stories Press, 2004.

————. *Journey to Nowhere: The Saga of the New Underclass*. New York: Hyperion, 1996.

Maimon, Solomon. *Solomon Maimon: An Autobiography*. Translated by J. Clark Murray. Urbana: University of Illinois Press, 2001.

Manseau, Peter. *Vows: The Story of a Priest, a Nun, and Their Son*. New York: Free Press, 2005.

Martin, William. *With God on Our Side: The Rise of the Religious Right in America*. New York: Broadway Books, 1996.

Marty, Martin E., and R. Scott Appleby. *The Glory and the Power: The Fundamentalist Challenge to the Modern World*. Boston: Beacon Press, 1992.

————, eds. *The Fundamentalism Project*. 5 vols. Chicago: University of Chicago Press, 1991–95.

McGirr, Lisa. *Suburban Warriors: The Origins of the New American Right*. Princeton, NJ: Princeton University Press, 2001.

Meerloo, Joost A. M. *The Rape of the Mind: The Psychology of Thought Control, Menticide, and Brainwashing*. Cleveland and New York: The World Publishing Company, 1956.

Mendelssohn, Moses. *Jerusalem: Or On Religious Power and Judaism*. Translated by Allan Arkush. Introduction and Commentary by Alexander Altmann. Lebanon, NH: University Press of New England, 1983.

Niebuhr, Reinhold. *The Irony of American History*. New York: Charles Scribner's Sons, 1952.

Niebuhr, Reinhold. *Justice and Mercy*. Edited by Ursula M. Niebuhr. New York: Harper & Row, 1974.

Nock, A. D. *Conversion: The Old and the New in Religion from Alexander the*

Great to Augustine of Hippo. Baltimore, MD: The Johns Hopkins University Press, 1998.

O'Leary, Stephen D. *Arguing the Apocalypse: A Theory of Millennial Rhetoric.* New York: Oxford University Press, 1994.

Ortega y Gasset, José. *The Revolt of the Masses.* Translated by Anthony Kerrigan. Edited by Kenneth Moore. Notre Dame, IN: University of Notre Dame Press, 1985.

Orwell, George. *1984.* New York: Harcourt Brace Jovanovich, 1977.

Palmer, Laura. *Shrapnel in the Heart: Letters and Remembrances from the Vietnam Veterans Memorial.* New York: Random House, 1987.

Paxton, Robert O. *The Anatomy of Fascism.* New York: Alfred A. Knopf, 2004.

Phillips, Kevin. *American Dynasty: Aristocracy, Fortune, and the Politics of Deceit in the House of Bush.* New York: Penguin Group, 2004.

Popper, Karl. R. *The Open Society and Its Enemies: The Spell of Plato.* Princeton: Princeton University Press, 1966.

Postman, Neil. *Amusing Ourselves to Death: Public Discourse in the Age of Show Business.* New York: Penguin Books, 1986.

Press, Bill. *How the Republicans Stole Christmas: The Republican Party's Declared Monopoly on Religion and What Democrats Can Do to Take It Back.* New York: Doubleday, 2005.

Prothero, Stephen. *American Jesus: How the Son of God Became a National Icon.* New York: Farrar, Straus and Giroux, 1985.

Riley, Naomi Schaefer. *God on the Quad: How Religious Colleges and the Missionary Generation Are Changing America.* New York: St. Martin's Press, 2005.

Robertson, Pat. *The New World Order.* Dallas: Word Publishing, 1991.

Rossing, Barbara R. *The Rapture Exposed: The Message of Hope in the Book of Revelation.* New York: Basic Books, 2004.

Rushdoony, Rousas John. *The Institutes of Biblical Law.* Dallas, TX: The Craig Press, 1973.

Saloma, John S., III. *Ominous Politics: The New Conservative Labyrinth.* New York: Hill and Wang, 1984.

Sargant, William. *Battle for the Mind: A Physiology of Conversion and Brain-Washing.* Cambridge, MA: ISHK, 1997.

Singer, Margaret Thaler. *Cults in Our Midst: The Continuing Fight Against Their Hidden Menace.* San Francisco: Jossey-Bass, 2003.

Smith, Christian. *Christian America?: What Evangelicals Really Want.* Los Angeles: University of California Press, 2000.

Smith, Chuck. *Calvary Chapel Distinctives*. Costa Mesa, CA: The Word for Today Publishers, 2004.

Smith, Wilfred Cantwell. *What Is Scripture: A Comparative Approach*. Minneapolis, MN: Fortress Press, 1993.

Spong, John Shelby. *Rescuing the Bible from Fundamentalism: A Bishop Rethinks the Meaning of Scripture*. New York: HarperCollins Publishers, 1991.

Stein, Stephen J. *The Encyclopedia of Apocalypticism, Vol. 3. Apocalypticism in the Modern Period and the Contemporary Age*. New York: Continuum, 1999.

Stern, Fritz. *The Politics of Cultural Despair: A Study in the Rise of the Germanic Ideology*. Berkeley: University of California Press, 1989.

Stern, Jessica. *The Ultimate Terrorists*. Cambridge, MA: Harvard University Press, 1999.

Strozier, Charles B. *Apocalypse: On the Psychology of Fundamentalism in America*. Eugene, OR: Wipf and Stock Publishers, 2002.

Theweleit, Klaus. *Male Fantasies, Vol. 1. Women, Floods, Bodies, History*. Translated by Stephen Conway. Minneapolis: University of Minnesota Press, 1987.

———. *Male Fantasies, Vol. 2. Male Bodies: Psychoanalyzing the White Terror*. Translated by Erica Carter and Chris Turner. Minneapolis: University of Minnesota Press, 1989.

Tillich, Paul. *The Shaking of the Foundations*. New York: Charles Scribner's Sons, 1948.

Todorov, Tzvetan. *The Conquest of America*. New York: HarperCollins, 1992.

———. *Facing the Extreme: Moral Life in the Concentration Camps*. Translated by Arthur Denner and Abigail Pollak. New York: Henry Holt and Company, 1997.

———. *Hope and Mercy: Lessons from the Twentieth Century*. Translated by David Bellos. Princeton, NJ: Princeton University Press, 2003.

Twain, Mark. *The Adventures of Huckleberry Finn*. New York: Charles L. Webster and Company, 1885.

Wallis, Jim. *God's Politics: Why the Right Gets It Wrong and the Left Doesn't Get It*. New York: HarperCollins Publishers, 2005.

Whitcomb, John C., and Henry M. Morris. *The Genesis Flood: The Biblical Record and Its Scientific Implications*. Phillipsburg, NJ: P & R Publishing, 1960.

White, Mel. *Stranger at the Gate: To Be Gay and Christian in America*. New York: Plume, 1995.

Wills, Garry. *Under God: Religion and American Politics*. New York: Simon & Schuster, 1990.

Winn, Denise. *The Manipulated Mind: Brainwashing, Conditioning and Indoctrination*. Cambridge, MA: Malor Books, 2000.

Wolfe, Alan. *The Transformation of American Religion: How We Actually Live Our Faith*. New York: Free Press, 2003.

Wright, Stuart A., ed. *Armageddon in Waco: Critical Perspectives of the Branch Davidian Conflict*. Chicago: University of Chicago Press, 1995.

Acknowledgments

This book was written with the generous and unstinting support of the Nation Institute, which allowed me to work unfettered for many months on this project. I am deeply grateful for this support and encouragement, especially that of Hamilton Fish, Taya Grobow, Janine Jaquet and Jonathan Schell, as well as Peggy Suttle and Katerina vanden Heuvel at *The Nation* magazine. I also owe a huge debt to Princeton University, where I teach in the Program in American Studies. R. Sean Wilentz and Judith S. Ferszt, as well as C. K. "Charlie" Williams, Elaine Pagels, Sam and Liz Hynes, and many of my dedicated and brilliant students always lent encouragement and advice. I am blessed with supportive and thoughtful friends and colleagues.

Pamela Diamond, for the second time, oversaw the research and organization of a book of mine with her usual skill, patience, dedication and good humor. I cannot imagine having to go through this without her. Rebecca Beyer, a talented reporter and writer, worked extensively on the book, carrying out some interviews and attending events. She was a close and valued collaborator. Elyse Graham and Amy Paeth, two of my students at Princeton, did tremendous and important research, especially under heavy time pressure in the closing days of production. Timothy Nunan, another Princeton student, did a fine job documenting creationist attacks on Charles Darwin and evolution. I benefited greatly from his research. Lisa Winn, Lauren Brown, James Arnold, Maria Guerrero-Reyes, Linda Kane, Kate Peters, Jason Proske, Colin Maier, Moya Quinlan-Walshe and Kathryn Tippett constituted our small army of transcribers. I turned over hours of tape to them and relied on their care and dedication to produce the transcripts. I owe a tremendous debt to those few who have been among the first to investigate and explain dominionism. They include Katherine Yurica, who produces the *Yurica Report,* available online; Frederick Clarkson, whose three-part series in PublicEye.org in March/June 1994 called "Christian Reconstructionism" was a groundbreaking piece of journalism and who continues to do important research into the movement; and Sarah Diamond, whose books, such as *Roads to Dominion: Right-Wing Movements and Political Power in the United States,* are indispensable.

I owe thanks for vital help and support from Bernard Rapoport and Peter Lewis, as well as Patrick Lannan, Ralph Nader, Jenny Frutchy, Joan Bokaer, Mariah Blake, Cristina Nehring, Ann and Walter Pincus, Lauren B. Davis, June Ballinger, Michael Goldstein, Anne Marie Macari, Robert J. Lifton, Richard Fenn, Fritz Stern, Robert O. Paxton, Charles B. Strozier, Irene Brown, Joe Sacco, Al Ross, the Reverend Mel White, the Reverend Davidson Loehr, the Reverend Ed Bacon, Bishop Krister Stendhal, the Reverend William Sloane Coffin, the Reverend Joe Hough, the Reverend Michael Granzen and the Reverend Terry Burke. The Reverend Coleman Brown, as he has done with all my books, read and critiqued each chapter. Coleman again let me rely on his profound insight and wisdom. As usual, he raised questions and offered critiques that often forced me to reconsider my position or go back to my research. Max Blumenthal, a friend and fine reporter, nursed me through much of this with sage help and advice. I would like to thank Marji Mendelsohn and Janice Weiss for guidance and research, as well as Tamar Gordon, whose advice and scholarship helped me head in the right direction. Tom Artin, as talented a jazz musician as he is a scholar and writer, went through every chapter, as did Eunice Wong, whose brilliance as an actor is matched by her intelligence, critical eye and talent as a writer. There are numerous passages in this book that she patiently reworked. These sections, which bear her imprint and wisdom, have a lucidity and clarity that eluded me. Eunice was my rock and foundation.

I often leaned for emotional support on my friend John "Rick" MacArthur, who keeps alive *Harper's* magazine, one of the great intellectual journals in America, as well as my friend the poet Gerald Stern, who appeared frequently as I was writing to drag me into the sunlight for lunch and impart needed encouragement.

My editors at Free Press, especially Dominick Anfuso and Wylie O'Sullivan, patiently edited, shaped and formed the text. I would also like to thank Michele Jacob. Lisa Bankoff of International Creative Management held my hand, for the fourth time, through this process of proposal to contract to delivery. She is a gift.

Index

abortion, 109, 122, 139
  condemnation of, 23, 40–43,
    47, 61, 85, 92, 138–39,
    144, 146, 195
  of converts, 42, 43–44, 137
  death penalty for, 23, 85, 155
  illegalization of, 21, 23, 43
  legalized, 22, 138–39
  sin of, 71
Adam and Eve, 12, 116, 117,
    120–21, 123, 124, 129, 175
Adams, James Luther, 197–204,
    205, 206, 207
Adventures of Huckleberry Finn, The
    (Twain), 207–9
Afghanistan, 30
Africa, 156
African-Americans, 4, 25, 27, 28,
    73, 140, 146–47, 157, 161,
    203–4
AIDS research, assault on, 126
Air Force, U.S., 32
Alabama Supreme Court, 28–29
American Humanist Association
    (AHA), 27
America's Providential History
    (Beliles and McDowell),
    15, 182–83
Amos, Book of, 37, 148
Ampt, Jean, 117
Anatomy of Fascism (Paxton), 18
Anatomy of Revolution, The (Brin-
    ton), 19–20
Angels in America (Kushner), 98

Antichrist, 5, 28, 91, 186, 187,
    188, 189, 190, 192, 194
anti-intellectualism, xvi, 13, 14
apocalyptic violence, 9, 24,
    28–33, 38, 47–48, 82,
    86–87, 203
  Antichrist in, 5, 28, 91, 186,
    187, 188, 189, 190, 192,
    194
  believers protected from, 33,
    36, 48, 121, 179, 186
  biblical justification of, 3–5,
    6–7, 35, 37
  as biblical prophecy, 187,
    188–89, 190–92
  in Book of Revelation, 4–5, 27,
    143, 147, 188–89
  collective suicide produced by,
    35–36
  genocidal killers inspired by,
    9, 34–35, 87
  and historical empires,
    190–92
  Islamic terrorism in, 192–94
  in Left Behind series, 186–87,
    189–90
  nonbelievers' destruction in,
    5, 6–7, 27, 33, 34–36, 37,
    44–45, 48, 87, 145, 147,
    149, 154, 179, 186, 189,
    191, 209
  presaging events of, 189
  purification by, 7, 34–36, 44,
    45, 154, 186

241

About the Author

Chris Hedges, a graduate of Harvard Divinity School, was a foreign correspondent for nearly 20 years. He was the bureau chief in the Middle East and the Balkans, and worked in other foreign posts, for *The New York Times* from 1990 to 2005. He worked previously for *The Dallas Morning News,* National Public Radio and *The Christian Science Monitor* in Latin America and the Middle East. He has reported from more than 50 countries. Hedges was a member of the *New York Times* team that won the 2002 Pulitzer Prize for Explanatory Reporting for the paper's coverage of global terrorism, and he received the 2002 Amnesty International Global Award for Human Rights Journalism. He holds a B.A. in English Literature from Colgate University and a Master of Divinity from Harvard Divinity School. Hedges has taught at Columbia University, New York University and Princeton University, where he is currently a Visiting Lecturer in the Council of the Humanities and the Program in American Studies as well as the Anschutz Distinguished Fellow. He has written for *Foreign Affairs, Granta, Harper's, Mother Jones* and *The New York Review of Books.* Hedges is the author of *War Is a Force That Gives Us Meaning*—a finalist for the National Book Critics Circle Award for Nonfiction. His other books are *What Every Person Should Know About War* and *Losing Moses on the Freeway: The 10 Commandments in America.* He lives in New Jersey.

AMERICAN FASCISTS

THE CHRISTIAN RIGHT AND THE WAR ON AMERICA

CHRIS HEDGES

A Conversation with Chris Hedges

ABOUT THIS Q&A

The following author question & answer is intended to help you find an interesting and rewarding approach to your reading of *American Fascists*. We hope this enhances your enjoyment and appreciation of the book.

A CONVERSATION WITH THE AUTHOR

The holy blitz rolls on.

The Christian Right is a "deeply anti-democratic movement" that gains force by exploiting Americans' fears, argues Chris Hedges. Salon talks with the former *New York Times* reporter about his fearless new book, *American Fascists*.

By Michelle Goldberg

Jan. 8, 2007. Longtime war correspondent Chris Hedges, the former *New York Times* bureau chief in the Middle East and the Balkans, knows a lot about the savagery that people are capable of, especially when they're besotted with dreams of religious or national redemption. In his acclaimed 2002 book, *War Is a Force That Gives Us Meaning*, he wrote: "I have been in ambushes on desolate stretches of Central American roads, shot at in the marshes of Southern Iraq, imprisoned in the Sudan, beaten by Saudi military police, deported from Libya and Iran, captured and held for a week by Iraqi Republican Guard during the Shiite rebellion following the Gulf War, strafed by Russian Mig-21s in Bosnia, fired upon by Serb snipers, and shelled for days in Sarajevo with deafening rounds of heavy artillery that threw out thousands of deadly bits of iron fragments." Hedges was part of the *New York Times* team of reporters that won a 2002 Pulitzer Prize for explanatory reporting about global terrorism.

Given such intimacy with horror, one might expect him to be aloof from the seemingly less urgent cultural disputes that dominate domestic American politics. Yet in the rise of America's religious right, Hedges senses something akin to the brutal movements he's spent his life chronicling. The title of his new book speaks for itself: *American Fascists: The Christian Right and the War on America*. Scores of volumes about the religious right have recently been published (one of them, *Kingdom Coming: The Rise of Christian Nationalism*, by me), but Hedges' book is perhaps the most furious and foreboding, all the more so because he knows what fascism looks like.

Part of his outrage is theological. The son of a Presbyterian minister and a graduate of Harvard Divinity School, Hedges once planned to join the clergy himself. He speaks of the preachers he encountered while researching *American Fascists* as heretics, and he's appalled at their desecration of a faith he still cherishes, even if he no longer totally embraces it. Writing of Ohio megachurch pastor Rod Parsley and his close associate, GOP gubernatorial candidate Ken Blackwell, he says, "[T]he heart of the Christian religion, all that is good and compassionate within it, has been tossed aside, ruthlessly gouged out and thrown into a heap with all the other inner organs. Only the shell, the form, remains. Christianity is of no use to Parsley, Blackwell and the others. In its name they kill it."

I first met Hedges at last spring's War on Christians conference in Washington, D.C., where Parsley, a wildly charismatic Pentecostal who loves the language of holy war, electrified the crowd. ("I came to incite a riot!" he shouted. "Man your battle stations! Ready your weapons! Lock and load!") It was shortly before the publication of my book, and as Hedges and I spoke, we realized we had similar takes on our subject. Both of us relied on Hannah Arendt's analysis of totalitarian movements in their early stages, and on some of the concepts that historian Robert O. Paxton elucidated in his book *The Anatomy of Fascism*. But where I, anxious not to be seen as hysterical, tried to treat these ideas gingerly, Hedges is unabashed and unsparing. His rage and contempt for the movement's leaders, though, is matched by sympathy for its followers, because he understands the despair, the desperate longing for community and even the idealism that often drives them.

Hedges spoke to me on the phone from his home in New Jersey.

Let's start with the title. A lot of liberals who write about the right see echoes of fascism in its rhetoric and organizing, but we tiptoe around it, because we don't want people to think that we're comparing James Dobson to Hitler or America to Weimar Germany. You, though, decided to be very bold in your comparisons to fascism.

You're right, "fascism" or "fascist" is a terribly loaded word, and it evokes a historical period, primarily that of the Nazis, and to a lesser extent Mussolini. But fascism as an ideology has generic qualities. People like Robert O. Paxton in *The Anatomy of Fascism* have tried to quantify them. Umberto Eco did it in *Five Moral Pieces,* and I actually begin the book with an excerpt from Eco: *Eternal Fascism: Fourteen Ways of Looking at a Blackshirt.* I think there are enough generic qualities that the group within the religious right, known as Christian Reconstructionists or dominionists, warrants the word. Does this mean that this is Nazi Germany? No. Does this mean that this is Mussolini's Italy? No. Does this mean that this is a deeply anti-democratic movement that would like to impose a totalitarian system? Yes.

You know, I come out of the church. I not only grew up in the church but graduated from seminary, and I look at this as a mass movement. I give it very little religious legitimacy, especially the extreme wing of it.

You say they would like to impose a totalitarian system. How

much of a conscious goal do you think that is at the upper levels of organizing with, say, somebody like Rod Parsley?

I think they're completely conscious of it. The level of manipulation is quite sophisticated. These people understand the medium of television, they understand the despair and brokenness of the people they appeal to, and how to manipulate them both for personal and financial gain. I look at these figures, and I would certainly throw James Dobson in there, or Pat Robertson, as really dark figures.

I think the vast majority of followers have no idea. There's an earnestness to many of the believers. I had the same experience you did—I went in there prepared to really dislike these people and most of them just broke my heart. They're well meaning. Unfortunately, they're being manipulated and herded into a movement that's extremely dangerous. If these extreme elements actually manage to achieve power, they will horrify [their followers] in many ways. But that's true with all revolutionary movements.

The core of this movement is tiny, but you only need a tiny, disciplined, well-funded and well-organized group, and then you count on the sympathy of 80 million to 100 million evangelicals. And that's enough. Especially if you don't have countervailing forces, which we don't.

If there's a historical period that's analogous to the situation we have now, it would come close to being the 1930s in the United States. Obviously we're not in a depression, but the situation for the working class is very bleak, and the middle class is under assault. There has been a kind of Weimarization of the American working class, and there's a terrible instability in the middle class. And if we enter a period of political and social instability, this gives this movement the opportunity it's been waiting for. But it needs a crisis. All of these movements need a crisis to come to power, and we're not in a period of crisis.

How likely do you think a crisis is?

Very likely. The economy is not in healthy shape. I covered al-Qaida for a year for *The New York Times*. Every intelligence official I ever interviewed never talked about if, they only talked about when. They spoke about another catastrophic attack as an inevitability. The possibility of entering a period of instability is great, and then these movements become very frightening.

The difference between the 1930s and now is that we had powerful progressive forces through the labor unions, through an independent and vigorous press. I forget the figure but something like 80 percent of the media is controlled by seven corporations, something horrible like that. Television is just bankrupt. I worry that we don't have the organized forces within American society to protect our democracy in the way that we did in the 1930s.

Since the midterm election, many have suggested that the Christian Right has peaked, and the movement has in fact suffered quite a few severe blows since both of our books came out.

It's suffered severe blows in the past too. It depends on how you view the engine of the movement. For me, the engine of the movement is deep economic and personal despair. A terrible distortion and deformation of American society, where tens of millions of people in this country feel completely disenfranchised, where their physical communities have been obliterated, whether that's in the Rust Belt in Ohio or these monstrous exurbs like Orange County, where there is no community. There are no community rituals, no community centers, often there are no sidewalks. People live in empty soulless houses and drive big empty cars on freeways to Los Angeles and sit in vast offices and then come home again. You can't deform your society to that extent, and you can't shunt people aside and rip away any kind of safety net, any kind of program that gives them hope, and not expect political consequences.

Democracies function because the vast majority live relatively stable lives with a degree of hope, and, if not economic prosperity, at least enough of an income to free them from severe want or instability. Whatever the Democrats say now about the war, they're not addressing the fundamental issues that have given rise to this movement.

But isn't there a change in the Democratic Party, now that it's talking about class issues and economic issues more so than in the past?

Yes, but how far are they willing to go? The corporations that fund the Republican Party fund them. I don't hear anybody talking about repealing the bankruptcy bill, just like I don't hear them talking about torture. The Democrats recognize the problem, but I don't see anyone offering any kind of solutions that will begin to re-enfranchise people into American society. The fact that they can't even get healthcare through is pretty depressing.

The argument you're now making sounds in some ways like Tom Frank's, which is basically that support for the religious right represents a kind of misdirected class warfare. But your book struck me differently—it seemed to be much more about what this movement offers people psychologically.

Yeah, the economic is part of it, but you have large sections of the middle class that are bulwarks within this movement, so obviously the economic part isn't enough. The reason the catastrophic loss of manufacturing jobs is important is not so much the economic deprivation but the social consequences of that deprivation. The breakdown of community is really at the core here. When people lose job stability, when they work for $16 an hour and don't have health insurance, and nobody funds their public schools and nobody fixes their infrastructure, that has direct consequences into how the life of their community is led.

I know firsthand because my family comes from a working-class town in Maine that has suffered exactly this kind of deterioration. You pick up the local paper and the weekly police blotter is just DWIs and domestic violence. We've shattered these lives, and it isn't always economic. That's where I guess I would differ with Frank. It's really the destruction of the possibility of community, and of course economic deprivation goes a long way to doing that. But corporate America has done a pretty good job of destroying community too, which is why the largest growth areas are the exurbs, where people have a higher standard of living, but live fairly bleak and empty lives.

In the beginning of the book, you write briefly about covering wars in Latin America, the Middle East and the Balkans. How did that shape the way you understand these social forces in America? What similarities do you see?

When I covered the war in the Balkans, there was always the canard that this was a war about ancient ethnic hatreds that was taken from Robert Kaplan's *Balkan Ghosts*. That was not a war about ancient ethnic hatreds. It was a war that was fueled primarily by the economic collapse of Yugoslavia. Milosevic and Tudman, and to a lesser extent Izetbegovic, would not have been possible in a stable Yugoslavia.

When I first covered Hamas in 1988, it was a very marginal organization with very little power or reach. I watched Hamas grow. Although I came later to the Balkans, I had a good understanding of how Milosevic built his Serbian nationalist movement. These radical movements share a lot of ideological traits with the Christian Right, including that cult of masculinity, that cult of power, rampant nationalism fused with religious chauvinism. I find a lot of parallels.

People have a very hard time believing the status quo of their existence, or the world around them, can ever change. There's a kind of psychological inability to accept how fragile open societies are. When I was in Pristina, the capital of Kosovo, at the start of the war, I would meet with incredibly well-educated, multilingual Kosovar Albanian friends in the cafés. I would tell them that in the countryside there were armed groups of the Kosovo Liberation Army, who I'd met, and they would insist that the Kosovo Liberation Army didn't exist, that it was just a creation of the Serb police to justify repression.

You saw the same thing in the café society in Sarajevo on the eve of the war in Bosnia. Radovan Karadzic or even Milosevic were buffoonish figures to most Yugoslavs, and were therefore, especially among the educated elite, never taken seriously. There was a kind of blindness caused by their intellectual snobbery, their inability to understand what was happening. I think we have the same experience here. Those of us in New York, Boston, San Francisco or some of these urban pockets don't understand how radically changed our country is, don't understand the appeal of these buffoonish figures to tens of millions of Americans.

But don't you feel like the tipping point is still quite a way off? Speaking personally, when I've read about totalitarian movements, I've always imagined that I'd know enough to pack up and go. That would seem to be a very premature thing to do here.

Well, most people didn't pack up and go. The people who packed up and left were the exception, and most people thought they were crazy. My friends in Pristina had no idea what was going on in Kosovo until they were literally herded down to the train station and pushed into boxcars and shipped like cattle to Macedonia. And that's not because they weren't intelligent or perceptive. It was because, like all of us, they couldn't comprehend how fragile the world was around them, and how radically and quickly it could change. I think that's a human phenomenon.

Hitler was in power in 1933, but it took him until the late '30s to begin to consolidate his program. He never spoke about the Jews because he realized that raw anti-Semitism didn't play out with the German public. All he did was talk about family values and restoring the moral core of Germany. The Russian revolution took a decade to consolidate. It takes time to acculturate a society to a radical agenda, but that acculturation has clearly begun here, and I don't see people standing up and trying to stop them. The Democratic policy of trying to reach out to a movement that attacks whole segments of the society as worthy only of conversion or eradication is frightening.

Doesn't it make sense for the Democrats to reach out to the huge number of evangelicals who aren't necessarily part of the religious right, but who may be sympathetic to some of its rhetoric? Couldn't those people be up for grabs?

I don't think they are up for grabs because they have been ushered into a non-reality-based belief system. This isn't a matter of, "This is one viewpoint, here's another." This is a world of magic and signs and miracles and wonders, and [on the other side] is the world you hate, the liberal society that has shunted you aside and thrust you into despair. The rage that is directed at those who go after the movement is the rage of those who fear deeply being pushed back into this despair, from which many of the people I interviewed feel they barely escaped. A lot of people talked about suicide attempts or thoughts of suicide—these people really reached horrific levels of desperation. And now they believe that Jesus has a plan for them and intervenes in their life every day to protect them, and they can't give that up.

So in a way, the movement really has helped them.

Well, in same way unemployed workers in Weimar Germany were helped by becoming brownshirts, yes. It gave them a sense of purpose. Look, you could always tell in a refugee camp in Gaza when one of these kids joined Hamas, because suddenly they were clean, their djelleba was white, they walked with a sense of purpose. It was a very similar kind of conversion experience. If you go back and read [Arthur] Koestler and other writers on the Communist Party, you find the same thing.

This is a question that I get all the time, and you've probably heard it too: Do you think Bush is a believer, or do you think he and his administration are just cynically manipulating their foot soldiers?

I think he's a believer, to the extent that this belief system empowers his own arrogant sense of privilege and intellectual shallowness. When you know right and wrong, when you've been mandated by God to lead, you don't have to ask hard questions, you don't have to listen to anyone else. I think that plays into the Bush character pretty well.

I think there are probably other aspects or tenets of this belief system that he finds distasteful and doesn't like. But in a real sense he fits the profile: a washout, not a very good family life—apparently his mother was a horror show—he was a drunk, allegedly used drugs, coasted because of his daddy, reaches middle age, hasn't done anything with his life, finds Jesus. That fits a lot of people in the movement.

What do you think of the argument, exemplified by David Kuo's book, *Tempting Faith,* that this administration has

duped the Christian Right and hasn't really given them much in exchange for their support?

It's given them a lot of money. It's given them a few hundred million dollars. I wouldn't call that nothing.

Kuo's argument is that Bush promised $8 billion for the faith-based initiative but that there was actually very little new funding. What's missing in what he says, I think, is that while there was little *new* money, there was a massive effort to shift money that was already appropriated from secular social services to evangelical groups. But if you believe, as Kuo apparently did, that compassionate conservatism really meant helping the poor, then Bush hasn't really done anything to further it.

Well, [Bush] never wanted to help the poor. That was just to sell us on a program—he didn't have any intention of helping the poor.

Did you start out to research this book with the intellectual framework that comes from Hannah Arendt and Karl Popper in mind?

Yes. I studied a lot of Christian ethics, a lot of Reinhold Niebuhr, Karl Barth, that's how I was formed, so when I covered conflicts as a foreign correspondent, the peculiarity of my education made me look at those conflicts a little differently. I was always very wary of utopian movements because I had it pounded into me that utopianism is a dangerous phenomenon, of the left or the right. I was very critical of liberation theology because it essentially endorsed violence to create a Christian society. The way that I articulated that was really through writers like Popper and Arendt. I needed Karl Popper and Hannah Arendt to get a lot of the despotic movements that I was covering, to give myself a vocabulary by which to explain these movements to myself. Even when I teach journalism classes I tend to make them read *The Origins of Totalitarianism* because I think it's such an important book. I've read the book seven or eight times.

When did you see its relevance to the Christian Right?

Because of my close coverage, or close connection with movements like Hamas or Milosevic, or even some of the despotic movements in Latin America like Efraín Ríos Montt in Guatemala, I'd already been conditioned to smell these people out. And then, of course, coming out of the church and coming out of seminary, the combination was such that as soon as I came back from overseas, I had a sense of who these people were. There was a strange kind of confluence from my experience as a reporter and my academic background that came together and gave me a kind of sensitivity to the Christian Right that maybe other people didn't have immediately. I don't know how much it's apparent, but it's an angry book.

That's very apparent.

Good. My father remains the most important influence on my life, and he was a Presbyterian minister, a devout Christian. I quote Reinhold Niebuhr saying, "Religion is a good thing for good people and a bad thing for bad people." I wouldn't describe myself as particularly pious but I certainly would describe myself as religious. And when I see how these people are manipulating the Christian religion for personal empowerment and wealth and for the destruction of the very values that I think are embodied in the teachings of Jesus Christ, I'm angry.

This article first appeared in Salon. com at *http://www.Salon.com.* An online version remains in the Salon archives. Reprinted with permission.